DEBUNKING THE SEVEN MYTHS THAT DENY THE HISTORICITY OF GENESIS, CREATION, AND NOAH'S FLOOD

*A video-based training program
to help students keep their faith in college*

Daniel A. Biddle, Ph.D.

The entire contents of this book (including videos) are available online: *www.genesisapologetics.com/sevenmyths*

Debunking the Seven Myths that Deny the Historicity of Genesis, Creation, and Noah's Flood: A video-based training program to help students keep their faith in college by Daniel A. Biddle, Ph.D.
Printed in the United States of America

ISBN-13: 9781690180111

Print Version October 2019

Download the FREE "Genesis Apologetics" Mobile App for Creation v. Evolution Videos!

Dedication

To my wife, Jenny, who supports me in this work. To my children Makaela, Alyssa, Matthew, and Amanda, and to your children and your children's children for a hundred generations—this book is for all of you.

We would like to acknowledge Answers in Genesis (*www.answersingenesis.org*), the Institute for Creation Research (*www.icr.org*), and Creation Ministries International (*www.creation.com*). Much of the content herein has been drawn from (and is meant to be in alignment with) these Biblical Creation ministries.

"Guard what has been entrusted to you, avoiding worldly and empty chatter and the opposing arguments of what is falsely called 'knowledge'—which some have professed and thus gone astray from the faith. Grace be with you."
—1 Tim. 6:20–21

"This is the Lord's doing; it is marvelous in our eyes."
—Psalm 118:23

Contents

About the Author

Dr. Daniel A. Biddle is president of Genesis Apologetics, Inc., a 501(c)(3) organization dedicated to equipping youth pastors, parents, and students with Biblical answers for evolutionary teaching in public schools. Daniel has trained thousands of students in Biblical Creation and evolution and is the author of several Creation videos, books, and other publications. Daniel holds a doctorate in the Behavioral Sciences from Alliant University in San Francisco, California, and has worked as an expert consultant and/or witness in over 100 state and federal cases in the areas of research methodologies and analysis.

About the Ministry

Genesis Apologetics (*www.genesisapologetics.com*) is a non-profit 501(c)(3) ministry that equips Christian students and their parents with faith-building materials that affirm a Biblical Creation worldview. We are committed to providing Christian families with biblically and scientifically accurate answers to evolution as taught in public schools. Our doctrinal position on Biblical Creation aligns with ministries such as Answers in Genesis, the Institute for Creation Research, and Creation Ministries International which take Genesis at face value, including its testimony of a miraculous creation and global Flood that occurred only thousands of years ago. Genesis Apologetics offers the following free online training resources:

- *Mobile App:* Search for "Genesis Apologetics" in the iTunes or Google Play stores.
- *www.debunkevolution.com*
- *www.genesisapologetics.com*
- YouTube Channel (**Genesis Apologetics**). Our channel includes over 100 videos that promote Biblical Creation.

9

Preface: On Roots and Batons

On Roots: Personal Reflections from my Daughter's Wedding

The day was June 10th and it came way too fast. The culmination of weeks of planning and setup were ready to be tested by 200 people convening to celebrate my daughter's wedding. Time is the great companion or foe that takes us through every situation in life—ready or not—and time had me on autopilot for the day's activities. Before I knew it, I was standing before the pastor and all the witnesses giving my daughter away.

But this day didn't have to come. They might have missed it, making other choices with relationships, occupations, friends, and most importantly, spiritual decisions that could have stood in the way of their wedding day ever coming. But come it did, and we were all grateful.

As the day progressed, I continued reflecting on the day's festivities: the flowers, the people who poured in their time and resources, and the gifts being showered into their lives. To some, the day's event could be chalked up to "luck": "Isn't it nice they met each other—what a lucky couple!" To others, it was just a "self-made" event—two people falling in love celebrating their special day with friends and family.

The more I reflected about these various perspectives, the clearer the reality came to me: It's all about *roots*. The outward and visible wedding that day—like the opening of a flower representing their new lives together—was all about roots. It was the quiet, God-centered choices that each of them made years before their wedding day that led to the now-visible outcome of their celebration together.

When we study the beauty of a flower we seldom think about its roots, but it's those very roots—hidden beneath the soil—that are responsible for the flower's expression of beauty and design. What we really see when we're looking at the flower is *what the roots are expressing*.

"Rooted" Vase by
Ashley Rowley
(Sister of the
Groom)

Membership and
Education Manager
at American
Museum of Ceramic
Art / AMOCA

These roots were established over time through the silent, unseen process of growing their lives in the Lord through His Word. This process later resulted in a once-in-a-lifetime celebration now seen by hundreds. To look at the wedding as luck or a self-made occurrence doesn't accurately represent what happened that day, especially according to scripture. Psalm chapter 1, verses 1–3:

> Blessed is the man
> Who walks not in the counsel of the ungodly,
> Nor stands in the path of sinners,
> Nor sits in the seat of the scornful;
> But his delight is in the law of the Lord,
> And in His law he meditates day and night.
> He shall be like a tree
> Planted by the rivers of water,
> That brings forth its fruit in its season,
> Whose leaf also shall not wither;
> And whatever he does shall prosper.

Right out of the gate, before the reader dives into the remaining 149 Psalms in the book, the writer establishes that the person who does not walk, stand, or sit in the counsel, path, or seat of the ungodly, sinner, or scornful person is *blessed*, meaning to *receive favor* from God, the maker of heaven and earth.

The passage continues to assure that the person whose delight is in the law (specifically the Torah, the first five books of the Bible) and who meditates day and night on its truths will be likened to a tree that is planted (i.e., rooted) by the rivers of water that brings forth fruit in its season and whose leaf shall not wither. The passage even promises that whatever this person does will prosper. The passage is saying that the person who separates themselves from the world and its ways and *saturates* themselves in God's Word will *thrive* (not forbidding, of course the persecutions and challenges that Scripture also assures believers). Breaking down the passage, there are three key terms to unpack: *delight, meditate,* and *law.* Let's review each.

The Hebrew term for delight is chêphets and means *to take pleasure or desire something concrete and valuable* and (by extension) a matter (as in having something in mind). Solomon certainly expressed this when he said in Proverbs 3:15 that [God's] wisdom is "more precious than jewels" and "nothing we desire" can compare with it. Note that this term *delight* is directed exclusively toward the law of God (more on this below).

The next key term is *meditates* (hâgâh in Hebrew) which in this context means to *ponder* or *imagine.* Given that the term delight precedes meditate, two key meanings emerge from this part of the passage: *reflection* and *saturation.* It's talking about soaking in Scripture. This goes well beyond blasting through a quick daily devotional. It means "stewing" in God's Word. Charles Spurgeon puts it this way:

> Oh, that you and I might get into the very heart
> of the Word of God, and get that Word into
> ourselves! As I have seen the silkworm eat into

the leaf, and consume it, so ought we to do with the Word of the Lord; not crawl ever its surface, but eat right into it till we have taken it into our inmost parts. It is idle merely to let the eye glance over the words, or to recollect the poetical expressions, or the historic facts; but it is blessed to eat into the very soul of the Bible until, at last, you come to talk in Scriptural language, and your very style is fashioned upon Scripture models, and, what is better still, your spirit is flavored with the words of the Lord.

Joshua 1:8 paints a good picture of this: "This book of the law shall not depart from your mouth, but you shall meditate on it day and night, so that you may be careful to do according to all that is written in it; for then you will make your way prosperous, and then you will have success."

The last key term is the law, or *Torah* in Hebrew. While Torah is specifically used to describe the first five books of the Bible (Genesis, Exodus, Leviticus, Numbers, and Deuteronomy), it is not a stretch to include the laws, commandments, precepts, and statutes throughout Scripture as well.

However, the Torah is specifically mentioned in this passage, so what's in the Torah? Well, Genesis 1–11 explains the historical account of Creation and judgement by the Flood. The remaining chapters explain the development of God's chosen people, the Israelites. Exodus explains the history regarding the redemption of Israel and freedom from slavery. Leviticus lays out the covenants and regulations necessary for abiding under God's laws, paving the way for the New Covenant brought by Christ. Numbers is more history, describing how the people of Israel tested God's patience, and He in turn tested their endurance and faithfulness. Deuteronomy is still more history and reiterates the laws given by God to the Israelites in previous books of the Torah.

Do you see the pattern? If someone told me to *meditate* on these five books, reading them for several hours and pondering their implications, I would come away with some central themes: God is God, He created just how He explained, His Word should be taken seriously and reverently, He is a just God requiring righteousness, and we are desperately in need of a Savior.

By meditating on the law as this Psalm advises, we're reflecting on the reality of the Creator and what He has done to begin everything and pull His people through history—His-story—as described in His Word. It's about worshiping and acknowledging God and all that He has done in His-story. How could the God who transmitted Scripture through human authorship be a reliable, trustworthy God we can count on if the hundreds of people listed by name, along with their children's names and the birth years, lifespans, and death years did not represent a reliable chain as the text represents?

Let's take this back to the wedding day. Where does this all connect? It's simple, but many may not see it. My daughter and her husband—years before they got married—made decisions to receive Christ. And *beyond taking that step*, they made decisions to *follow* Christ and *build their lives upon His Word*, which begins with the law (Torah)—which includes the very *historical foundation* of the Christian faith. It includes the ground-level worldview-shaping understanding of the loving Creator-God and the account of our origins that He laid down in His authoritative Word.

Christ reminds us of the importance of ordering our lives after His Word in the Parable of the Sower:

> Behold, a sower went out to sow. And as he sowed, some seed fell by the wayside; and the birds came and devoured them. Some fell on stony places, where they did not have much earth; and they immediately sprang up because they had no depth of earth. But when the sun was up they were scorched, and because they had no

root they withered away. And some fell among thorns, and the thorns sprang up and choked them. But others fell on good ground and yielded a crop: some a hundredfold, some sixty, some thirty. He who has ears to hear, let him hear! ... Therefore hear the parable of the sower: When anyone hears the word of the kingdom, and does not understand it, then the wicked one comes and snatches away what was sown in his heart. This is he who received seed by the wayside. But he who received the seed on stony places, this is he who hears the word and immediately receives it with joy; yet he has no root in himself, but endures only for a while. For when tribulation or persecution arises because of the word, immediately he stumbles. Now he who received seed among the thorns is he who hears the word, and the cares of this world and the deceitfulness of riches choke the word, and he becomes unfruitful. But he who received seed on the good ground is he who hears the word and understands it, who indeed bears fruit and produces: some a hundredfold, some sixty, some thirty. (Matthew 13)

Why do the seeds in this parable grow to be fruit-bearing plants? It's all because they have *roots*. The trusting Christian—the one with roots—actually believes that the Words of the Creator are trustworthy, so much so that they can allow the seeds of the Word to penetrate their inner beings. Believe it or not, many people who attend church today have no idea about the real truth, history, and inspiration of God's Word because they have *stewed* and *meditated* in the world and all its smoke-and-mirror offerings about creation and humanity. In many cases, their conscious and subconscious doubts have choked the Word from growing in their lives.

Here is the key—people are only going to allow the seeds of God's Word to penetrate the depths of their beings if they believe them to be true. They must trust it. A seed will only grow to its full potential if the soil is fertile, ready, and tilled. It must be *receptive to the seed* for the seed to do its work. Likewise, people are not going to allow God's Word to have the transformative, life-shaping, worldview-making potential if they don't believe it to be true in the most practical of ways.

Yes, even the metaphors carried in mythical writings can impact us and shape who we are. But God's Word—specifically the Torah—is not metaphor. The Torah, beginning with Genesis, includes history, dates, and genealogies about our early beginnings. It is this very history that describes our brokenness and the curse of sin that requires a redeemer, Christ. Taking God's Word at face value changes a person. It places God's Word (not man's word) at the center of their worldview—the lens through which they see the world and the governing filter for how we got here and our purpose on earth. A flower does not blossom and express its beauty because of the flower—it does so because of the *roots*. A flower's outward expression of beauty is a direct reflection of what is happening in the unseen part of the flower—its roots. And for Christians, this stands true as well, and it *all starts in Genesis*.

Makaela & Christian Hushaw (Wedding Day)
(Christy Johnston Photography)

On Batons

I was 18 years old and like many young men that age, I wanted a girlfriend. While I was trying to "wait for God's best" in my life (starting with college and career building), I was often tempted with taking the short-cut to what I thought I needed, which in this season was a relationship. One night—growing tired of waiting for God to "send me that special someone"—I decided to take things into my own hands and found myself hanging out with a not-so-godly young lady at a park.

I came home to grab some things before venturing off with my new potential girlfriend, and passed by my mom in the kitchen, mumbling, "I'm tired of waiting for God's best for me—I've found my own girlfriend." After grabbing my things and passing by her again, she said something that stopped me dead in my tracks: "That's fine Danny… just remember that Esau gave up his entire inheritance for a bowl of soup" (Genesis 25:29–34).

I am convinced to this day that my mom's words changed the rest of my life, even leading up to my daughter's wedding, her future kids, and onward it goes. That's the power of God's Word in action. No other words from any other book could have done this. My mom said this because she was rooted in God's Word. She passed the baton.

Joyce Biddle: Passing the Baton of God's Word between Generations (Christy Johnston Photography)

Those who plant their roots deeply into God's Word—beginning in Genesis—will be blessed. Yes, we'll also go through many struggles in life, but these can actually lead to our *roots growing deeper*. There is no greater reward than seeing the baton of faith passed from generation to generation. We live in interesting times as Christians, but the *remnant* of God's followers are still strong, and growing stronger.

If you drop the baton, there's always hope!

We all struggle. We all make choices we regret. When it comes to the topic of being rooted and passing the baton, I've had some close calls.

While attending theology class in seminary I remember the professor stating, "The Hebrew text in Genesis clearly points to a recent creation and the creation days being ordinary days, but 'science' points to an old earth—so you guys go figure it out..." While I hardly knew it at the time, this teaching placed a ball and chain on my faith, leaving me with lingering questions like: "Why would God be so clear about the history of Genesis dating back recently to Adam just thousands of years ago if 'science' disproves it so readily? What other key topics in the Bible cannot be taken at face value? Why would God be so clear in narrating Genesis history—with birth/lifespan/death years given for 87 patriarchs in Genesis if it wasn't trustworthy history?" These questions did to my faith what they do to many Christians today: they created *cognitive dissonance*—the friction that emerges when wrestling between two apparent "truths." They also prevented the seed of God's truths from growing deeply into my heart and mind, held back by subconscious doubt.

Stuck in this place for most of my early parenting years, my oldest two kids received mixed messages from me about God's Word and the reliability of Scripture. When they were barraged with evolutionary teaching in public school (250 pages and 50 classroom hours in my state) and they looked to me for answers, I spoke out of both sides of my mouth.

Questions like "Dad, what about the dinosaurs?" were answered with, "Well, Christians have two perspectives on this topic: if the earth is old, dinosaurs were created millions of years before humans, were not present when Adam lived, were not named by Adam as the Bible describes, and were not part of mankind's dominion mandate. However, if the earth is young, dinosaurs were created just thousands of years ago, were present when Adam was created, were named by him as the

19

Bible describes, and were part of mankind's dominion mandate."

This wasn't what they were hearing in public school. In classes starting in 5th grade onto their high school years, their textbooks and every museum they visited had one consistent line about the dinosaurs: millions of years, evolution, and extinction, with humans not even in the picture, having arrived millions of years later.

When faced with such mixed viewpoints, my kids, like other students are likely to respond in one of three ways: 1) The truth about the creatures that once filled the planet is so obscure that dad and the Bible don't provide an answer; 2) the answer exists but dad doesn't know it; or 3) the answer to this question that I hear from the world (TV, movies, children's books, public school, and museums and state parks) is correct and more believable than the answer given by dad and the Bible, and the Bible can't be trusted for answering basic questions about how life got here and the truth about earth history. It's only an ancient book useful today for morality and spiritual guidance.

Unfortunately, it's the third response that most Christian students in public school receive today, resulting in a weakened faith—most of the time without even knowing it. Their minds never join the faith walk of their hearts. Even if they believe that Jesus is real from an experience standpoint, which is common in churches today, God's Word is powerless in their lives because they don't yet believe that it is historically or scientifically accurate and reliable. After training thousands of students through our ministry, we see this *all the time.*

It's sad—while many churches today lock Genesis in the closet because it's "controversial," the world has no problem drowning students in the lie of evolution. I wonder why the enemy battles so fiercely over origin-related matters? I think this book explains why.

It's not until the student realizes there are two completely opposite narratives—God's history recorded in His Word and the godless evolution-based framework of the world—and only *one of them is true,* that full life

20

transformation occurs. This is because the life-empowering seeds of the Bible will not transform their hearts if they are prevented from taking root by their *doubting minds, being indoctrinated by the world's ideas.* Remember, Scripture states that Satan's system of deception *has and will span the entire world* (see 1 John 5:18–19, 2 Thessalonians 2:9–10, and Revelation 20:3).

Now that I'm on the other side of my "Creation Awakening," I have developed the correct answer about the question above, and the Lord gave me time to inscribe these truths into the minds and hearts of my family:

> The Bible is the true source of knowledge and guidance for all of life. While it doesn't give us detailed answers about all of biology, the Bible is crystal clear that all life was created in six days, with land creatures created on Day 6 before humans, then humans were created as God's final capstone of Creation and named all the animals, and took dominion over them. Animals did not have the fear of man until after the Flood (Genesis 9:2). God describes (in Job 40) the largest creature he ever made—*Behemoth*, a sauropod dinosaur—as the *Chief* of His creation, the grandest, most magnificent land creature ever created.[1] We find dinosaurs and other creatures today buried all over the earth by Noah's Flood, a judgment we deserved because of our rebelliousness towards God. This judgment buried the dinosaurs in North America across a 13-state region (known as the Morrison Formation, and the Cretaceous layers that top it) and the evidence for this recent burial is obvious and widespread, including soft tissue still found in their bones today, the habitat in which they were buried, and the manner in which we find

their disarticulated bones buried in water-laid sediments.

Fortunately, I was "awakened" to the truth and historicity of God's Word with enough parenting time remaining to set the record straight with all my kids before they left home. Now grounded with a tap root that penetrates deep into the trustworthiness of God's Word all the way back to Genesis, I can look them intently in the eyes and affirm that I trust God's Word and they can too—every Word of it. What impact do you think it has on kids when their father demonstrates transparent trust in God's Word? I think it has a big impact. Looking back through the Bible, a "grounded father's blessing"[2] is a big deal. I had supportive parents, but not a biblical patriarchal blessing. Many do not.

To help ground them further, I took them on research trips to Montana, Canada, and other places to see and touch the evidence of God's judgment on earth that came by Noah's Flood. On one such trip my daughter and I were standing by an outdoor dinosaur burial exhibit in Canada where a hadrosaur was still *in situ*—left exactly where it was found, buried by the Flood waters. A dad and his son stood behind us and pressed the button to play the audio recording from the secular museum explaining how "millions and millions of years ago" this dinosaur tried to swim across a swollen river during a tropical storm and drowned (somehow along with a 13-mile stretch of other dinosaurs, mammals, and sea life that met the *same fate* at the *same time*).

After hearing the explanation, Makaela had her "wake-up" moment. She turned to me—with the two strangers standing just feet away—and gave me 5-minute verbal storm about how the secular explanation made no sense whatsoever. We were surrounded by a catastrophic burial stretching at least 13 miles where over 32,000 specimens (only 300 complete) from 35 species, 34 genera, and 12 families of dinosaurs were somehow buried by hundreds of feet of mud along with fish, turtles, marsupials, amphibians, and countless clams.

We walked back to the car and the man who overheard my daughter's 5-minute "my eyes are now opened" speech approached me in the parking lot. Expecting him to confront me about my daughter's "Creationist rant," I was shocked when the opposite happened. He explained that he grew up as a Christian, but lost his faith while attending college to become a licensed geologist (his current occupation). His next words blew me away: "Your daughter's 5-minute explanation about the Flood and the dinosaur fossil record made more sense to me than the explanations I received over several years of studying to become a geologist. I am now returning to my faith…" He went on to explain how the millions of years, evolution, and dinosaur burial evidence never made sense to him, now especially so after learning more about the biblical framework surrounding dinosaurs.

I had two more "coincidental" meetings with him in different locations over the next two days, where we continued the dialogue about making biblical sense over the fossil record. Who could imagine what a young boy pushing the play button at a museum exhibit could do one hot day in Canada?

This book is necessary because students deserve to know that the Bible presents the true case about Earth's past, as well as its future. Secular colleges—and even many Christian colleges—teach that the Bible is not real history. Fortunately, Answers in Genesis retains a list of colleges that stand firm on the "Genesis is real history" position.[3] It's encouraging to know that this list includes some of the larger Christian institutions.

The 18 inches that separate the head from the heart can represent a chasm of faith that is never crossed by many. Today's students want to know: When does the truth begin in the Bible? On the first page? How many pages need to be turned until truth begins? May this book help you on your journey.

Introduction

Suggested Videos:

Seven Myths https://genesisapologetics.com/sevenmyths/
Theistic Evolution: https://youtu.be/uTogDQ5vIXg

The sci-fi thriller movie *Matrix* (1999) popularized the "blue pill/red pill" metaphor in today's culture. The original phrase from the movie is:

> You take the blue pill, the story ends. You wake up in your bed and believe whatever you want to. You take the red pill, you stay in Wonderland, and I show you how deep the rabbit hole goes. Remember, all I'm offering is the truth. Nothing more.

The metaphor derived from this movie juxtaposes two choices: The red pill represents a life of harsh knowledge, desperate freedom, and the brutal truths of reality; whereas the blue pill represents a life of luxurious security, tranquil happiness, and the blissful ignorance of the harsh realities of life, basking in an (essentially dishonest) illusion.[4]

Believe it or not, we live in a world where this metaphor actually applies—at least when it comes to our worldview regarding our origins, purpose in life, and what happens after death. Let me explain.

The world surrounds us with the "conventional paradigm"—a matrix—about our origins and the history of life on earth. This reality matrix is reinforced by education, movies, television, museums, and secular institutions. This matrix entirely discounts the credibility of Biblical history as plainly written. In its place, it teaches that the universe came into being by natural processes apart from the supernatural actions of a personal Creator God. Natural processes alone brought all things into existence, beginning with the elements, stars, and galaxies. Plants, animals, and human beings are all ultimately products of random chance events that unfolded over the multi-billion-year evolutionary history of life on Earth. Because of this, life has no ultimate meaning or purpose, and morality is basically relative. We are ultimately accountable to no one for our choices, because when we die, we will cease to exist. This paradigm represents a reinforced, false reality that keeps many from awakening to the truth of Creation, leaving them in the dark blindness Satan uses to "deceive the whole world" (see 1 John 5:18–19, 2 Thessalonians 2:9–10, and Revelation 20:3).

Sadly, this worldview has also slipped into many Christian colleges that have morphed Biblical truth to be relevant to the culture of today—sacrificing clear biblical truth on the "altar" of relevance and sometimes attraction. There are seven key "myths" that make up this matrix:

1. "While the Bible may be 'inspired,' by God, it's not 'inerrant' and parts of it are just myth."
2. "The Bible's account of Creation is only metaphorical, the six creation days were not ordinary days, and creation really unfolded over millions of years."
3. "Genesis 1 and 2 provide two different accounts of creation."
4. "Adam and Eve were not real people, only allegorical figures in the story of human evolution."
5. "The Bible's account of Noah's Flood is just myth and was drawn from writings from the Ancient Near East."
6. "Moses did not actually write the first five books of the Bible."
7. "Dinosaurs died out millions of years ago, did not walk with man, and are not mentioned in the Bible."

In today's culture where many seem to be okay with a "marketplace of ideas" that spread across a "spectrum of truth," the Bible stands out—presenting a clear record of who created us, when we were created, and the current state of humanity, and then offers Christ as our sole redeemer. Let's review why these seven topics actually matter.

First, Jesus said we should "love the Lord our God with all our heart, soul, strength, and mind" (Matthew 22:37). While we see plenty of Christians today who are passionate about their faith, sometimes they are not committed to the validity and truth of the Bible, denying its obvious claims about Creation, the Flood, and the many other miracles that even Christ Himself taught as real, historical events. Sometimes their hearts are on board, but their minds are dragging far behind, loaded down with a secular worldview that weakens their Christian walk.

Because these competing views create dissonance in their minds, many Christians are living a half-hearted faith—some without even knowing it. Many times, this problem gets compounded when they attend Christian colleges that place the Bible on equal footing with Ancient Near East mythology, spin the Creation and Flood accounts every which way, and turn Adam and Eve into myths or allegories.

To cope with these challenges, many Christians become theistic evolutionists, hoping to reconcile their Christianity with what their professors or classmates believe. The challenge with this is that evolution over millions of years is totally irreconcilable with Scripture (see "Theistic Evolution" discussion below and video here: _www.genesisapologetics.com/theistic_).

Other students deal with these challenges by compartmentalizing their Christianity as their "spiritual" side, or even identifying as "New Testament" Christians. This is all because they don't believe that the Christian faith is based on real history, beginning with the first page of the Bible.

Consider this: Would Christians live out their faith with more boldness if they really believed that the Bible is true—both theologically and historically? If their hearts, souls, and minds were "all in"? What would happen if Jesus came to earth and took 100 doubting Christians into a theater and showed a movie that replayed history from the beginning—Creation week, the Flood, and major biblical events that happened after—all the way to today. Would those Christians leave the theater and return to life as usual? Certainly not. This is because evidence that confirms God's Word translates into a *committed belief* in one's mind, and this belief emboldens Christians to live faith-filled lives.

Fully believing and obeying God's Word also opens the door to blessing. No—we're not promoting prosperity teaching here. We're talking about what happens when a person makes a conscious decision to order their lives after Biblical teaching and makes choices that align with God's Word. For "God will not be mocked: whatsoever a man sows, that he will also reap" (Galatians 6:7). We're talking about Christians getting onto the right tracks for their lives and journeying to their ideal destinations because they're living their lives in ways that honor God and His Word.

Today's youth are only going to follow God's Word if they believe it to be true in its claims. No one's going to submit to a book of fairy tales. This is exactly why Biblical apologetics is important—beginning with the first book of the Bible.

Look at it this way[5]: Christians believe that Jesus rose from the dead. How do we know it happened? We weren't there. We can't go back and watch a re-run of it. We get that belief from the Bible. But wait—scientists today would say that a person can't rise from the dead, so shouldn't we reinterpret this event and say that it wasn't really a bodily resurrection? Same with the Virgin birth? The miracles Christ performed? Most Christians would say, "Of course not." But that's exactly what a lot of Christians do with Genesis—it's the same thing. Many Christians have no problem affirming the New Testament miracles of Christ, but when we get to the Creation account in Genesis where He created in six days, created man from dust and Eve from his side, many say, "Oh no—science says otherwise, so it can't be so!" They don't believe what the Bible says because of what modern scientists say, so they reinterpret the Bible. Once we unlock that door, we unleash the same attack that Satan made on Eve, questioning: "Did God really say?" (Genesis 3:1)

This "did God really say" attack was so effective in the Garden that the enemy still uses it today. Evolution over millions of years. Ape men. No life after death. These ideas lead people to question, doubt, then ultimately reject God's Word. If people won't believe the history of the Bible, this undermines the authority of the Bible, and the Gospel is *based in that very authority*.

If we cannot trust the Bible's history, why would we believe what it says about salvation? If people won't believe Genesis 1, why believe John 3:16? Jesus even said, "I have spoken to you of earthly things and you do not believe; how then will you believe if I speak of heavenly things?" (John 3:12) These challenges represent a key stumbling block to the Gospel of Jesus Christ for many people today.

The Bible also stresses that we should not be "cheated" by those in the world who tout philosophies that follow the traditions and basic principles of this world, rather than on Christ and His Word (Colossians 2). Indeed, the wisdom of God has made foolish the wisdom of this world, since, "the world through wisdom did not know God" (1 Corinthians 1:21), with many being led astray and deceived by the "so called science" of each generation (1 Timothy 6:20). Such "wisdom of this world" draws back into the mystery of unseen, unproven deep time to frame the theory of evolution—far beyond when we can use *true science*—that which we can observe, measure, and repeat—to test such ideas. Rather, such theories are comprised of inferences and speculations rooted in a person's worldview—*historical* science.

Finally, these topics are not important so we can have the satisfaction of winning arguments. Rather, they are important because believing in the clear message of the Bible firmly grounds and roots a person's faith—allowing them to build their lives in the solid, rich ground of God's Word and base their life decisions and choices in ways that are aligned with the Bible.

28

Theistic Evolution: What's Wrong with the Idea That God Used Evolution to Create Everything?

In a nutshell, theistic evolution is the belief that God used evolution to bring about the variety of life on Earth over millions of years. The Bible plainly disagrees with theistic evolution. More and more student-aged Christians are becoming theistic evolutionists—especially those who attended public schools and did not receive much biblical training at home or in church.

One of the most common testimonies we hear from high schoolers goes something like this: They become Christians at a young age, but they don't get much training in doctrine, especially creation-evolution related topics. After being saturated in public school evolutionary teaching (and not hearing the Biblical Creation view from parents or church leaders), they start developing *cognitive dissonance*—the tension that develops when holding two contradictory beliefs. They begin questioning: "I know that God exists, but they seem to present so much credible evidence for evolution at school, and it seems like the 'smart scientists' tend to believe it." Many take the shortest route to resolving this mental tension by adopting a worldview that is somewhere between their Christian faith and evolution. Without even knowing it, they have just adopted the view of theistic evolution and compromised their trust and reliance on the Bible.

In one subtle play, the enemy replaces belief in an all-powerful God who spoke creation into existence with a "god" who creates life through a slow, random, murderous process of death and suffering. If true, the Bible wouldn't really mean what it says. Should we trust a god who lied to us about our beginnings? Those who pretend there's nothing wrong with this, downgrade the Bible and suspend reason. Exposing six fatal flaws with theistic evolution resolves the issue by leaving the Genesis record standing tall.

The Seven Fatal Flaws of Theistic Evolution

We've distilled the major problems of theistic evolution into a list of the top seven. As we'll see, the problems with theistic evolution are not just some abstract theological problems—they bring a serious impact on the daily lives of believers. After all, our beliefs form the roots of our actions and the sum of our actions make up our lives and our choices.

Adam Versus Apes: Theistic Evolution Denies the Biblical Creation of Adam and Makes Apes Our Ancestors

The Bible is clear that Adam was created supernaturally by God, in God's own image and likeness, out of the dust of the Earth (Genesis 1:26 and following). We are not made in the image of some lower ape-like creature, and the "image" of God and His "likeness" certainly does not match that of an ape.

Genesis gives us a strong clue that we did not evolve from any type of "lower life form" or ape-like ancestor. Adam's first order from God was to study and name all the animal *kinds*. After doing this, Adam noticed that none of them represented a suitable "match" for his "kind" (humans) (Genesis 2:20). God's solution was to draw a helper/companion from Adam's own side and create Eve. Adam's response to this was: "This is now *bone of my bones, and flesh of my flesh*; she shall be called Woman, because she was *taken out of Man*" (Genesis 2:23, emphasis added).

How is it possible that we evolved from ape-like creatures if Adam had single-handedly studied and named all the animal kinds on earth and determined there wasn't a single creature—chimps included—that resembled his *kind*? Christians who ascribe to theistic evolution simply cannot reconcile monkey-to-man evolution with the Bible.

Making this idea even worse, evolution holds that humans exist as they are today because our particular line of ape-like ancestors out-lasted and even out-killed other varieties. This is a far cry from humans being specially created out of the

30

dust of the Earth in the image of a loving and intentional God. Jesus Himself clearly disagreed with the ideas that millions of years of human evolution occurred by stating, "But *from the beginning* of the creation, God 'made them male and female'" (Mark 10:6, emphasis added).

The Biblical Order of Creation

The basic order of the Creation account in Genesis 1 disagrees with modern, man-made ideas of how evolution supposedly unfolded (see Table 1).

Table 1. Differences between the Bible and Evolution.

Bible	Evolution Theory
Earth before the sun	Sun before the earth
Oceans before land	Land before oceans
Land plants first	Ocean life first
Fish before insects	Insects before fish
Plants before sun	Sun before plants
Birds before reptiles	Reptiles before birds
God created man instantly after all other animals were created, animals vary and adapt only within "kind"	The process of death created man, and evolution is still occurring, though invisible because it takes deep time

Table 1 lays out how the Biblical order of Creation is opposite to how evolution supposedly happened.

Theistic Evolution Makes Death, and not God, Our Creator

No matter which "version" of evolution one holds to—whether naturalistic evolution without a God or theistic evolution with a process started by God and left to run its course, or progressive creation where God uses cosmological and geological evolution while occasionally wiping out and creating new life forms along the way—the core problem with all versions of evolution is its proposal that the process of *death is set up as the creator of life.* Each version of evolution has a bloody and competitive process of "survival of the fittest" as the creator of new life forms. Each starts from lower life forms and eventually leads to man over millions of years. There are some serious problems with this view, and it could not differ more from the biblical account! What kind of all-powerful God would need to use a cruel, experimental process to bring about the variety of life on earth?

The idea of *punctuated equilibrium* (a view even held, in some form, by many progressive creationists) holds that God advances evolutionary development by isolated episodes of rapid speciation between long periods of little or no change. In other words, God used "random, wasteful, inefficiencies" to create the world into which Adam was placed.[6] What kind of God couldn't get it right the first time, so He had to experiment with hapless life forms?

To the contrary, the Bible holds that God initially created everything perfect, and then our sin initiated the process of death, suffering, and bloodshed. How could God look upon all His Creation and call it "very good" (Genesis 1:31) if animals were tearing each other apart to survive for millions of years before Adam? Why would an all-powerful, loving, merciful God need to use a blood-filled, clumsy, and random process to populate the Earth with animal variety? God's initial Creation was perfect, but we messed it up! Theistic evolution violates clear Bible statements and clearly seen attributes of God throughout the Bible.

Theistic Evolution Places Death before Sin

Perhaps the most serious problem with theistic evolution is that it has man coming on the scene after billions of years of death-filled evolution has taken place. This makes the brutal "survival of the fittest" process God's idea instead of the consequence of sin. In contrast, according to the Bible, when man appears in Creation he is perfect and sinless and there's no such thing as death. Death does not come into the picture *until man sins* ("but of the tree of the knowledge of good and evil you shall not eat, for in the day that you eat of it you shall surely die," Genesis 2:17). It was this very penalty of death for sin that Christ came to pay with His death on the cross! According to Romans 6:23, "the wages of sin is death but the gift of God is eternal life in Christ Jesus our Lord." So, you can't have death of mankind before the Fall of man and have a logical foundation for the Gospel (see also Romans 5:12 and 1 Corinthians 15:22). If death already existed all around Adam, God's warning of death as a consequence for eating the forbidden fruit would have been meaningless and idle.

In addition to God clearly warning Adam that "death will come" if he sins, two stark truths in Genesis address this important "death before sin" topic.

First, animals did not eat each other at the beginning of Creation, and thus there was no "survival of the fittest" or "natural selection" process available to drive evolution. Humans and animals originally ate vegetation:

> And God said, 'See, I have given you every herb that yields seed which is on the face of all the earth, and every tree whose fruit yields seed; to you it shall be for food. Also, to every beast of the earth, to every bird of the air, and to everything that creeps on the earth, in which there is life, I have given every green herb for food' (Genesis 1:29–30).

God did not endorse humans using animals as food until *after* the Flood: "Everything that lives and moves about will be food for you. *Just as I gave you the green plants, I now give you everything*" (Genesis 9:3, emphasis added). Further, God put the fear of man into animals *after* the Flood because they would be a food source from that point forward: "And the fear of you and the dread of you shall be on every beast of the earth, on every bird of the air, on all that move on the earth, and on all the fish of the sea" (Genesis 9:2).

Second, how could God look over the billions of years of blood-filled "survival of the fittest" evolution until it finally reached man and then call Creation "very good" (Genesis 1:31)? This would make Adam's sin and the curse of death meaningless! If death was used to create Adam and Eve, what was the real consequence of sin?

Figure 1. Is this a "very good" creation? Carnivory entered the world after sin.

God's original creation was perfect. The first chapter of Genesis states six times that what God had made was "good" and the seventh time that "God saw everything that He had made, and indeed it was *very* good" (Genesis 1:31). Now, however, we can look at the world around us and see there has been an obvious change. Many animals live by predation. Lions eat their prey while still alive. Bears eat young deer shortly after they are born. Surely that isn't what a good and loving God would describe as "very good."

The Believer Loses the Power That Comes from Fully Believing in God's Word

Put simply, there is power that comes from fully believing in the Word of God. A straightforward reading of the Bible's account of origins as laid out in Genesis 1 and 5 and Exodus 20:11—without spin or interpreting it through man's lens of "science"—will lead an honest reader to six days of Creation just thousands of years ago. If God really used evolution to create everything, He could have simply told Moses to write it down that way! But He didn't, and the Creation account reads much differently than how it might read if evolution took place over millions of years. The Bible is clear in several places that God "spoke" creation into existence (every time before creative acts in Genesis as well as elsewhere in the Bible—e.g., Psalm 33:4–11).

Compromising on God's Word by agreeing with theistic evolution robs Christians of the power that comes from standing fully on the Word of God and claiming its authority. When Dr. Charles Jackson with Creation Truth Foundation was asked, "Do you meet many Christians at college who are drifting away from the faith?" his response was eye-opening:

They're more than being drifted away from the faith; there's a current that's created under them that pulls them away from the faith. When you put a question mark after any Bible verses that don't have them there already (or verses that give a disclaimer like, 'this is a mystery'), like 'in six days the Lord God created heaven and earth and all that's in them' (Exodus 20:11), instantly you have a quantum drop in the joy and power of the Christian walk—all of the gifts of God in you—you can feel it. It's like someone pulled the plug and you are running on battery now, and a low battery at that. [7]

There is a close association between the Word of God and the Power of God (Hebrews 4:12, 6:5; Matthew 22:29). Can a Christian live a power-filled life and walk in God's will while denying the Word of God? Christians will live a more power-filled life when they strongly align what they believe and how they live to the Word of God. Every stanza of Psalm 119 mentions the Word in some way for this reason.

Denying God's special creation and not believing that He created the world by His Word (Hebrews 11:3; Psalm 33:6) creates a deep crack in the foundation of a Christian, even in ways that are sometimes not known by the person doubting. John Macarthur[8] adds to this discussion by stating:

> Christians will get out there, saying "Boy, we're against abortion, and we're against homosexuality, and we're against Jack Kevorkian because he's murdering people, and we're against euthanasia, and we're against genocide and, you know, we're against the moral evils of our society, etc." Why are we against those things? Can you tell me why? Why are we against those things? Give me one reason. Here it is, because they're forbidden in Scripture. Is that not true? The only reason we're against abortion is because God's against it. How do we know that? Because it's in the Word of God. The reason we're against homosexuality, adultery, etc. is because of the Bible. You see, we stand on the Scripture. But the problem is we don't want to stand on the Scripture in Genesis. So we equivocate on whether the Bible is an authority at all. What do you think the watching world thinks about our commitment to Scripture? Pretty selective, isn't it?

Theistic Evolution Has Christ Dying for the Sins of a Mythical Adam

The genealogies in Genesis 5 and 10 and Luke 3 lead directly back to Adam, the first man created by God. But if these genealogies don't lead to a real Adam who sinned, then who do they lead to? Because the "sinner" Adam and the Savior Jesus are linked together in Romans 5:16–18, any theological view which mythologizes Adam undermines the biblical basis of Jesus' work of redemption.

The Bible Claims to Be Revelation from God and If Theistic Evolution is True, the Bible Is Wrong

The Bible claims to be revelation from God. It also lays out a clear picture of Creation—animals created from dust, after their kinds, and subject to humans. If God channeled His Word to humans with clarity, and this seems to be the case, then He certainly "got it wrong" if evolution happened. God failed in communicating how He created, He lied, or He was just plain wrong.

Is the God of the Universe incapable of conveying to lowly humans what actually happened at Creation? Is He who formed the ear not capable of clear communication? Does He not bear some responsibility to ensure that Scripture is written accurately so that we can understand these important things?

If God created through the process of evolution over long ages, He could have told us that, but He didn't. He gave us an account that gives a young earth chronology and specifically told us multiple times—including personally inscribing in the Ten Commandments—that He created all things in six days.

This is really an issue of God's credibility and ability to communicate. Either God is capable of giving us an accurate account of what happened or He is not. And if He is capable and the account was still wrong, then this implies that God purposely gave us erroneous information. In short, this would make God a liar.

Myth 1: "While the Bible may be 'inspired,' by God, it's not 'inerrant' and parts of it are just myth"

Suggested Videos:

Myth 1: https://genesisapologetics.com/myth-1/
The Bible and Isaiah 53: https://youtu.be/qAH_-Du2428
The Bible and History: https://youtu.be/6okZJlw84lo

Overview

Inerrancy refers to God's original Word having no errors. Inerrancy is important because the question of ultimate authority is of the highest importance to the Christian. It's not just a theological or philosophical issue—it's one that permeates our lives, thoughts, attitudes, perspective, and ultimately our behaviors.

We can't offer the world a *reliable gospel* if it comes from an *unreliable Scripture*. How can we offer the truth on any issue if we're suspicious of errors everywhere? For example, airline pilots will ground their planes even with the most minor of faults, knowing that one flaw can destroy confidence in the whole machine. If you pick your car up after being serviced and find out they missed something simple, wouldn't that call into question the rest of their work?

The entire core message of the Gospel, including sin, redemption, and forgiveness, is rooted in Genesis history. If these core events are not true, how can we trust the theology behind them? Did Jesus die for the sins of a mythical Adam who lived in a mythical garden?

The Bible itself claims to be much more than myth—it claims to be God's Word delivered through human authors to all humankind. Passages like 2 Peter 1:21 and 2 Timothy 3:16 assure us that God Himself authored the Scriptures. The process by which God produced the Scriptures is sometimes called the inspiration of Scripture, because 2 Timothy 3:16 says that, "All Scripture is given by the *inspiration* of God" (emphasis added). The Greek word translated "given by the inspiration of God" is *theopneustos*, literally, "God-breathed." God "breathed out" the Words of the Bible! Because of this, everything it says is completely reliable, making it the only sure foundation for the Christian in all matters of faith and life (2 Timothy 3:17). Psalms 119:89 also makes clear that God's Word is "fixed" or "settled" in Heaven.

Jesus confirms this by saying that not even a dot on a letter will pass away from God's Word until heaven and earth pass away. He also prayed to the Father saying, "Sanctify them by Your truth. Your word is truth." Jesus also confirmed that Moses produced the Torah, rather than it being a compilation of Ancient Near East mythology as some colleges teach today. Jesus referred to the Old Testament over 40 times and *every time* He treated it as real history, including Creation, the Flood, Sodom and Gomorrah, Jonah and the fish, and the account of Cain and Abel. To Jesus, the Bible was clearly inerrant, inspired, *and* historical.

The New Testament writers were so convinced that the writings of the Old Testament were the actual words of God that they even claimed "Scripture says" when the words quoted actually came directly from God. In Romans 9, Paul accepted that God delivered His Word directly to Moses. Paul also treats Isaiah's words as God Himself speaking.[9] In Acts 4, both Peter and John affirmed the creation account in the 4th commandment written by God. The believers who heard Peter and John also acknowledged that David wrote Psalm 2 *by the Holy Spirit.*

Having established that Scripture teaches that it is God's authoritative Word, let us now consider some of the ways we can evaluate the validity of the Scriptures. First, we will look at the New Testament.

There are some classic historical tests we can use to demonstrate the validity of the New Testament writings: First, we can determine whether *what we have today matches what was written originally.* Second, we can evaluate whether *the recorded events describe true, historical events.* Let's see how the Bible holds up to each of these tests.

Putting the Reliability of Scripture to the Test

One way to apply the first test is to look at the *time gap* between the original writing and the copies that still exist today. Ancient manuscripts like the New Testament were written on fragile material such as papyrus.[10] This required ancient writers to continually make new copies. Copying documents by hand is a time-consuming, laborious task, and understandably, errors sometimes creep into copies. Over time, as copies are made of copies, deviations from the original text due to copying errors can accumulate. However, the closer the copy is to the original, the greater chances that it more accurately represents the original.

Table 2. How the New Testament Compares to Other Ancient Writings.[11]

Author/Work	Date Written	Earliest Copies	Time Gap	Num. Copies
Homer (Iliad)	800 BC	400 BC	400 yrs.	643
Herodotus (History)	480–425 BC	AD 900	1,350 yrs.	8
Thucydides (History)	460–400 BC	AD 900	1,300 yrs.	8
Plato	400 BC	AD 900	1,300 yrs.	7
Demosthenes	300 BC	AD 1100	1,400 yrs.	200
Caesar (Gallic Wars)	100–44 BC	AD 900	1,000 yrs.	10
Tacitus (Annals)	AD 100	AD 1100	1,000 yrs.	20
Pliny (Natural) Secundus (History)	AD 61–113	AD 850	750 yrs.	7
New Testament (Frag)	AD 50–100	AD 114	50 yrs.	5,366
New Testament (Books)		AD 200	100 yrs.	
New Testament (Most Content)		AD 250	150 yrs.	
New Testament (Complete)		AD 325	225 yrs.	

Table 2 reveals two important facts. First, when we evaluate the number of New Testament manuscripts we have compared to other famous works of antiquity, the Bible exceeds them all with 5,366 manuscripts![12] Adding the copies from other languages (such as Latin, Ethiopic, and Slavic) results in more than 25,000 manuscripts that pre-date the 15th century printing press! By comparison, the runner-up historical text (Homer's Iliad) has only 643.[13] Having more copies means that we can have greater certainty that the words of the New Testament have been preserved accurately because we can compare copies with one another and correct for copying mistakes. Second, we can also see that the time span between the original and these copies is closer than any other work compared. There is more.

Even if all the copies of the Bible from AD 350 to today were destroyed, the entire New Testament (except for only 11 verses)[14] could be reconstructed *using only quotations* by the Early Church Fathers in the first few hundred years after Christ! This is because the Church Fathers frequently quoted large sections of Scripture in their letters to each other.

Next, we can test to see if *what was written down actually happened.* The gospels written by Matthew, Mark, and John were written with or by *direct eyewitnesses* of the events in Jesus' life. Luke, a physician, wrote the account of Jesus' life for Theophilus, a high-ranking official.[15] Luke said: "Many have undertaken to draw up an account of the things that have been fulfilled among us, *just as they were handed down to us by those who from the first were eyewitnesses and servants of the word.*" Luke continues to state that he carefully vetted his account of Jesus' life and ministry: "With this in mind, since I myself have carefully investigated everything from the beginning, I too decided to write an orderly account for you, most excellent Theophilus, so that you may know the certainty of the things you have been taught."

Other New Testament writers had similar testimonies: First John 1:3 states: "We proclaim to you what we have seen and heard, so that you also may have fellowship with us..."

Second Peter 1:16 says: "For we did not follow cleverly devised stories when we told you about the coming of our Lord Jesus Christ in power, but we were eyewitnesses of His majesty."

We should also consider that 11 of the 12 disciples died terrible deaths—being killed for their unchanging testimony of who Christ was—and of His resurrection. They were so sure that Christ was who He claimed to be that they signed their testimonies with their own blood! Who would die for a resurrection that never happened? Paul said that without the resurrection, "we are of all men the most pitiable," if indeed they suffered persecution for a falsehood.

It's also incredible that numerous Bible prophecies have come true over the years—even prophecies that we now can confirm were written *before* the actual events occurred. For example, Isaiah 53 specifically foretold Christ's trial, crucifixion, and burial.

Isaiah 53 and the Dead Sea Scrolls

In 1947, shepherds chasing a lost sheep in the caves above the Qumran Valley northwest of the Dead Sea made one of the most significant archaeological discoveries of our time— the Dead Sea Scrolls. Over 900 scrolls were found in numerous clay jars, and 200 of the scrolls include numerous sections and fragments of every book in the Old Testament except Esther.

One of the most significant scrolls is called the "Great Isaiah Scroll," which includes the same Book of Isaiah that we have today in modern bibles but dates to 125 BC.[16] The Isaiah Scroll is significant for two reasons: (1) it was written before Christ was yet born, and it includes Chapter 53 which contains clear prophecies about the torture, death, burial, and resurrection of Christ; and (2) its discovery now allows us to compare three versions of the Bible representing different time periods: Pre-Christ Dead Sea Scroll, AD 930, and today. Table 3 provides a word-by-word comparison of these three versions so you can see for yourself how reliable the transmission process has been through the millennia:

Table 3. Comparison of Isaiah 53 between the Dead Sea Scrolls, the Aleppo Codex, and the Modern Bible.[17]

Verse	Dead Sea "Great Isaiah" Scroll (125 BC)	Aleppo Codex (AD 930)	Modern Translation (NIV)
1	Who has believed our report and the arm of YHWH [(1)] to whom has it been revealed?	Who would have believed our report? And to whom hath the arm of the LORD been revealed?	Who has believed our message and to whom has the arm of the LORD been revealed?
2	And he shall come up like a suckling before us and as a root from dry ground there is no form to him and no beauty to him and in his being seen and there is no appearance that we should desire him.	For he shot up right forth as a sapling, and as a root out of a dry ground; he had no form nor comeliness that we should look upon him, nor beauty that we should delight in him.	He grew up before him like a tender shoot, and like a root out of dry ground. He had no beauty or majesty to attract us to him, nothing in his appearance that we should desire him.
3	He is despised and rejected of men, a man of sorrows and knowing grief and as though hiding faces from him he was despised and we did not esteem him.	He was despised, and forsaken of men, a man of pains, and acquainted with disease, and as one from whom men hide their face: he was despised, and we esteemed him not.	He was despised and rejected by men, a man of sorrows, and familiar with suffering. Like one from whom men hide their faces he was despised, and we esteemed him not.
4	Surely our griefs he is bearing and our sorrows he carried them and we esteemed him beaten and struck by God and afflicted.	Surely our diseases he did bear, and our pains he carried; whereas we did esteem him stricken, smitten of God, and afflicted.	Surely he took up our infirmities and carried our sorrows, yet we considered him stricken by God, smitten by him, and afflicted.
5	and he is wounded for our transgressions, and crushed for our iniquities, the correction of our peace was upon him and by his wounds he has healed us.[(2)]	But he was wounded because of our transgressions, he was crushed because of our iniquities: the chastisement of our welfare was upon him, and with his stripes we were healed.	But he was pierced for our transgressions, he was crushed for our iniquities; the punishment that brought us peace was upon him, and by his wounds we are healed.
6	All of us like sheep have wandered each man to his own way we have turned and YHWH has caused to light on him the iniquity of all of us.	All we like sheep did go astray, we turned every one to his own way; and the LORD hath made to light on him the iniquity of us all.	We all, like sheep, have gone astray, each of us has turned to his own way; and the LORD has laid on him the iniquity of us all.
7	He was oppressed and he was afflicted and he did not open his mouth, as a lamb to the slaughter he is brought and as a ewe before her shearers is made dumb he did not open his mouth.	He was oppressed, though he humbled himself and opened not his mouth; as a lamb that is led to the slaughter, and as a sheep that before her shearers is dumb; yea, he opened not his mouth.	He was oppressed and afflicted, yet he did not open his mouth; he was led like a lamb to the slaughter, and as a sheep before her shearers is silent, so he did not open his mouth.

43

8	From prison and from judgment he was taken and his generation who shall discuss it because he was cut off from the land of the living. Because from the transgressions of his people a wound was to him.	By oppression and judgment he was taken away, and with his generation who did reason? for he was cut off out of the land of the living, for the transgression of my people to whom the stroke was due.	By oppression and judgment he was taken away. And who can speak of his descendants? For he was cut off from the land of the living; for the transgression of my people he was stricken.
9	And they gave wicked ones to be his grave and [3] rich ones in his death although he worked no violence neither deceit in his mouth.	And they made his grave with the wicked, and with the rich his tomb; although he had done no violence, neither was any deceit in his mouth.	He was assigned a grave with the wicked, and with the rich in his death, though he had done no violence, nor was any deceit in his mouth.
10	And YHWH was pleased to crush him and He has caused him grief. If you will appoint his soul a sin offering he will see his seed and he will lengthen his days and the pleasure of YHWH in his hand will advance.	Yet it pleased the LORD to crush him by disease; to see if his soul would offer itself in restitution, that he might see his seed, prolong his days, and that the purpose of the LORD might prosper by his hand:	Yet it was the LORD's will to crush him and cause him to suffer, and though the LORD makes his life a guilt offering, he will see his offspring and prolong his days, and the will of the LORD will prosper in his hand.
11	Of the toil of his soul he shall see {+light+} and he shall be satisfied and by his knowledge shall he make righteous even my righteous servant for many and their iniquities he will bear.	Of the travail of his soul he shall see to the full, even My servant, who by his knowledge did justify the Righteous One to the many, and their iniquities he did bear.	After the suffering of his soul, he will see the light [of life] and be satisfied; by his knowledge my righteous servant will justify many, and he will bear their iniquities.
12	Therefore I will apportion to him among the great ones and with the mighty ones he shall divide the spoil because he laid bare to death his soul and with the transgressors he was numbered, and he, the sins of many, he bore, and for their transgressions he entreated.	Therefore will I divide him a portion among the great, and he shall divide the spoil with the mighty; because he bared his soul unto death, and was numbered with the transgressors; yet he bore the sin of many, and made intercession for the transgressors.	Therefore I will give him a portion among the great, and he will divide the spoils with the strong, because he poured out his life unto death, and was numbered with the transgressors. For he bore the sin of many, and made intercession for the transgressors.

Notes: (1) The tetragrammaton (YHWH) is one of the names of the God of Israel used in the Hebrew Bible. (2) There is a scribal thumb print over lines 10 to 12 in the Dead Sea "Isaiah" Scroll (lines 10–12 include verses 5–7 in modern Bibles). However, while this obscures some letters, all letters are "reconstructible with certainty" (see: *http://www.ao.net/~fmoeller/qum-44.htm*); (3) a scribbled word probably the accusative sign "eth."

While variation exists between versions due to translational differences, Table 3 shows that scribes maintained an incredibly high degree of similarity between copies over millennia. In fact, regarding this specific chapter in Isaiah, renowned Christian philosopher and apologist Norman Geisler writes:

> Of the 166 words in Isaiah 53, there are only 17 letters in question. Ten of these letters are simply a matter of spelling, which does not affect the sense. Four more letters are minor stylistic changes, such as conjunctions. The remaining three letters comprise the word "light" which is added in verse 11, and does not affect the meaning greatly. Furthermore, this word is supported by the Septuagint and IQ Is [first cave of Qumran, Isaiah scroll]. Thus, in one chapter of 166 words, there is only one word (three letters) in question after a thousand years of transmission—and this word does not significantly change the meaning of the passage.[18]

How is this possible? How can these three different documents—being translated and transcribed over a 2,000-year timeframe—have such *incredible* similarity? One explanation is simply that God watched over the process. Practically speaking, He used many incredible scribes to do it. For example, the Talmudists (Hebrew scribes and scholars between AD 100 and AD 500) had an incredibly rigorous system for transcribing biblical scrolls. Samuel Davidson describes some of the disciplines of the Talmudists in regard to the Scriptures:[19]

> A synagogue roll must be written on the skins of clean animals, prepared for the particular use of the synagogue by a Jew. These must be fastened together with strings taken from clean animals.

Every skin must contain a certain number of columns, equal throughout the entire codex. The length of each column must not extend over less than 48 or more than 60 lines; And the breadth must consist of thirty letters. The whole copy must be first-lined; And if three words be written without a line, it is worthless. The ink should be black, neither red, green, nor any other color, and be prepared according to a definite recipe. An authentic copy must be the exemplar, from which the transcriber ought not in the least deviate. No word or letter, not even a yod, must be written from memory, the scribe not having looked at the codex before him... Between every consonant the space of a hair or thread must intervene; Between every new parashah, or section, the breadth of nine consonants; Between every book, three lines. The fifth book of Moses must terminate exactly with a line; But the rest need not do so. Besides this, the copyist must sit in full Jewish dress, wash his whole body, not begin to write the name of God with a pen newly dipped in ink, and should a king address him while writing that name, he must take no notice of him.

Why is Isaiah 53 so important to Christians? It's important because Isaiah 53 includes at least 12 highly specific prophecies regarding the life, death, and resurrection of Christ. The details in this chapter would not be nearly as important if they were written after Christ's birth, but the fact that we can confirm that the chapter was in fact written before Christ proves beyond reasonable doubt both the accuracy and Divine authorship of the Bible. Consider these 12 prophecies, originally written by Isaiah about 700 years before Christ was even born, alongside references of their New Testament fulfillments:

1. He would not be widely believed (John 1:10–12).
2. He would not have the look of Majesty (Luke 2:7).
3. He would be despised and suffer (Matthew 26:67–68; 27:39–43).
4. He would be concerned about health needs (Matthew 8:17) and would die for our sins (1 Peter 2:24).
5. His pain/punishment would be for us (Matthew 28:20; Romans 4:25).
6. He would not respond to charges (Matthew 26:63).
7. He was to be oppressed and killed (Matthew 26:65–68).
8. He was associated with criminals during life and at death (Matthew 27:38, 27:57–60).
9. He would be buried in a rich man's tomb (Isaiah 53:9).
10. He would be crushed, suffer, and die, yet live (Luke 23:44–48, 24:36–44).
11. He would bear our sins (1 Peter 2:24).
12. He would have a portion with the great (Philippians 2:8–11).

Now that we have the Dead Sea Scrolls, we can confirm that these prophecies were *written before Christ even walked the earth*! How could anyone fulfill each of these prophecies, many of which happened after Christ's death and were clearly out of His control (i.e., if He wasn't God)? Finally, consider these prophecies about Christ that were all penned before He was born, and their fulfillments:[20]

Table 4. Forty-three (43) Prophecies Fulfilled by Jesus.

Prophecies About Jesus	Old Test. Scripture	New Testament Fulfillment
Messiah would be born in Bethlehem.	Micah 5:2	Matthew 2:1; Luke 2:4–6
Messiah would be born of a virgin.	Isaiah 7:14	Matthew 1:22–23; Luke 1:26–31
Messiah would come from the line of Abraham.	Genesis 12:3, 22:18	Matthew 1:1; Romans 9:5
Messiah would be a descendant of Isaac.	Genesis 17:19, 21:12	Luke 3:34
Messiah would be a descendant of Jacob.	Numbers 24:17	Matthew 1:2
Messiah would come from the tribe of Judah.	Genesis 49:10	Luke 3:33; Hebrews 7:14
Messiah would be heir to King David's throne.	2 Sam. 7:12-13; Isa. 9:7	Luke 1:32–33; Romans 1:3
Messiah's throne will be anointed and eternal.	Ps. 45:6–7; Daniel 2:44	Luke 1:33; Hebrews 1:8–12
Messiah would be called Immanuel.	Isaiah 7:14	Matthew 1:23
Messiah would spend a season in Egypt.	Hosea 11:1	Matthew 2:14–15
Children would be massacred at Messiah's birthplace.	Jeremiah 31:15	Matthew 2:16–18
A messenger would prepare the way for Messiah.	Isaiah 40:3–5	Luke 3:3–6
Messiah would be rejected by his own people.	Psalm 69:8; Isaiah 53:3	John 1:11; John 7:5
Messiah would be a prophet.	Deuteronomy 18:15	Acts 3:20–22
Messiah would be preceded by Elijah.	Malachi 4:5–6	Matthew 11:13–14
Messiah would be declared the Son of God.	Psalm 2:7	Matthew 3:16–17
Messiah would be called a Nazarene.	Isaiah 11:1	Matthew 2:23
Messiah would bring light to Galilee.	Isaiah 9:1–2	Matthew 4:13–16
Messiah would speak in parables.	Ps.78:2–4; Is. 6:90	Matthew 13:10–15, 34–35
Messiah would be sent to heal the brokenhearted.	Isaiah 61:1–2	Luke 4:18–19
Messiah would be a priest after Melchizedek's order.	Psalm 110:4	Hebrews 5:5–6
Messiah would be called King.	Ps. 2:6; Zech. 9:9	Matt. 27:37; Mark 11:7–11
Messiah would be praised by little children.	Psalm 8:2	Matthew 21:16

Messiah would be betrayed.	Ps. 41:9; Zech. 11:12–13	Luke 22:47; Mt:14–16
Messiah's betrayal money used to buy a potter's field.	Zechariah 11:12–13	Matthew 27:9–10
Messiah would be falsely accused.	Psalm 35:11	Mark 14:57–58
Messiah would be silent before His accusers.	Isaiah 53:7	Mark 15:4–5
Messiah would be spat upon and struck.	Isaiah 50:6	Matthew 26:67
Messiah would be hated without cause.	Psalm 35:19, 69:4	John 15:24–25
Messiah would be crucified with criminals.	Isaiah 53:12	Matthew 27:38; Mark 15:27–28
Messiah would be given vinegar to drink.	Psalm 69:21	Matthew 27:34; John 19:28–30
Messiah's hands and feet would be pierced.	Ps. 22:16; Zech. 12:10	John 20:25–27
Messiah would be mocked and ridiculed.	Psalm 22:7–8	Luke 23:35
Soldiers would gamble for Messiah's garments.	Psalm 22:18	Luke 23:34; Matthew 27:35–36
Messiah's bones would not be broken.	Exodus 12:46; Ps.34:20	John 19:33–36
Messiah would be forsaken by God.	Psalm 22:1	Matthew 27:46
Messiah would pray for his enemies.	Psalm 109:4	Luke 23:34
Soldiers would pierce Messiah's side.	Zechariah 12:10	John 19:34
Messiah would be buried with the rich.	Isaiah 53:9	Matthew 27:57–60
Messiah would resurrect from the dead.	Ps.16:10; Ps. 49:15	Matthew 28:2–7; Acts 2:22–32
Messiah would ascend to heaven.	Psalm 24:7–10	Mark 16:19; Luke 24:51
Messiah would be seated at God's right hand.	Psalm 68:18, 110:1	Mark 16:19; Matthew 22:44
Messiah would be a sacrifice for sin.	Isaiah 53:5–12	Romans 5:6–8

Summary

These are some of the reasons why tens of thousands of ministry professionals have signed the Bible Petition, affirming that the Bible alone, and in its entirety, is the infallible written Word of God in the original text and is, therefore, inerrant in all that it affirms or denies on whatever topic it addresses.[21]

This leaves us at a crossroads: either the Bible is divinely inspired and true in all it says including historical events, or it is not. It can't be true and untrue at the same time. What gives us the right to pick and choose which parts we want to believe? If the Bible is not based in real history but claims to be historical, it's not authoritative, and if it's not authoritative, why follow and obey it? If it is not true, then there's no reason to submit to it. Since the Bible is true, however, it has authority over all matters of life.

When Christians understand that the Scripture is inerrant *and* historically valid, their faith and their minds are fused together—like two pieces of a puzzle. This provides a solid foundation for their faith in the work of Christ as revealed in the Words of Christ, resulting in a solid foundation for their faith, a real faith that produces good fruit.

Study Questions

1. Why is it important that the Gospel (the "good news" of salvation through Christ) is based on the Bible as a whole being reliable, all the way back to Genesis?

   _____

   _____

   _____

   _____

   _____

   _____

   _____

   _____

2. Read 2 Peter 1:21, 2 Timothy 3:16, and Psalms 119:89. How are these passages similar? Connected?

   _____

   _____

   _____

_____

_____

_____

_____

_____

3. Jesus regarded the Old Testament accounts of Creation (Mark 10:6, Matthew 19:4), Noah's Flood (Matthew 24:36–44), and other supernatural events such as Sodom and Gomorrah and Jonah and the Great Fish as actual, historical events. He also prayed to the father saying, "Sanctify them by Your truth. Your word is truth" (John 17:17) and confirmed that Moses produced the Torah (the first five books of the Bible). How does that impact how we should view these accounts in the Bible?

_____

_____

_____

_____

_____

_____

_____

_____

4. How do the Dead Sea Scrolls confirm that Scripture has been reliably transmitted over the centuries? How do they reveal that Scripture was *inspired*?

_____

_____

_____

_____

_____

_____

_____

_____

5. How does Isaiah 53 confirm that Jesus was the Messiah?

_____

_____

_____

_____

_____

_____

_____

_____

_____

Myth 2: "The Bible's account of Creation is only metaphorical, the six creation days are not ordinary days, and creation really unfolded over millions of years"

Suggested Videos:

Myth 2: https://genesisapologetics.com/myth-2/
Six Days: https://youtu.be/pjx88K8JTY8
Young/Old Earth: https://youtu.be/QzEzkrMdgIs
The Bible and History: https://youtu.be/6okZJlw84lo
Radiometric Dating: https://youtu.be/fg6MfnmxPB4

The Bible clearly says that God created in six days just thousands of years ago. However, the secular narrative (based on radiometric dating), claims the earth is billions of years old. Does radiometric dating debunk the Bible's timeline? Does it really make any difference what someone believes about the age of the earth? We'll answer these important questions in this chapter.

Significance of Believing in a "Young Earth"

Most students who have graduated from Christian colleges can name at least four different views of the Genesis Creation account: the literal/historical "young earth" view, the Day-age view, Progressive Creation, and the Gap Theory. Unfortunately, many of these same students would also likely say "we don't really know because we weren't there" and/or "it doesn't really matter what you believe."

Sadly, these couldn't be further from the truth. First, as we will see below, we *can* reliably know when God created because He's clearly told us in His Word. Second, it really *does* matter what we believe because our beliefs shape our actions, attitudes, and choices.

How we regard God's Word (authoritatively or just as a guidebook) has direct implications on how we live our lives. Today's students want to know: If truth doesn't start on the first page, then how many pages do I need to turn in the Bible until I run into truth?" If truth doesn't start on the first page, the rest is up for grabs.

Honest readers will admit that the text clearly means what it says in Genesis 1: *God created in six normal days.* Readers who spend time investigating the genealogies listed in Genesis 5, 10, and 11 will also admit that it's a *historical* narrative with *real* people, real dates, and real lifespans that lead directly back to Adam, the first human who was miraculously created out of the dust by God. In fact, in just the first 11 chapters of Genesis, 87 patriarchs are given along with their birth, lifespan, or death years! Sounds like a history book, doesn't it?

Why would God give us these genealogies? Certainly, He knew that people today would read them and ponder the historicity of these early accounts. Let's face it: people who regard the historicity of these accounts and their implications (a recent creation made "out of nothing" by God) develop a much different worldview about life, origins, and our purpose than those who do not believe these accounts. These beliefs shape our choices, attitudes, and behaviors. Indeed, the Bible lays out the foundation for understanding all of life with a much different story than the world does!

Readers will also notice that there's certainly no way to insert millions of years within or between these genealogies. While scholars may quibble about hundreds of years and the ancient texts upon which our modern bibles are based may differ by a couple thousand years, honest readers will admit there's certainly no room for millions of years. Without filtering what's clearly written in Genesis through secular science textbooks, the reader is left with a young earth.

If one submits to the *authority* of Scripture, relying on Scripture to tell them about the basic framework of the history of the world, their origins, and their purpose, their lives will radiate outward from these understandings. Their entire worldview will be different from someone who does not believe. For example, to a Christian who holds that Genesis 1 is literal history:

- God is the all-powerful Creator who spoke Creation into existence (Psalm 33:9, Hebrews 11). Each person will give an account to this all-powerful Creator.
- God started out everything "very good" without bloodshed and disease, but man's sins brought death, corruption, bloodshed and disease. Cancer is man's fault, not God's.
- God did not use a slow, random, murderous process of natural selection and survival of the fittest to bring the many types of life on earth into existence.
- The fossil record reflects God's judgement on a world turned corrupt after the Fall.
- Racism has no foundation because there aren't millions of years for the human line to splinter off into various "races." A recent dispersion at the Tower of Babel means all people groups are closely related, separated by only hundreds of generations.

Submitting to biblical truth—beginning in Genesis—results in all these benefits and more. A person whose worldview is anchored to biblical foundations will also be constantly reminded that they are *in the world but not of the world*, and that the world has fallen into the deception of the enemy (1 John 5:19). They will see the lie of "deep time" espoused in the majority of secular schools, media outlets, and state parks. These two perspectives are very different: It's either death and suffering over millions of years before Adam or a perfect creation marred by original sin just thousands of years ago. Scripturally, death does not come before sin—it was sin that brought death to God's perfect creation—a curse in which we are still living (Romans 8).

Despite the stark contrast between these two viewpoints, many Christians attempt to reconcile them, accepting one of the "hybrid" perspectives mentioned at the beginning of this chapter. To be clear, a person can be saved by the blood of Jesus and still believe in deep time, so we're not making belief in a recent creation the test of one's salvation. But if they believe in long ages, they will not likely grow fully in their faith because their roots may be prevented from penetrating into the deepest parts of Scripture—the parts that happened *when we weren't there to see them.* These are the parts that require the most faith and trust in His Word to believe.

Replacing the obvious history of Scripture with the millions-of-years narrative from the world undermines the authority of Scripture and erases the logical foundation for the Gospel of Christ because it places death (the consequence of sin) before sin. Just try to explain the Gospel to someone without referring to a *historical* view of Genesis. It is a difficult (if not impossible) task.

Many who buy into the idea of long ages have not thought about the consequences, the worst of which is simply this: *it undermines the gospel.* Understanding how does not take long and can be done by asking a few questions:

1. Were death, suffering, and disease part of God's "very good" creation for billions of years? (Genesis 1:27–30).
2. If there was no first man Adam to bring sin into the world, then why do we need the last Adam to free us from the penalty and curse of sin? (Romans 5:12–21)
3. If God made Adam and Eve "from the beginning of creation," then how are we to account for billions of years before man's supposed emergence through evolution? (Mark 10:2–9)
4. The Bible records that Adam was created in the image of God (Genesis 1:28) and that this image was passed down to his descendants (Genesis 5:3). If we do not all descend from Adam, how can we bear the image of God? Only those who bear the image of God can be

saved (1 Corinthians 15:49), and thus only descendants of Adam can be saved.

Many Christians feel pressured to be accepted by the mainstream and thus buy into the idea of millions of years. Some just haven't fully thought through why they believe the way they do. Most of the time they really don't know how much it's costing them and their families.

Because I "converted" to a Biblical Creationist late in life, my two older children were raised by Christian parents who had "undeclared" positions on origins. Their questions about the dinosaurs and cavemen were always prefaced with "if the earth is young, the answer is... but if the earth is old, the answer is..." With this type of conditional answer to many of life's very basic questions, what they were really hearing was "maybe dad doesn't know," or (even worse) "maybe the Bible, which is supposed to be the most definitive book for me to build my life upon, doesn't have an answer, or perhaps it even doesn't even have the correct answer." Fortunately, I had the opportunity to re-solidify their faith before they went to college.

Blessings will come to those who completely embrace the whole Scripture. For example, Jesus said, "For whoever is ashamed of Me *and My words*, of him the Son of Man will be ashamed when He comes in His own glory, and in His Father's, and of the holy angels" (Luke 9:26).

The Book of Psalms is likely one of the most frequently read books of the Bible. The very beginning of this book starts out by stating those who believe in and meditate on the Torah (the first five books of Bible, led by Genesis) will be blessed in every way:

> Blessed is the man who walks not in the counsel
> of the ungodly, nor stands in the path of sinners,
> nor sits in the seat of the scornful; But his delight
> is in the law [Torah] of the Lord, and in His law
> he meditates day and night. He shall be like a
> tree planted by the rivers of water, that brings

forth its fruit in its season, whose leaf also shall not wither; and whatever he does shall prosper. (Psalms 1:1–3).

The Bible presents the unchangeable, perfect, and true Words of God Himself, including what God says about the history of our world—history that occurred before the Great Flood of Noah's time thousands of years ago. Since the Bible says that God cannot lie and that He even honors His Word along with His own name, we ought to treat Scripture with the reverence it deserves.[22]

How does Scripture Teach a "Young Earth"?

Determining the age of the earth using the Bible is a straightforward, two-step process: (1) Determine whether the six days in Creation Week were *ordinary days*. This leads us to Adam, who was supernaturally created by God (i.e., he didn't evolve) on the Sixth Day of Creation; (2) Determine how long ago Adam lived using the genealogies in Genesis.

We know that the six days in Genesis 1 were *ordinary days* (not six long ages) because the Hebrew word for day (*yom*) is qualified with "*evening*," "*morning*," and a *number* for each of the six days in the Creation Week. When *yom* is used with any of these qualifiers throughout Scripture, it always means an *ordinary day*. We'll take an in-depth look at this topic in this section.

Determining *how long ago* Adam lived is a straightforward process because Genesis records the **fathering age** and total **lifespan** of Adam's descendants all the way to Abraham and his sons (most directly; in some cases indirectly).[23] Summing the lifespans in these genealogies leads to Creation Week either about 6,000 or 7,600 years ago (based on the Masoretic or Septuagint texts, respectively[24]). We'll take a closer look at these genealogies below.

In addition to these interlinking and overlapping genealogies, the Genesis account itself provides two clues that lead to our understanding that Adam and Eve were the first humans who were created immediately after God had created everything else. The first clue is God's commission given to humans to take *dominion* over (that is, to wisely manage) everything God made during Creation Week. The second is God bringing the animals to Adam "to see what he would call them" (the *kinds* of animals, not every species) (Genesis 2:20). Thus, the Genesis account itself forbids inserting millions of years of animal death and life (e.g., some "dinosaur era") before Adam and Eve were present to take dominion over Creation and name the animal kinds.

The Days in Genesis 1

The Hebrew word for "day" (*yom*) is used over 2,000 times in the Old Testament. In some instances, it means a period of time or an era, but in the vast majority of instances it means an ordinary day.

In the first chapter of Genesis, it's clear that *yom* means an ordinary day. The first time *yom* is used in the Bible is Genesis 1:5: "God called the light Day, and the darkness He called Night. And the **evening** and the **morning** were the first **day**" (v. 5). Notice that in marking the end of the First Day of Creation Week, the word day (*yom*) is qualified by "evening," "morning," and a number (day one). This pattern— evening/morning/number—repeats for each of the six days in Genesis 1, so the entire Creation Week is described by days that are qualified as ordinary days.

The word *yom* is used over 400 times in the Old Testament along with a number, like "first day." In every case, it always means an ordinary day. *Yom* is used with the word "evening" or "morning" 23 times, and "evening" and "morning" appear together without *yom* 38 times, and in all 61 instances the text refers to an ordinary day. It seems God wanted to make it clear to us. He said "evening" and "morning," then a day with a number.

Because God is all-powerful, He could have just created everything in an instant, but He didn't. He chose to take six days because He was setting up a *system of days* and a context for our lives and how the world works.

Genesis 1:14 states that God established "lights in the firmament of the Heavens to divide the day from the night" and that they would be used for "signs and seasons, and for days and years." Here, two of the most basic units of time—days and years—are *linked*, their duration being determined by the fixed movements of the earth in reference to the sun.

Need further convincing? Consider that God wrote the Ten Commandments *with His own hand* (Exodus 31:18, "He gave Moses two tablets of the Testimony, tablets of stone, *written with the finger of God.*"). When God wrote the Fourth Commandment, He stated:

> For in six days the Lord made the heavens and the earth, the sea, and all that is in them, and rested on the seventh day. Therefore, the Lord blessed the Sabbath day and hallowed it. (Exodus 20:11).

Here are the six days again—this time in the Ten Commandments no less—and *written by the hand of God.* What do you think God wanted the Israelites to believe when He said this? Long ages or real days? God was talking about the Sabbath, which is one day a week. If God meant "thousands of years" when He said "day," then that would make for a really long work week! It seems from this passage that *God told us what to believe,* and how to model our lives: six days of work followed by a day of rest.

Our weeks have been like this ever since the beginning. After all, we don't have a five-day week, do we? Back in the 1920's the Soviets tried a five-day week and a six-day week, but it was a major failure. So, they went back to a seven-day week. The seven-day week seems to be hardwired into human existence—as if God designed us to work six days and take a rest on the seventh.

Taking a careful look at the context of the Ten Commandments, it wouldn't make much sense if nine out of the Ten Commandments were literal and one was figurative. How could lying, adultery, and stealing be figures of speech? They were all rather black and white—just like the days of Creation. We certainly don't work for six long ages, but six days, then we rest. God gave us a day of rest to reset our internal clocks. God didn't have to give us that seventh day, but He knew we needed it.

When fending off scholars who were developing the idea that God really didn't create everything in six days (but rather only a single day), the famous reformer Martin Luther warned: "When Moses writes that God created heaven and earth and whatever is in them in six days, then let this period continue to have been six days, and do not venture to devise any comment according to which six days were one day. But if you cannot understand how this could have been done in six days, then grant the Holy Spirit the honor of being more learned than you are."[25]

Doesn't the Bible Say That "a Day to the Lord Can Be like a Thousand Years"?

Many Christians ask, "Doesn't the Bible say that 'a day to the Lord can be like a thousand years.'" Second Peter 3:8 actually says that "one day is with the Lord *as* a thousand years, and a thousand years *as* one day." This passage is talking about God's judgment and His patience with man's rebellion. It's not talking about Creation Week.

Notice that the verse says one day is *as* a thousand years. It's a *simile* showing that God is *outside* of time, because He is the *Creator* of time. We know that those who use this verse to say that one day in Creation Week took one thousand years are forcing that view onto the Bible since they never assert the last part of the verse: that a thousand years of Old Testament history all happened in one day.

This passage is saying that God is outside of time and is unaffected by it, but to man, a day is still a day. It's not defining a day, because it doesn't say, "a day *is* a thousand years." It's not even talking about the days of Creation. Rather, both times—a day and a thousand years—are described from God's perspective because "with the Lord" these times are the same. The verse is saying that with God, time has no meaning, because He is eternal, outside of the dimension of time that He created. So a thousand years, a day, and a second all are the same to Him. He sees all of history *simultaneously*.

Because *yom* is used over 2,000 times in the Old Testament, it's important to look at the context in which it is used. In the passage in Peter, the writer is referring to Psalm 90:4, which says, "For a thousand years in Your sight are like yesterday when it is past, and like a watch in the night," yet a night watch does not last 1,000 years, does it? Here, 1,000 years is just a figure of speech, a comparison to make something more vivid. In context, 2 Peter 3 is saying that although it may seem like a long time to us, the Lord still keeps His promises.

If the days in Genesis 1 were thousand-year periods (or longer), then we are presented with a major logistical problem involving plants and pollinators. Genesis 1 says that God made the plants on day *three*, while flying insects like bees were created on the *fifth* day. How could the plants created during the third thousand-year time period survive and reproduce without pollinators until the fifth thousand-year time period? It really makes the most sense to interpret the days in Genesis 1 as literal, approximately 24-hour days, with all of the inter-dependent parts of Creation working as a whole.

How Do We Get a 6,000-Year-old Earth from the Bible?

Genesis 5 lists ten patriarchs that lived before Noah's Flood. For each of these patriarchs, their age

before having the son named, the years they lived **after** having a son, and their **total** years are listed:

Genesis 5: The Family of Adam

And Adam lived **130** years, and begot a son in his own likeness, after his image, and named him Seth. After he begot Seth, the days of Adam were 800 years; and he had sons and daughters. So all the days that Adam lived were 930; and he died. Seth lived **105**, and begot Enosh. After he begot Enosh, Seth lived 807, and had sons and daughters. So all the days of Seth were 912; and he died. Enosh lived **90** years, and begot Cainan. After he begot Cainan, Enosh lived 815 years, and had sons and daughters. So all the days of Enosh were 905 years; and he died. Cainan lived **70** years, and begot Mahalalel. After he begot Mahalalel, Cainan lived 840 years, and had sons and daughters. So all the days of Cainan were 910 years; and he died. Mahalalel lived **65** years, and begot Jared. After he begot Jared, Mahalalel lived 830 years, and had sons and daughters. So all the days of Mahalalel were 895 years; and he died. Jared lived **162** years, and begot Enoch. After he begot Enoch, Jared lived 800 years, and had sons and daughters. So all the days of Jared were 962 years; and he died. Enoch lived **65** years, and begot Methuselah. After he begot Methuselah, Enoch walked with God 300 years, and had sons and daughters. So all the days of Enoch were 365 years. And Enoch walked with God; and he was not, for God took him. Methuselah lived **187** years, and begot Lamech. After he begot Lamech, Methuselah lived 782 years, and had sons and daughters. So all the days of Methuselah were 969 years; and he died. Lamech lived **182** years, and had a son. And he called his name Noah, saying, "This one will comfort us concerning our work and the toil of our hands, because of the ground which the Lord has cursed." After he begot Noah, Lamech lived 595 years, and had sons and daughters. So all the days of Lamech were 777 years; and he died. And Noah was **500** years old, and Noah begot Shem, Ham, and Japheth.

Let's take a closer look at this passage focusing on Adam, the first one listed in Genesis 5:

Age Before Having First Son	Years Lived After Having a Son	Total Years
And Adam lived **130** years, and begot a son in his own likeness, after his image, and named him Seth.	After he begot Seth, the days of Adam were **800** years;	So all the days that Adam lived were **930**; and he died.

Notice that three numbers are given for Adam: his age before having Seth (130), the years he lived after fathering Seth (800), and his total lifespan (930 years). Because these three sets of numbers are provided for all ten patriarchs before the Flood, it's easy to assemble an inter-connected, overlapping chain that goes straight back to Adam, the very first man created:

Table 5. Genesis 5 Genealogies.

Order	Patriarch	Age at Birth of Named Son	Years Lived After Son	Total Age	Sum of Years
1	Adam	**130**	800	930	130
2	Seth	**105**	807	912	235
3	Enoch	**90**	815	905	325
4	Cainan	**70**	840	910	395
5	Mahalalel	**65**	830	895	460
6	Jared	**162**	800	962	622
7	Enoch	**65**	300	365	687
8	Methuselah	**187**	782	969	874
9	Lamech	**182**	595	777	1056
10	Noah	**500**	450	950	1556

Notice that adding the ages in the "age at birth of named son" column sums to a total of 1,556 years (as shown in the far-right column). Because Noah was 600 years old when the Flood came (Genesis 7:6), adding 100 years to Noah's age in the table

(500) places the Flood at 1,656 years after Creation. Genesis 10 and 11 provide the next set of genealogies that allow us to move up the timescale to Abraham who lived about 2,000 BC, as shown in the chart below.

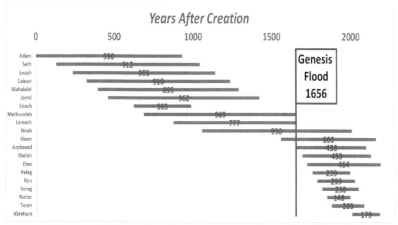

Figure 2. The First 20 Patriarchs since Creation.

Notice that the lifespans of the pre-Flood patriarchs overlapped. Their lifespans also declined in a systematic way over time. These give us confidence that Genesis records an accurate timeline (see our FAQ: Lifespans Before the Flood: How Did People Live to Be 900 Years Old Before the Flood?[26]). The time that elapsed from Adam, the first man created on the Sixth Day of Creation Week, to Abraham was about 2,000 years. The time from Abraham to the time of Christ is about another 2,000 years. The time from Christ until now is another 2,000 years. So, the straight chronology from the Bible places Creation about 6,000 years ago.

Scholars have debated possible gaps in these genealogies for years, but even if there were gaps in these genealogies, we cannot insert them without basically rewriting the text to fit our own preferences. Further, such gaps may allow for hundreds of additional years, but certainly not thousands or millions!

Even many secular historians would agree with Christian scholars that Abraham lived about 2,000 BC, or about

4,000 years ago. If that's true, with Abraham being the 20th patriarch after Adam listed in the line-up provided in Genesis, we can't have multiple thousands of years' worth of missing genealogies based on the (evolutionary) idea that "modern" humans emerged from other hominid species tens or hundreds of thousands of years ago!

For example, some creation views (e.g., Progressive Creation) agree with the evolutionary timeline that places the evolution of modern humans *at least* 50,000 years ago (most estimates are higher).[27] But even with this conservative position, there would be 44,000 years of "missing" genealogies in Genesis (4,000 genealogy years from Genesis, plus the 2,000 years from Christ to present)! Just how can one fit an extra 40,000+ years into the 4,000 years shown on Figure 2 (ten times the number of years accounted for in the Bible)? Under this model, the Bible's genealogies would not be a reliable record.

An additional consideration with the lifespans in Genesis is that many of them *overlap*, so there's not a lot of room for gaps. Further, the Genesis genealogies are repeated or referenced in other parts of the Bible, including the books of 1 Chronicles, Jude, Matthew, and Luke. This shows that the New Testament and Old Testament's human authors also believed in the Genesis genealogies as *real history*.

Finally, consider the fact that Jesus referred to the Old Testament over 40 times. Every single time He treated the Old Testament literally and historically. For instance, in Mark 10:6 Jesus mentioned that God created man and woman at the "beginning of Creation"—not long ages after Creation. Jesus also references other Old Testament accounts as true events, such as Noah's Flood, the destruction of Sodom and Gomorrah, Jonah and the great fish, and many others.

Despite what some would say, the Bible's Creation account is not so vague that it's subject to each person's unique spin. The Bible clearly narrates how God created everything over a six-day period. What else could God have meant when He wrote with His own hands—and in the 10 commandments no less—that He created in six days, and even wanted us to

66

model our lives after the same weekly cycle? Did Jesus or any of the New Testament writers "update" what God said? Certainly not—He wanted us to believe—back then and still today—that He created in six days.

Wait a Minute! Doesn't "Science" Prove the Earth is Billions of Years Old?

Secular scientists date the Earth to about 4.5 billion years old by using selected radiometric dating results. Ultimately, what they call "deep time" serves as the very *foundation* of evolution theory. High school biology books openly acknowledge this necessary connection:

> Evolution takes a long time. If life has evolved, then Earth must be very old. Geologists now use radioactivity to establish the age of certain rocks and fossils. This kind of data could have shown that the Earth is young. If that had happened, Darwin's ideas would have been refuted and abandoned. Instead, radioactive dating indicates that Earth is about 4.5 billion years old—plenty of time for evolution and natural selection to take place.[28]

But as we show here, geologists do not use radioactivity to establish the age of certain rocks. They instead use selected radioactivity results to confirm what they need to see. As discussed in previous chapters, this viewpoint, being secular, contradicts God's stated Word in Genesis and even the Ten Commandments, where He wrote with His own hand that He created the heavens, Earth, sea, and all that is in them in six days (Exodus 20:11).

Belief in deep time rests upon evolution's required time. That's sure putting a lot of faith in something that can't be tested through *direct observation*. After all, plenty of assumptions go into the calculations.

The **Technical Appendix** provides a section that reviews the details behind radiometric dating, but keep in mind that only two key "fatal flaws" are necessary to debunk the inferences made by radiometric dating.

The **first fatal flaw** is that it relies upon *untestable assumptions*. The entire practice of radiometric dating stands or falls on the veracity of four *untestable* assumptions. The assumptions are untestable because we cannot go back millions of years to verify the findings done today in a laboratory, and we cannot go back in time to test the original conditions in which the rocks were formed. If these assumptions that underlie radiometric dating are not true, then the entire theory falls flat, like a chair without its four legs.

The **second fatal flaw** clearly reveals that at least one of those assumptions must actually be wrong because radiometric dating *fails to correctly date rocks of known ages*. For example, in the case of Mount St. Helens, we watched rocks being formed in the 1980s, but when sent to a laboratory 10 years later for dating, the 10-year-old rocks returned ages of hundreds of thousands to millions of years. Similarly, some rocks return radiometric "ages" twice as old as the accepted age for earth. Most rocks return conflicting radiometric "ages." In these cases, researchers select results that match what they already believe about earth's age (see the **Technical Appendix** for details of this study and several others like it).

Study Questions

1. Why is it important to rely upon God's Word the Bible to inform us about the distant past that we cannot see, test, or repeat (e.g., Creation)?

   _____

   _____

   _____

   _____

   _____

_____
_____
_____
_____
_____

2. What clues from Scripture lead to the conclusion that the six days of Creation Week were "ordinary" days?

_____
_____
_____
_____
_____
_____
_____

3. How can we stunt our growth as Christians if we turn what God wrote as history into a mythical account?

_____
_____
_____
_____
_____
_____
_____
_____

4. How do the genealogies in Genesis chapters 5 and 11 allow for us to estimate the age of Creation?

_____
_____
_____
_____
_____

_____

_____

_____

_____

5. What are the two "fatal flaws" with radiometric dating?

_____

_____

_____

_____

_____

_____

_____

6. If God really created over millions of years by allowing chance processes and "survival of the fittest" to bring about new "kinds" of creatures, what would that say about God's character?

_____

_____

_____

_____

_____

_____

_____

_____

Myth 3: "Genesis 1 and 2 provide two different accounts of creation"

Suggested Videos:

Myth 3: https://genesisapologetics.com/myth-3/

Many professors today promote the idea that Genesis 1 and 2 provide two different, even contradictory, accounts of Creation. At first blush, this may seem to be the case. But taking a careful look reveals something different. Let's find out why. Before we start, first consider that both chapters are inspired *and* historical—at least Jesus believed so when He quoted from both Genesis 1 and 2 in Matthew 19.

Looking at the big picture helps us understand how Genesis is laid out. While our Bibles today break Genesis into 50 chapters, the original text is actually broken into 11 sections, called *toledotes* (pronounced: "Toll-Dotes") which means "to bear" or "to generate" in Hebrew.

Genesis 1 provides the introduction—the overview of the creation of the entire universe in six days, which precedes the first toledote that begins in Genesis 2 verse 4: "These are the generations of the heavens and of the earth…" Genesis 1:1 through 2:3 provides a complete overview of the six days of Creation in a step-wise way, with each creation day starting out with "God said," followed by His creative works on that day, then concluded by "there was evening and morning" and a mention of the numerical day.

Genesis 2 is not concerned with the *steps* of the overall Creation account, but rather focuses on the events of Day 6, including the creation of Adam, the Garden of Eden and its river systems, Adam's instructions for the Garden, naming the animals, the creation of Eve, and the institution of marriage. *None* of these details are in the first Chapter of Genesis; they are saved for the second chapter that sets the stage for the third, which is the fall of man and the curse of sin, both of which happened in the Garden. The second chapter also does not mention important Creation events from the first chapter, such as the creation of earth, atmosphere, oceans, sea creatures, land, and the sun and stars—*showing that it was not attempting to be a second account of creation.* These two chapters actually tie into each other, with each chapter providing important details not in the other.

Some say that it appears that plants were created *after* people in Genesis 2, apparently conflicting with the Genesis 1 account of plants being made on Day 3 and man on Day 6. Genesis 2:5–7 says: "Before any plant of the field was in the earth and before any herb of the field had grown. For the Lord God had not caused it to rain on the earth, and there was no man to till the ground; but a mist went up from the earth and watered the whole face of the ground. And the Lord God formed man of the dust of the ground..."

In this passage, these verses call the plants: "plants *of the field*" and "herbs *of the field.*" These terms are more specific than the "grass, herbs, and trees" described in Day 3 of Genesis 1 because none of these are accompanied with the "of the field" description. Hebrew scholar Dr. Mark Futato defines "plants of the field" as "wild shrubs of the steppe or grassland" and "herbs of the field" as "cultivated grain."[29] Both make sense, especially given the context that describes there being "no man to till the field" and no rain yet.

Then, in the very next chapter we see it is these very "herbs of the field" that are cursed with "thorns and thistles" that Adam would have to till and farm "by the sweat of his brow" as a consequence of the Fall (Genesis 3:17–18). Indeed, because of Adam's sin, he would no longer have it easy. Instead of eating from abundant fruit trees in the garden, he would need to till the ground, contend with thorns and thistles, and grow crops for food.

The next contention that some people bring up with the Genesis 2 account is that verse 19 states, "Out of the ground the Lord God formed every beast of the field and every bird of the

72

air, and brought them to Adam to see what he would call them." It's the word "formed" which gets people thinking the animal kinds were created right then and there—after man, and before woman—unlike the sequence in Chapter 1 where humans were created last. So, were the animals created *after* Adam? Actually, they weren't. The verse is simply stating the source and origin of the animal kinds, which were formed from dust and spoken into existence by God.

Also notice that God put Adam in charge over all the animals, taking dominion over all Creation. In Hebrew, the precise tense of a verb is determined by the *context*. Genesis 1 makes it clear that the animals were created *before* Adam, so Hebrew scholars would have understood the verb "formed" to mean "had formed" or "having formed," which is how many Bible translations state this passage (including Tyndale's translation, which predates the King James).

Moreover, Hebrew verbs focus on *completeness of action*, not past/present/future temporality. So, they do not have "tense" like English verbs. Instead, the past/present/future of an action verb is determined by context. Thus, in context with Genesis 1, Genesis 2:19, which uses a verb that denotes *completion of actions*, can be translated as "Now the Lord God *had formed* out of the ground all the beasts of the field and all the birds of the air."[30] Given this, the apparent disagreement with Genesis 1 disappears completely.

The extra details in the Genesis 2 account demonstrate several things. First, the account affirms Genesis 1 in *every way*, without contradiction. Second, we find that Genesis 1 and 2 are *complementary* rather than *contradictory*. Chapter 1 may be understood as Creation from God's perspective; it is the "big picture," an overview of the whole and the sequence of God's created works: light, atmosphere, vegetation, sun and stars, birds and fish, land animals and man. Chapter 2 views the more important aspects from man's perspective and expounds upon Day 6 events with details like the names of the first man and woman, their relationship with Creation, where they were first placed (in the Garden of Eden), naming the animals, and setting the stage for the events that would later occur in the garden.

Looking at it this way, the first two chapters of Genesis provide a cohesive and detailed account of Creation. They certainly don't represent two different accounts of Creation. They were produced by Moses, cited by Jesus, and referred to as authoritative by New Testament writers.

Study Questions

1. What are the primary differences between Genesis 1:1–2:4 and Genesis 2:5–25?

   _____

   _____

   _____

   _____

   _____

   _____

   _____

   _____

   _____

   _____

2. Why do you think Genesis 1 and 2 are laid out in such a way that Genesis 1 provides an overview and Genesis 2 narrows in on Day 6 events?

   _____

   _____

   _____

   _____

   _____

   _____

   _____

   _____

Myth 4: "Adam and Eve were not real people, only allegories used to describe the first humans"

Suggested Videos:

Myth 4: https://genesisapologetics.com/myth-4/
Human-Chimp DNA: https://youtu.be/Rav8sfuJFYc
Lucy Videos: www.genesisapologetics.com/lucy

Many professors in secular and even some Christian colleges place the Genesis Creation account on equal footing with mythological writings from the Ancient Near East. Indeed, one can look back in history and find many different accounts of human origins. What makes the Genesis account stand apart? Is there scientific evidence that supports the Bible's account of human origins? Let's look and find out.

First, the Bible is *very clear* about human origins: Genesis lays out who made us (God, or *Elohim* in the Hebrew), what we were made from (dust), how we were made (divinely spoken into existence), who we were made like (in God's image), our role in Creation (dominion), and our marital covenant for family. Scripture even includes when we were created during Creation week (Day 6) and the time in history, about 6,000 years ago based on the genealogies in Genesis.

Next, Scripture is *consistent* about this account, with every Bible contributor in both the Old and New Testaments holding to the same description of how we came to be, spanning 66 books over 1,500 years written by 40 writers in 3 languages on 3 continents. Billions of people over the millennia have regarded the Bible's account of origins as historical and quite literal. Were they all wrong?

Scripture is clear that that Adam was the *first man*[31] and Eve the *first woman*, the mother of the human race (Genesis 3:20). The Apostle Paul inseparably connects Jesus to Adam, with Jesus coming to redeem us from the curse of sin and death brought by Adam.[32] Paul also describes how Adam and Eve specifically—as individuals—fell into temptation.[33] The Gospel of Luke even connects Christ's genealogy to Adam and Adam's sons who lived after him. How could *that* be mythical?

Without a real Adam, a real garden, a real tree, and a real enemy that led Adam and Eve into sin, the consequences for sin laid out in Genesis 3 has *no foundation*. And without this, the Gospel and the entire New Testament has *nothing* to stand on. Because of the sinful nature we inherited from Adam, we are all in need of a Savior. That's the very foundation of the Gospel and the New Testament. Did Jesus die for the sins of a mythical Adam? Certainly not.

Unlike ancient mythological writings, the Bible makes the unique claim to be inspired so the pages of Scripture can be relied upon as *Words from God Himself*. The Jewish people and Christians have regarded Scripture with this level of reverence for millennia. In addition, Romans 1 says that all of Creation—including humans—are an obvious testimony to God's creative powers and invisible attributes, so people are without an excuse.

One of the most obvious evidences that humans are created is found in our hearing system.[34] Evolution is supposed to be a mindless, random process that takes place over millions of years. If this is the case, how did the human hearing system arise, with its five separate components that *don't function without the others*? Five separate parts to our hearing system all work in unison to enable us to hear, and *none* of the five make *any* sense by themselves. What good is an outer ear (engineered for capturing sound waves) if there's not an ear drum to capture the sound wave pulses? What good is a pulsing ear drum without the three tiny bones behind it that use leverage to amplify the sound signal by a factor of 1.7 and connect to a water-charged cochlea filled with fluid? The cochlea converts the mechanical leverage to a hydraulic system that amplifies the signal another 22 times. And what good is all of this without the 20,000 tiny hair cells (stereocilia) inside the cochlea that convert the fluid movement into an electrochemical signal that we can immediately comprehend as speech?

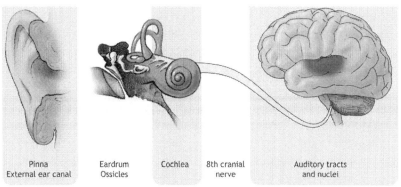

| Pinna | Eardrum | Cochlea | 8th cranial | Auditory tracts |
| External ear canal | Ossicles | | nerve | and nuclei |

Figure 3. Five Components of Human Hearing.[35]

Creationists see this as an intentional design by a Divine Creator. Evolutionists see this as the result of time + chance + mutations + natural selection. Which explanation makes more sense? What creature would have devoted its genes and energies to crafting non-functional ear parts for generations while it waited for the fifth precise part to spontaneously appear?

The eye might even be more convincing, containing hundreds of parts that had to be assembled to create the overall purpose and function for seeing. Random chance certainly doesn't have the intelligence needed for assembling different parts into a cohesive, inter-dependent system for sight to work.

Genetics and a Recent Creation[36]

A substantial amount of scientific evidence supports the recent creation described in the Bible. Little-known natural timeclocks from geology, paleontology, physics, and astronomy agree.[37] However, what does the field of genetics and modern genomics, one of the most rapidly advancing areas of science, have to offer in this regard? As it turns out, new discoveries using the tools of modern biotechnology also showcase recent creation and events associated with the global flood.

Genetics allow us to test the *predictions* of creation science versus evolution. Creation science predicts that the genomes of all the different kinds of living creatures were created perfect *in the beginning*. However, due to the curse on creation—related to man's sin and rebellion—combined with the damaging effects of time, we should see degradation, corruption, and the *loss* of genetic information. While evolutionists do recognize that information loss occurs in short scales, the long-term, grand Darwinian model predicts just the opposite of creationists. They believe that over vast amounts of time, genomes evolved and became *more* complex—gaining new information through random mutational processes. New results support biblical creation in unforeseen ways.

DNA

DNA is the most sophisticated information storage system in the known universe—nothing comes even close. In fact, over 10,000 DNA molecules can fit on the head of a pin and unfolding just one of them reveals six feet of instructions capable of building who you are. Stretching out DNA in the trillions of cells in your body could reach to the sun and back hundreds of times, while the combined weight of all this DNA would not be heavier than an egg.[38]

Perhaps you've heard that humans and chimps share 98% of their DNA.[39] But did you know that when they made this comparison, they ignored 18% of the chimp genome and 25% of the human genome?[40] Plus, the chimp genome is over 6% larger than ours! When they give the 98% similarity figure, it's based on cherry-picked DNA regions that were similar. Of course, humans and chimps have similar DNA; they're both mammals living in the same world with similar requirements for biological life. Our DNA is also similar to several other creatures. See the **Technical Appendix** for a more detailed discussion on this topic.

Mitochondrial DNA

Mitochondrial DNA (mtDNA) is unique because it comes only from the mother's egg, making it useful for tracing maternal ancestry. Since DNA was sequenced in 1981, researchers have been studying the mutation rates in mtDNA to try and estimate when different groups of people possibly diverged. Evolutionary researchers have based these timelines on the assumption that humans and chimps shared a common ancestor about five million years ago.

That date was based on counting the mtDNA and protein differences between all the great apes and timing their divergence using dates from fossils of one great ape's ancestor. This evolutionary assumption counts on the mtDNA mutation rate of about one mutation every 300 to 600 generations, or one every 6,000 to 12,000 years.[41]

Do these evolutionary assumptions hold up? Actually, recent studies have shown that the *actual, observed* mutation rates are *much faster* than the rates *assumed* by evolution theory, causing researchers to re-think the mtDNA clock they depend on for forensic investigations. This discovery was published in Nature Genetics by Dr. Parsons and his colleagues who investigated the mtDNA of 357 individuals from 134 different families representing 327 generational "events," which are counted by the number of times that mothers passed on mtDNA to their offspring. Parson's team showed that mutation rates actually occur at a rate of 1 every 33 generations, which was twenty-fold higher than estimates based on the theoretical 5-million-year timeline between chimps and humans.

This faster mutation rate discovery has stood fast even as the number of families in the study has doubled. For example, Howell's team analyzed mtDNA from 40 members of a family, finding an overall divergence rate of one mutation every 25 to 40 generations. Howell remarked that "Both of our studies (his and Parsons) came to a remarkably similar conclusion." Based on these findings, Howell warned that phylogenetic studies—studies that try to estimate the evolutionary branching between animal kinds—have "substantially underestimated the rate of mtDNA divergence."

As one science writer puts it, "evolutionists are most concerned about the effect of a faster mutation rate. For example, researchers have calculated that "mitochondrial Eve"—the woman whose mtDNA was ancestral to that in all living people—lived 100,000 to 200,000 years ago in Africa. Using the new clock, she would be a mere 6,000 years old."[42] This of course fits well within the Bible's timeline.

Based on their updated work, "identifying 220 soldiers' remains from World War II to the present," Parsons and Holland now have "new guidelines—adopted by the FBI as well—to account for a faster mutation rate." Studies have also confirmed that there was a massive DNA variability explosion that happened on earth just thousands of years ago, within the time frame of Noah's Flood and the Babel dispersion that occurred afterwards.

Human Origins and Fossils

If human evolution was true, we should find millions, thousands, hundreds, or even just a dozen "in-between" creatures alive today. But the score for these "transitional forms" today is *zero*. Not one creature lives today that can be branded half-ape and half-human. Instead, apes produce apes and humans produce humans, just like the Bible describes.

While college labs have replicas of supposed examples of transitions in the fossil record, careful study reveals they are either ape or human. Also, consider the fact that there are very, very few such "examples" (as pointed out below). Second, there are significant problems with the ape-to-human transition fossil icons that are used to support evolution's case (see discussion on the leading icon, Lucy, in the section below).

If "molecules-to-man" evolution was true, we would expect evidence of millions of in-between creatures that were still evolving along the ape-to-human progression. This was even a question that Charles Darwin, the 19th century promoter of evolution, asked about the historical fossil record. He wrote, "By evolution theory, innumerable transitional forms must have existed." He then asked, "Why do we not find them embedded in countless numbers in the crust of the earth?"[43] And, if human evolution were true, wouldn't we expect plenty of obvious "transitional creatures" between apes and humans in the crust of the earth? Darwin also asked, "Why is not every geological formation and every stratum full of such intermediate links? Geology assuredly does not reveal any such finely graduated organic chain." He followed this question by saying this was the "most obvious and serious objection which can be urged against the theory."[44] In other words, Darwin knew that his theory would be weakened if researchers in the future did not dig up millions of "in-between" creatures. According to Ian Tattersall, the Director of the American Museum of Natural History, if one were to collect all the alleged transitions between humans and apes, "You could fit it all into the back of a pickup truck if you didn't mind how much you jumbled everything up."[45] That's certainly not the footprint we expect evolution to leave behind.

What do we find today? Millions of ape-human half-breeds? No. In fact, we see over seven billion people on the planet who are all obviously human in every sense. Though some physical and many cultural differences display God's creativity, we are all the same kind—sons and daughters of Adam and Eve. People from various regions of the world can have families together. And what do we find in the crust of the earth after digging up billions of fossils for over 150 years since Darwin posed his "big questions" above? We find a handful of fossil creatures that better fit either the apes or human categories than they do the evolutionary category of ape-human transition.

It seems that Darwin wanted a *clear line of evidence* showing "half-way-in-between" ape-human creatures. We should have millions of their bones in earth's sediments. Yet we do not find them. What we see instead is what God said: mankind is made in the image and likeness of God, able to think, plan, worship, pray, and create. We also see variations *between* people groups as the Bible mentioned both in the Old (Genesis 9:18–19) and New Testaments.

For example, consider Acts 17:26–27, which records Paul's gospel presentation to pagans. It says, "And He has made from one blood every nation of men to dwell on all the face of the earth, and has determined their pre-appointed times and the boundaries of their dwellings, so that they should seek the Lord, in the hope that they might grope for Him and find Him, though He is not far from each one of us."

God made humans in His likeness, breathed His breath of life in them, and gave them charge over all of His Creation— just as we still see today. We see today just what the Bible specified ten times in the very first chapter: that all living creatures would reproduce and fill the earth each after their own kind.

About Lucy: The Leading Ape-to-Human Icon

Now we turn to the leading human evolutionary icon of today: Lucy. The year 1974 welcomed the famous "Lucy," a fossil form that bears the name *Australopithecus afarensis*. Lucy is arguably the most famous human evolution icon ever displayed in public school textbooks. Pictures and dioramas of Lucy inhabit countless museums and thousands of articles and dissertations.

Donald Johanson discovered Lucy in Ethiopia, Africa, and she quickly grew to be known as the supposed "missing link" between man and ape. At only about 3-1/2 feet tall and only about 60 pounds, she's very close to the size of small apes today.[46] The scientific name *Australopithecus* simply means "southern ape." Southern ape is a very appropriate name because, as you'll learn below, Lucy was just that—an ape!

Although public school textbooks often state that Lucy was our ancestor and they feature human-like drawings of her, the fossil evidence tells quite a different story. Over 40 years of Lucy research and about 20 more discoveries of her kind have raised new questions about its supposed evolutionary connection. Evolutionary research journals have substantiated ten fatal flaws regarding the claim that Lucy and her species are really our early ancestors.[47]

Fatal Flaw #1: Lucy's Skull

Even though only a few fragments of Lucy's skull were found, they revealed that her skull was about the same size as a chimpanzee. As Donald Johanson himself said, "Her skull was almost entirely missing. So knowing the exact size of Lucy's brain was the crucial bit of missing evidence. But from the few skull fragments we had, it looked surprisingly small."[48] Later estimates reveal that Lucy's brain was just one third the size of a human brain, which makes Lucy's brain the same size as the average chimpanze brain.[49]

Sir Solly Zuckerman, chief scientific advisor to the British government, said that the "*Australopithecine* skull is in fact so overwhelmingly ape-like, as opposed to human that the contrary position could be equated to an assertion that black is white."[50]

The skull in Figure 4 shows a rendition of what Lucy's skull may have looked like. Notice that the brown parts are what they found; the white parts used to fill in most of the skull are imagined. Notice its sloped and ape-like. It's also the size and shape that closely resembles a modern bonobo (a cousin to the chimp).

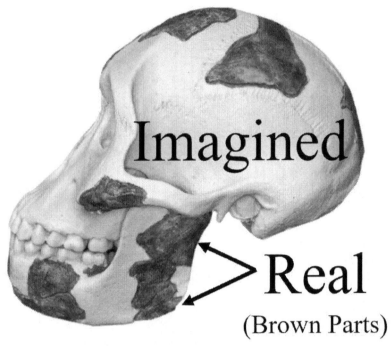

Figure 4. Lucy's Skull Reconstruction.[51]

Leading paleontologist, Dr. Leakey, stated, "Lucy's skull was so incomplete that most of it was 'imagination made of plaster of Paris,' thus making it impossible to draw any firm conclusion about what species she belonged to."

The Foramen Magnum

The foramen magnum is a hole in the bottom of a skull where the top of the spinal cord enters. The angle at which the spinal cord entered the foramen magnum of Lucy's species is nearly identical to a chimp's—indicating that Lucy's species walked hunched-over on all fours.[52]

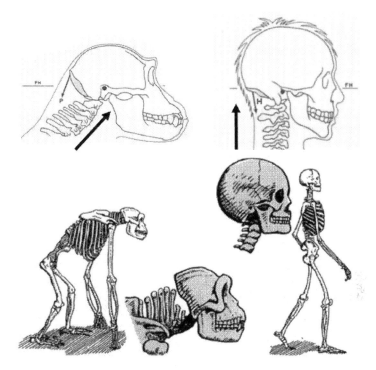

Figure 5. Foramen Magnum Angle and Walking Angle
Comparison (Chimps to Humans).[53]

One study conducted by evolutionary scientists showed
that the angle of the foraman magnum of Lucy's species was
"well below the range for our sample of modern humans but
overlaps the low end of the range for position between modern
apes and humans, but closer to the former (chimpanzees,
specifically)."[54]

Fatal Flaw #2: Lucy's Semicircular Canals

Humans have three semicircular canals embedded deep
within our ears that are integrated with our brains, heads, and
eyes to keep us balanced as we move. Apes' semicircular canals
orient to their up-tilted heads. To investigate how these
semicircular canals are involved in the movement of various

creatures, scientists have studied them in depth using advanced scanning techniques and making measurements of their different structures. *Australopithecines*, as well as other living and non-living apes, all have semicircular canals that fit ape-oriented heads that fit bodies designed for walking on all fours, whereas humans semicircular canals match upright, two legged locomotion.

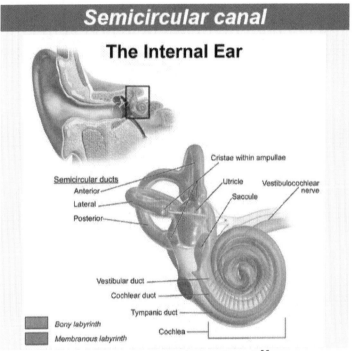

Figure 6. Semicircular Canal.[55]

In particular, they learned that the semicircular canals of *Australopithecines* were best suited for "facultative bipedalism,"[56] which means walking occasionally on two feet, just like many apes walk today. While this study focused on *Australopithecus africanus*—and Lucy's species has been labeled *Australopithecus afarensis*—they are anatomically similar.[57]

What about Lucy's species specifically? Dr. Bernard Wood conducted a study that revealed that the semicircular canals of Lucy's species "were more like those of chimpanzees than of modern humans. The fluid-filled semicircular canals are crucial in maintaining balance, and so all three lines of evidence suggest that the locomotion of *Australopithecus afarensis* was *unlikely to have been restricted to walking on two feet*"[58] (emphasis added).

Another report in the leading secular science journal *Scientific American*[59] reviewed the research conducted on a baby *Australopithecus afarensis*, stating: "Using computed tomographic imaging, the team was able to glimpse her semicircular canal system, which is important for maintaining balance. The researchers determined that the infant's semicircular canals resemble those of African apes and other *Australopithecines* (such as *Australopithecus africanus*). This, they suggest, could indicate the *Australopithecus afarensis* was not as fast and agile on two legs as we modern humans are."

One fascinating aspect of semicircular canals is that, while they all work together, each of them provides a separate sense of directional balance: "The superior canal detects head rotations on the anterior-posterior (side-to-side movement, like tilting the head toward the shoulders) axis. The posterior canal detects rotations on the sagittal plane (forward and backward movement, like sit-ups). The horizontal canal senses movement on a vertical basis, as the head rotates up-and-down on the neck."[60]

It just so happens that the two same canals that are most involved for helping us walk upright are the two canals that are *statistically significantly different*[61] between humans and chimps. Lucy's species clearly identifies with chimps. Dr. Spoor noted that two of the three semicircular canals in particular coordinate "upright bipedal behavior" because they are involved in "movements in the vertical plane" (i.e., upright walking). [62] Drs. Day and Fitzpatrick agree with this, stating: "The anterior and posterior canals of the human vestibular organs are enlarged in size relative to the horizontal canal whereas the three canals are more equal in size in other species. The significance of this is that the anterior and posterior canals are orientated to sense rotation in the vertical planes, *the movements that are important for controlling upright balance*"[63] (emphasis added).

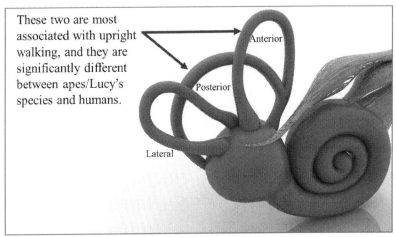

These two are most associated with upright walking, and they are significantly different between apes/Lucy's species and humans.

Anterior

Posterior

Lateral

Figure 7. Semicircular Canals.

What difference does this make? Well, think about it this way: If you had your semicircular canals surgically replaced with a chimp's, at the very least, you'd be really disoriented! Your head would feel level only when you were looking to the sky. You wouldn't be able to run with as much ease as you have now, since the same two semicircular canals that are significantly different between apes and humans help stabilize your head when running.[64]

Fatal Flaw #3: Lucy's Mystery Vertebra

In 2015, press releases started coming out and showing that, even after 40 years of study involving hundreds of scientists, one of Lucy's bones (a vertebra) didn't even belong to her![65] In fact, it didn't even belong to Lucy's species, but was from a *Theropithecus*, a type of baboon. Does that make you wonder if we're really dealing with bones from a single individual with Lucy? Especially when Lucy was put together from hundreds of bone fragments that were found scattered along a hillside?[66]

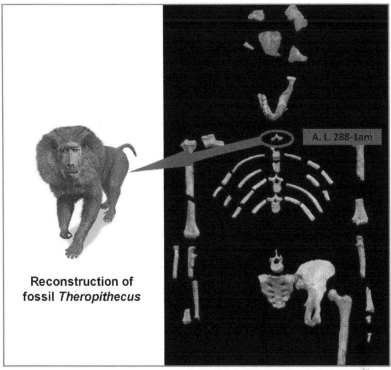

Figure 8. Incorrect Vertebra included in Lucy's Fossil.[67]

Fatal Flaw #4: Lucy's Pelvis

Next, we have Lucy's pelvis, which Johanson's team believed was "broken apart and then fused together during later fossilization..." which caused it to "be in an anatomically impossible position" and to "flare out like a chimp's pelvis."[68]

Their solution to this problem was to use a power saw to cut it apart and then piece it back together! After "fixing" the pelvis, they noted: "It was a tricky job, but after taking the kink out of the pelvis, it all fit together perfectly, like a three-dimensional jigsaw puzzle. As a result, the angle of the hip looks nothing like a chimp's, but a lot like ours..."[69]

Even secular scientists who hold to evolution have problems with Lucy's pelvis reconstruction, stating "We think that the reconstruction overestimates the width of this [pelvis] area, creating a very human-like sacral plane,"[70] and another stated, "The fact that the anterior portion of the iliac blade faces

laterally in humans but not in chimpanzees is obvious. The marked resemblance of AL 288-1 [Lucy] to the chimpanzee is equally obvious."[71] Charles Oxnard, evolutionist and author of the *Order of Man*, stated that her bones seemed to show that she was a "real swinger... based on anatomical data, *Australopithecines* must have been arboreal [tree-dwelling] ... Lucy's pelvis shows a flare that is better suited for climbing than for walking."[72] Isn't it interesting how these remarks from evolutionary scientists never make their way into public school textbooks? Instead, Lucy is typically shown walking upright, as shown in Figure 9.

Figure 9. Lucy in Public School Textbooks.[73]

Fatal Flaw #5: Lucy's Locking Wrists

Lucy had locking wrists like quadruped apes, not like humans.[74] This has been widely reported in both scientific journals as well as the general media. For example, even the *San Diego Union Tribune* reported, "A chance discovery made by looking at a cast of the bones of 'Lucy,' the most famous fossil of *Australopithecus afarensis*, shows her wrist was stiff, like a chimpanzee's, Brian Richmond and David Strait of George Washington University in Washington, D.C., reported. This suggests that her ancestors walked on their knuckles."[75] The study conducted by these scientists concluded: "Measurements of the shape of wristbones (distal radius) showed that Lucy's type were knuckle walkers, similar to gorillas."[76]

When interviewed about their study (published in *Nature*) they stated: "It suddenly occurred to me that paleoanthropologists had never looked at the wrists of Lucy or other important early human ancestors discovered since the early papers were published...." so while they were visiting the Smithsonian, they went to the cast collection, inspected Lucy's radius [forearm bone], and found that she had the "classic knuckle-walking feature." This became obvious when they "saw a ridge of bone on the lower forearm that prevented Lucy's wrist, like that of a chimpanzee or gorilla, from rocking backward, but allowed it to lock in an upright position for easy knuckle-walking."[77] Figure 10 highlights this "locking wrist" feature they found on Lucy's bones.

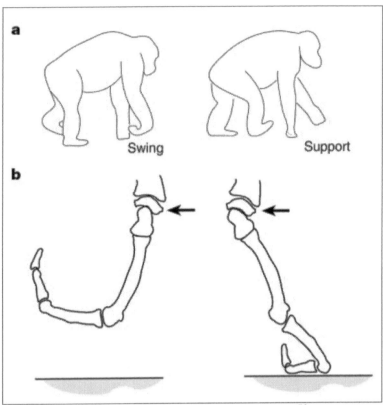

Figure 10. Lucy's Locking Wrist.[78]

The study conducted by Richmond and Strait revealed that Lucy had the same concave arm bone that joined with her convex wrist, creating a locking system that allowed for both swinging and stable knuckle-walking (as shown in Figure 11).

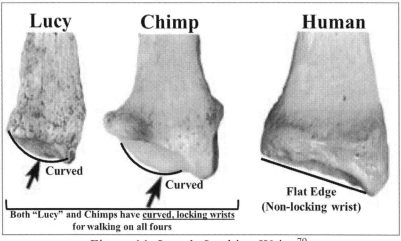

Figure 11. Lucy's Locking Wrist.[79]

Figure 11 shows a close-up view from the study. The arm bone on the far left is from Lucy; the one in the middle is from a chimp; and the one on the far right is human. Notice how Lucy's bone matches the chimp's—they both have the concave shape that allows the wrist to lock into place for knuckle walking. Humans do not have any angle for this whatsoever because we're not designed for walking on our hands!

Fatal Flaw #6: Lucy's Curved Fingers

Next, we'll take a look at the fingers of Lucy's species. Comparison of various apes, humans, and Lucy's species' finger curvatures reveal some major differences. Even evolutionary scientists have admitted that the curved fingers of Lucy's species were best suited for swinging in trees.[80] One study statistically compared various finger measurements from several different types of apes against humans, and grouped the fingers of Lucy's species in the same category as chimps and bonobos, and far away from human's straight fingers (see Figures 12 and 13).

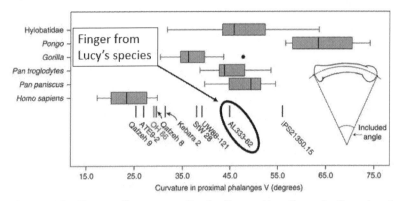

Figure 12. Finger Curvature Study Revealing Lucy's Species Is Categorized with Apes and Gorillas.[81]

Figure 13 shows a finger from one of Lucy's kind, showing significant curvature compared to human fingers, which are not curved.

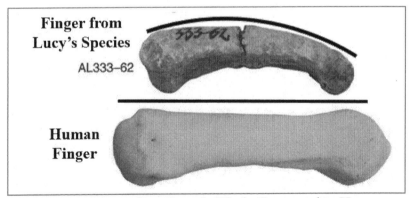

Figure 13. Finger from Lucy's Kinds Compared to Human Finger.[82]

Other examples of *Australopithecine* apes had curved fingers and ape-like limb proportions that point toward her kind as living in trees, so the same was probably true of Lucy.[83]

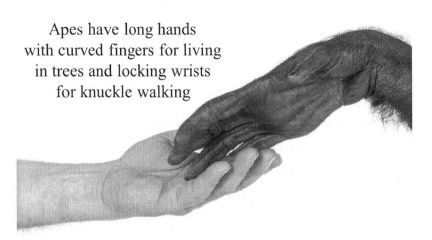

Apes have long hands
with curved fingers for living
in trees and locking wrists
for knuckle walking

Figure 14. Human and Chimp Hands.

Fatal Flaw #7: Lucy's Short Little Legs

Some evolutionary scientists have argued that Lucy's legs were much too short for upright walking. Some say she walked with a "bent-hip, bent-knee" method; some say she might have "shuffled"; some say she walked on all fours; some say she was bipedal. For example, Dr. Bill Jungers at the Stony Brook Institute in New York argued that "Lucy's legs were too short, in relation to her arms, for her species to have achieved a fully modern adaptation to bipedalism."[84] Drs. Stern and Sussman advocated that Lucy's species would have walked "bent-hip, bent-knee" method, much like a living chimpanzee, because of the number of skeletal features in their skeletons which are functionally associated with arboreality in living apes (e.g., curved phalanges, long trunk but short legs, etc.).[85] Dr. Hunt argued that the most efficient behavior for Lucy's species would have been "bipedal posture augmented with bipedal shuffling" as a consequence of anatomical compromise between the needs of terrestrial bipedality and arboreal climbing.[86]

Without any of Lucy's species alive today, one cannot know for certain how they moved around. But that hasn't stopped several scientists—from both the evolution and creation camps—from speculating about it. As we have reviewed in this section, however, plenty of evidence *from evolutionary scientists* indicates she likely walked on all fours (including her semicircular canals, skull, locking wrists, curved fingers, and now, her short legs).

Fatal Flaw #8: The Widespread Exaggeration of Lucy's Human-like Appearance

Lucy was originally found in *hundreds* of pieces before she was painstakingly glued together in the way they believed she was before she died. Even though many of the first reports that came out after Lucy was discovered stated that Lucy's skeleton was "40% complete,"[87] Lucy's discoverer (Johanson) clarified this in a book published 22 years after Lucy was found, stating: "Lucy's skeleton consists of some 47 out of 207 bones, including parts of upper and lower limbs, the backbone, ribs and the pelvis. With the exception of the mandible [lower jaw] the skull is represented only by five vault fragments, and most of the hand and foot bones are missing."[88] This computes to actually **23%** of the complete skeleton (47 ÷ 206), not "about 40%."

Numerous artists have drawn Lucy with human feet even though the fossil lacked both hand and foot bones. Frustratingly for those who care about truth, these illustrations continue to ignore subsequent finds, revealing that *Australopithecines* had curved ape fingers and grasping ape feet. Figure 15 shows how Lucy is represented at public exhibits, such as those found at the St. Louis Zoo and Denver Museum of Nature and Science.

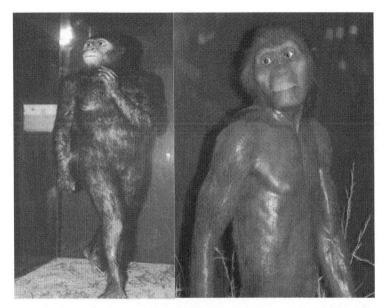

Figure 15. Lucy at Public Exhibits (Zoos and Museums). Lucy at the St. Louis Zoo (Left) and at the Denver Museum of Nature and Science (Right).[89]

Most Lucy models show her with white sclera of the eye visible, even though 100% of all apes alive today have eyes that look dark because the sclera is not visible. Do you think this was done to make her look more human-like?

It's amazing how they can find hundreds of bone fragments scattered across a hillside in a nine-foot radius[90] that supposedly lay in the soil for over 3 million years and reconstruct a human-like Lucy, complete with eyewhites displayed in museums around the world! At least one bone belonging to a completely different animal was mistaken for Lucy's for over 40 years. Were there others?

Figure 16. Making Lucy Look Human from Hundreds of Bones Fragments, Glue, and Imagination.

To further exaggerate Lucy's human-like appearance, some Lucy models don't even have hair! (see Figure 17).

Figure 17. Hairless Lucy Walking with her "Family," including Incorrect (Human) Feet and Hands. [91]

Fatal Flaw #9: Gender

A great deal of debate has emerged even over Lucy's gender, with some scientists arguing that the evidence shows she was actually a male! Articles with catchy titles have emerged such as "Lucy or Lucifer?[92] and more recently, "Lucy or Brucey?"[93] If evolutionists are so certain that we evolved from Lucy-like creatures, but they can't seem to even determine the gender of the leading human evolution icon, what other assumptions are being made?

Fatal Flaw #10: Falling out of a Tree to Her Death

Now we move onto the most recent news about Lucy. In 2016 the University of Texas had a team of orthopedic surgeons reveal the findings of a study that evaluated the numerous "compression" and "greenstick" fractures in Lucy's skeleton. A greenstick fracture goes by this name because it's the type of bone break that occurs under compression or fast bending—much like a green stick would break when such force is applied.

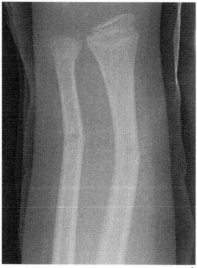

Figure 18. Greenstick Fracture.[94]

This team determined that Lucy most likely died while falling 40 feet out of a tree traveling 35 miles per hour, and was "conscious when she reached the ground" because of the way she tried to break her fall. Even the lead study scientist, John Kappelman, remarks, "It is ironic that the fossil at the center of a debate about the role of arborealism (living in trees) in human evolution likely died from injuries suffered from a fall out of a tree."[95] Yes, it is quite ironic that Lucy, the supposed human ancestor who walked on two feet, died while falling 40 feet out of a tree.

But they've even offered a "rescuing device," stating that "because Lucy was both terrestrial and arboreal, features that permitted her to move efficiently on the ground may have compromised her ability to climb trees, predisposing her species to more frequent falls." So, to save the embarrassment of the "bipedal ape" dying by falling out of a tree, they believe that she must have fallen out of a tree because she wasn't used to living in them anymore." That's quite a reach for a creature that supposedly lived over 3 million years ago!

Figure 19. Lucy, the Supposedly Bipedal Ape, Falling 40-Feet from a Tree to Her Death.[96]

Lucy Summary

In summary, consider these conclusions about Lucy that were drawn from leading evolutionary scientists:

- Dr. Charles Oxnard (professor of anatomy) wrote, "The *Australopithecines* known over the last several decades ... are now irrevocably removed from a place in the evolution of human bipedalism ... All this should make us wonder about the usual presentation of human evolution in introductory textbooks."[97]
- Dr. Solly Zuckerman heads the Department of Anatomy of the University of Birmingham in England and is a scientific adviser to the highest level of the British government. He studied Australopithecus fossils for 15 years with a team of scientists and concluded, "They are just apes."[98]
- Dr. Wray Herbert admits that his fellow paleoanthropologists "compare the pygmy chimpanzee to 'Lucy,' one of the oldest hominid fossils known, and finds the similarities striking. They are almost identical in body size, in stature and in brain size."[99]
- Dr. Albert W. Mehlert said, "the evidence... makes it overwhelmingly likely that Lucy was no more than a variety of pygmy chimpanzee, and walked the same way (awkwardly upright on occasions, but mostly quadrupedal). The 'evidence' for the alleged transformation from ape to man is extremely unconvincing."[100]
- Marvin Lubenow, Creation researcher and author of the book *Bones of Contention,* wrote, "There are no fossils of Australopithecus or of any other primate stock in the proper time period to serve as evolutionary ancestors to humans. *As far as we can tell from the fossil record,*

101

when humans first appear in the fossil record they are already human"[101] (emphasis added).

- Drs. DeWitt Steele and Gregory Parker concluded: "Australopithecus can probably be dismissed [from human evolution] as a type of extinct chimpanzee."[102]

In reality, the remains of these ape-like creatures occur in small-scale deposits that rest on top of broadly extending flood deposits. They were probably fossilized after Noah's Flood, during the Ice Age, when tremendous rains and residual volcanic explosions buried Ice Age creatures.[103] Answers in Genesis provides a rendition of what Lucy most likely looked like (Figure 20).

Figure 20. What Lucy Most Likely Looked Like
(Answers in Genesis Presentation Library).

Conclusion

If there's no historical Adam, there's no Gospel. If Adam and the Fall are not historical, then Jesus died for a mythological problem and He is a mythological savior offering us a mythological hope. Atheists also understand the problem of a mythical Adam and Eve: "No Adam and Eve means no need for a savior. It also means that the Bible cannot be trusted as a source of unambiguous, literal truth. It is completely unreliable, because it all begins with a myth, and builds on that as a basis. No fall of man means no need for atonement and no need for a redeemer."[104]

God made us on the sixth day of creation to name and take dominion over the entire animal kingdom. This happened just thousands of years ago. God sent His Son to redeems us from the Fall that happened when our real forefather sinned. We have been mercifully brought into a place of grace, forgiveness, and rest if we accept His sacrifice by confessing our sins and surrender our lives to Him.

Study Questions

1. What is the significance of Adam and Eve being created on the Sixth Day of Creation, and being charged to name and "take dominion" of all other created life? How does this differ from the theory of Evolution and where that places humanity?

2. What are the leading evidences from genetics/DNA research that substantiate a young creation?

_____

_____

_____

_____

_____

_____

_____

3. When it comes to the totality of the fossils that supposedly show ape-to-human evolution, Ian Tattersall, the Director of the American Museum of Natural History, stated: "You could fit it all into the back of a pickup truck if you didn't mind how much you jumbled everything up." What does this say about the evidence that we evolved from ape-like creatures over millions of years? Would you expect more fossils if evolution was true? Fewer?

_____

_____

_____

_____

_____

_____

_____

_____

4. What are the top characteristics that point to Lucy being only an extinct ape?

_____

_____

_____

_____

_____

_____

_____

_____

5. The theory of evolution asserts that we have no designer
    and ultimately no purposes. We just exist. How is this
    different from the Bible's case for Creation?

    _____

    _____

    _____

    _____

    _____

    _____

    _____

    _____

    _____

Myth 5: "The Bible's account of Noah's Flood is just myth and was drawn from writings from the Ancient Near East"[105]

Suggested Videos:

Myth 5: https://genesisapologetics.com/myth-5/
Noah's Flood Evidence: https://youtu.be/zd5-dHxOQhg
The Fossil Record: https://youtu.be/qHRYnm_J4ts

To investigate the myth that the Biblical Flood account is on par with "other myths" from the Ancient Near East, we'll look at the mechanism and process that best explains the Flood (Catastrophic Plate Tectonics, or "CPT"), the seaworthiness of the Ark (compared to the Ark from flood myths such as Gilgamesh), and answer common questions like "How could Noah fit all of the animals on the Ark?" and "How could all of the animals disperse around the world after the Flood?" We'll conclude by overviewing some of the worldwide flood legends and evaluating whether Noah's Flood was worldwide or local.

Catastrophic Plate Tectonics ("CPT")

The Bible records that the Flood commenced by the "fountains of the great deep" *breaking open*. The Hebrew term used for this is bâqa' (pronounced "baw-kah") which means to "cleave, rend, or break and rip open; to make a breach." This "cleaving and breaking/ripping open" couldn't describe what we see on the planet today any better.

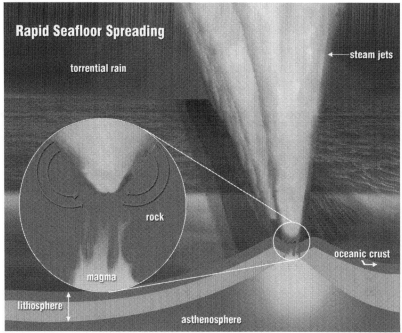

Figure 21. Fountains of the Great Deep Breaking Open (the Beginning of Noah's Flood).[106]

In 1994 six PhD scientists published a research paper titled, "Catastrophic Plate Tectonics: A Global Flood Model of Earth History,"[107] that substantiated this biblical aspect of the Flood. Their research revealed that fast-moving, subducting oceanic plates were responsible for the continents breaking apart and spreading to their current locations, in contrast to the evolutionary ideas of slow continental drift and equally slow seafloor spreading. Ongoing research in this area has shown that the model helps explain volcanoes, mountain ranges, the shapes and positions of continents, and the generation of global tsunamis that explain rock layers.

Genesis Apologetics worked with many of these leading Flood geologists to produce YouTube videos that visualize how CPT played such a large role in Noah's Flood.[108] Readers interested in a more technical explanation behind the catastrophic nature of the Flood are encouraged to view Dr.

Steve Austin's presentation titled, "Continental Sprint: A Global Flood Model for Earth History."[109]

Much of the fundamental research on the topic of CPT has been undertaken by Dr. John Baumgardner over the past 40 years. As a professional scientist, Dr. Baumgardner is known for developing TERRA, a finite element code designed to study flow of rock within the Earth's mantle. In 1997, US News and World Report described him as "the world's pre-eminent expert in the design of computer models for geophysical convection."[110] Baumgardner has applied TERRA to demonstrate that the Earth's mantle is indeed vulnerable to runaway instability and that this instability is capable of resurfacing the planet in the time span of just a few months. We'll review many of Baumgardner's findings below.

Brief summary of plate tectonics concepts

Scientists of both creation and evolutionary persuasions conclude that new ocean crust forms at ocean rift zones where two tectonic plates are moving apart. The plates in the rift migrate apart, magma rises to fill the gap, is cooled by ocean water, and solidifies to make a strip of new ocean crust. The two plates are each like a conveyor belt that moves away from the rift zone along one edge and usually toward a subduction zone along the other edge. At the subduction zone, the moving plate plunges into the mantle beneath and thus disappears from the surface.

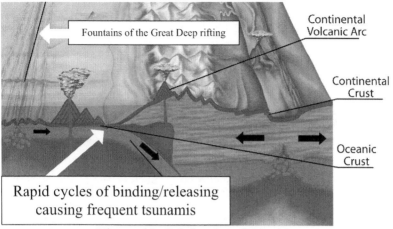

Figure 22. Subduction Overview.

The main difference between the creationist and secular understanding is that, in creationist understanding, during the Flood plate speeds were about five miles-per-hour instead of just a few inches per year, as they are measured to be today. The much higher speed is why the process during the Flood is referred to as *Catastrophic* Plate Tectonics.[111]

What evidence is there for plate tectonics?

The evidence supporting the concept of plate tectonics is overwhelming. Let's quickly tour some of the key evidences, starting first with the "big picture," then investigating some of the physical evidences in more detail.

Evidence 1: The continents fit together like puzzle pieces

One of the clearest evidences is that the continents fit together like puzzle pieces. While many school textbooks credit Alfred Wegener, a meteorologist, with the "discovery" that the continents "drifted" from an original super-continent (Pangea or similar configuration) to their current location, it was actually a creation scientist who brought this to light much earlier. His name was Antonio Snider-Pellegrini (1802–1885), a French geographer and scientist, who theorized about the possibility of continental drift. In 1858, Snider-Pellegrini published his book, La Création et ses mystères dévoilés ("The Creation and its Mysteries Unveiled") which included the image in Figure 23.

Figure 23. Snider-Pellegrini made these two maps in 1858, showing his interpretation of how the American and African continents once fit together before becoming separated.

Snider-Pellegrini based his theory on the Genesis Flood, the obvious shape and fitting of the continents, and the fact that plant fossils found in both Europe and the United States were identical.[112]

Modern mapping technologies and the help of bathymetric maps that reveal the shapes and contours of the continental shelf and the ocean floor allow us to clearly see that the continents were once connected and later torn apart. Figure 24 shows what earth looks like with all the ocean water removed. Without the oceans, the deep shelves on each side of the continents become visible and we can see how the continents fit together like puzzle pieces to shape an earth that used to be mostly a single land mass.

Interestingly, this perfectly fits the Genesis account: "Then God said, 'Let the waters under the heavens be gathered together into one place, and let the dry land appear'; and it was so. And God called the dry land Earth, and the gathering together of the waters He called Seas. And God saw that it was good" (Genesis 1:9–10). This is especially obvious when looking at the matching jagged edges of lower South America and Africa (see Figure 24).

Figure 24. Lower South America Matching Africa.[113]

We can also see how a notch of submerged land off the grand banks of Newfoundland fits nearly perfectly into a slot north of Spain (see Figure 25).

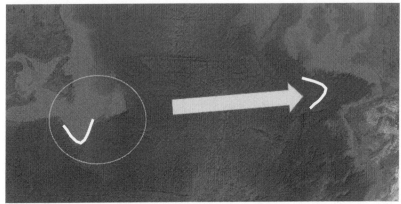

Figure 25. Submerged land off the Grand Banks of
Newfoundland fitting into a Slot North of Spain (Google Earth).

From a Biblical standpoint, the continents fit together so
well because of the catastrophic linear rifting that occurred
when the fountains of the great deep were "cleaved" and pulled
apart only a few thousand years ago.

Evidence 2: The Oceanic Ridge System

The oceanic ridge system covers more than 40,000 miles
and circles the earth 1.6 times over.

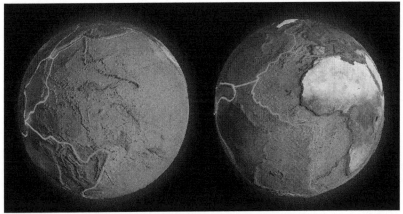

Figure 26. Oceanic Ridge System.

The Mid-Atlantic Ridge (MAR) represents one of the largest rifts left behind by the global seafloor spreading process. It looks like a giant baseball seam running around the face of the earth.

Figure 27. Mid-Atlantic Ridge (MAR).[114]

The MAR is part of the longest mountain range in the world and includes perpendicular faults along its entire length, known as transform faults, showing the formation of new seafloor involved a pulling apart of the ocean basin. The sharpness of the faults and the abrupt edges indicate that little time has expired since their formation. The raised and sloped features on each side of the rift also testify to the hot and buoyant rock that still lies beneath it. From a Biblical standpoint, the formation of the Atlantic basin occurred quickly during the Flood and then slowed down greatly to about an inch per year, as GPS measurements today indicate.

Evidence 3: Ring of Fire

The Ring of Fire is a 25,000-mile horseshoe-shaped string of oceanic trenches in the Pacific Ocean basin where about 90% of the world's earthquakes and a large fraction of the world's volcanoes occur.[115] It is also where most of the plate subduction is taking place today. From a Biblical perspective, this long belt of volcanoes and earthquakes marks the location where vast amounts of ocean plate was rapidly subducted into the earth's interior during the Flood. Today, by comparison, the speed of subduction is extremely slow, and the resulting earthquakes and tsunamis are dramatically less frequent.

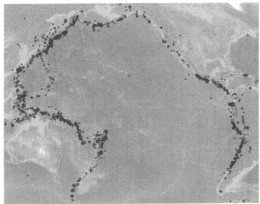

Figure 28. USGS 1900-2013 Earthquakes in the Ring of Fire.[116]

How is CPT different from the secular understanding of plate tectonics?

CPT is basically the expression at the earth's surface of a recent, massive, and rapid overturn of rock inside the region inside the Earth known as the mantle, which is the 1,800-mile thick layer of rock between the Earth's core and its crust. Regions of cooler rock in the upper part of the mantle have a natural tendency to sink downward toward the bottom, and regions of warmer rock at the bottom have a natural tendency to rise upward toward the surface. When conditions are right, this natural tendency for rising and sinking can "run away," such that both rising and sinking become faster and faster—up to a billion times faster. The force responsible for driving this behavior is simply gravity. From a Biblical perspective, the runaway episode responsible for CPT occurred during the Flood described in Genesis 6–8.

The possibility that runaway behavior might occur in the mantle was discovered decades ago in laboratory studies[117] that explored how mantle minerals deform at mantle temperature and stress conditions. These basic experiments revealed that mantle minerals weaken by factors of more than a billion for stress levels that can readily arise inside the earth. Computer experiments[118] later confirmed that episodes of runaway overturn in the mantle are inevitable under the right conditions because of this inherent weakening behavior demonstrated in these laboratory experiments.

What might be the consequences at the earth's surface of a runaway overturn event in the mantle? One notable consequence is that the tectonic plates at the earth's surface get caught up in the rapid flow of rock within the mantle beneath. In particular, the ocean plates that are currently diving into the mantle at the deep-ocean trenches during the overturn did so at a spectacularly accelerated pace. Likewise, in zones known today as spreading ridges (such as the Mid-Atlantic Ridge) where tectonic plates are moving apart from one another, the speed of separation during the overturn was dramatically higher.

Just how much faster would the plate motions during such an overturn event be compared with what is occurring today? This can be estimated based on the time frame provided in the Bible's account of the Flood and on the amount of plate motion associated with the part of the rock record that contains fossils of the plants and animals buried in the Flood. From these numbers one obtains a plate speed on the order of five miles-per-hour. A typical plate speed today, as measured by GPS, is on the order of a couple inches per year. The ratio of these two speeds is about one billion to one.

What are other noteworthy consequences of such rapid plate motions? One is that water on the ocean bottom in the zones where plates were moving apart so rapidly was in direct contact with the molten rock which was rising from below to fill the gap between the plates. This molten rock at about 1300° C converted the ocean water to steam at extremely high pressure. This steam organized to form in a linear chain of intense supersonic jets along the entire midocean ridge system. As these jets pierced the layer of ocean water above where they were formed, they entrained massive amounts of liquid seawater, which was lofted high above the Earth. This liquid water then fell back to the surface as rain. Hence, a direct consequence of rapid plate motions was persisting rain over much if not most of the earth.

A second prominent consequence of rapid plate motion was a rising sea level that flooded the land surface with ocean water. The rising sea level resulted from a decrease in the volume of the ocean basins. Behind that decrease was the loss of original cold ocean plate as it plunged into the mantle at an ocean trench and its replacement with new and much warmer ocean plate produced by seafloor spreading at a mid-ocean ridge. The new plate was on average 500–1000° C warmer than the cold plate it replaced. Because warm rock of a given mass has more volume than cold rock of the same mass, the ocean floor above new ocean floor was 0.6–1.2 miles higher than was the old ocean floor. As more and more new ocean floor was generated at mid-ocean ridges, while more and more of the

116

original ocean floor was removed by recycling into the mantle, the global sea level relative to the land surface rose by thousands of feet. Hence, a notable result of rapid plate motion was a rising sea level and a dramatic flooding of the continents by ocean water.

A third major consequence of the rapid plate motion is the generation of a huge number of giant tsunamis. In today's world, at an ocean trench where an oceanic plate is steadily slipping into the mantle, the adjacent overriding plate generally is locked against it and is bent downward as the other plate slides into the mantle (see Figure 29). As this motion proceeds, the overriding plate is deformed more and more in a spring-like manner until a stress limit is exceeded. At this point the two plates unlock, significant slip between the plates occurs, and the overriding plate returns to its original shape. Such an unlocking and slip event usually produces an earthquake. If the slip event is large enough it also can launch a tsunami. During the Flood, when plate speeds were a billion times higher than today, it is almost certain that this same locking and unlocking phenomenon also prevailed. The higher plate speeds and the huge amount of seafloor recycled into the mantle would have generated vast numbers of huge tsunamis. Conservative estimates are in the range of 50,000–100,000 or more tsunamis, with wave heights in the range of hundreds of feet or higher.

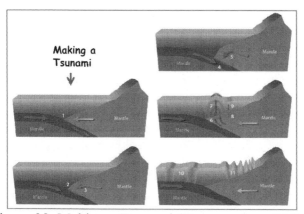

Figure 29. Making a Tsunami (Baumgardner, 2018).

Numerical experiments undertaken by Dr. Baumgardner to model the erosion and sediment deposition aspects of this sort of tsunami activity show that it is readily capable of producing the observed continent sediment record. This work is described in a recent paper titled, "Understanding how the Flood sediment record was formed: The role of large tsunamis."[119] Figure 30 shows a plot from this simulation that includes the plate motions.[120] Hence, a third major result of rapid plate motion is the formation of the observed layer-cake pattern of fossil-bearing sediments across the continents.

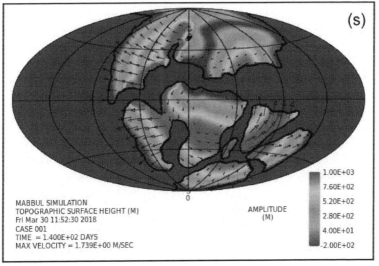

Figure 30. Plot from Dr. John Baumgardner's CPT Tsunami Simulation.[121]

Dr. Baumgardner's simulation allows us in a limited way to rewind time to gain some insight into what happened during the year-long Genesis Flood. Below we'll review some of the major physical evidences that support CPT.

Physical evidences that support the reality of CPT

Evidence 1: Catastrophic Subduction

The oceanic plates that rapidly subducted under the continents during the Flood are still visible! Seismic images of the mantle reveal a ring of unexpectedly cold rock at the bottom of the mantle, beneath the subduction zones that surround the Pacific Ocean. This structure is obtained using a technique known as seismic tomography that folds together data from 10,000 or more seismograms at once.

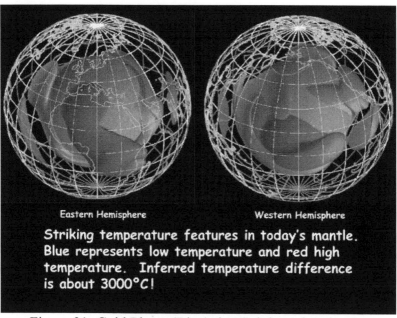

Eastern Hemisphere   Western Hemisphere

Striking temperature features in today's mantle. Blue represents low temperature and red high temperature. Inferred temperature difference is about 3000°C!

Figure 31. Cold Plates (Blue) that Subducted under the Continents During the Flood.[122]

Evidence 2: The Fossil Record

The action of CPT caused the oceanic plates to subduct rapidly under the land masses and generate cycles of tsunamis that brought staggering quantities of sediment onto land that wiped out every living creature in their paths, burying them in the muddy layers we still see today. These types of tsunamis still occur, although much less frequently and on a smaller scale. The moving sea floor subducts, snags under the land masses, and then releases, creating mud-filled tsunamis that carry debris and sea life onto land, sorting them in layers.

Giant, high-frequency tsunamis that were occurring during the Flood explain why today we see dinosaur graveyards around the world, including 13 states in the middle of America, containing dead dinosaurs mixed with marine life (see Figure 32). What type of Flood could do this? Just how much water would it take to bury millions of land creatures under hundreds of feet of mud and sand in the Morrison Formation (a 13-state, 700,000 square mile area)?

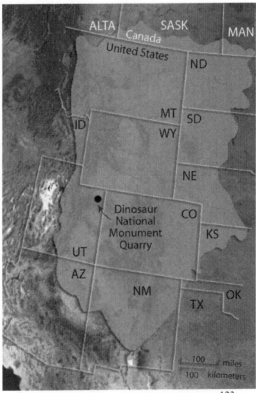

Figure 32. Morrison Formation.[123]

Just how did so many land creatures get buried together with marine life, with 97% of the dinosaurs found disarticulated,[124] and many of the remaining 3% that are found intact discovered in mud and sand layers with their necks arched back, suffocating as they died?[125]

A global inundation that covered most of North America is no secret to secular geologists, but they call it something different: the "widespread Late Cretaceous transgression"[126] (essentially technical jargon for "worldwide flood"). Studies have revealed that "a sea level rise of 310 meters is required to flood the Cretaceous layers based on their current elevation." The challenge for secular geologists, however, is that the maximum thickness of the fossil layers produced by a 310-meter sea level rise is only about 700 meters, but in North America, nearly 50 percent of the Cretaceous layers contain strata *thicker* than 700 meters.

Sediment transport via highly turbulent tsunami-driven flow described in Baumgardner's published work logically seems to be required to account for these thick layers. These layers also suggest that the continents also had to *downwarp* locally during this global inundation, as Baumgardner's modeling likewise suggests. This is what CPT predicts and what the Flood would have done. There's just no way that rising sea levels alone can explain the fossil record in North America— mechanisms much more powerful and catastrophic *had to be involved.*

Evidence 3: Fossil Correlation[127]

By comparing fossils of small organisms found on the ocean floor with fossils of the same organisms on different continents, it has been possible to determine when the ocean crust formed in terms of the fossil sequence found in the continental sediments. What has been discovered, both from a creationist as well as from a secular understanding, is that much of the continental fossil record was already in place before any

121

of the present-day ocean crust had come into existence. For example, all the trilobite fossils had already been deposited, plus all the older coal deposits (Pennsylvanian System coals) had already been formed before any of the present-day ocean crust had formed.

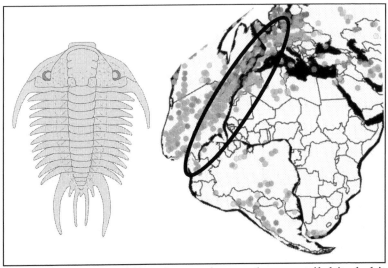

Figure 33. Reassembling the continents shows a trilobite habitat torn apart by the Flood.

The fossil record (e.g., certain trilobite species) that now straddles both sides of the MAR testify to the rapid nature of this catastrophe, with millions of the same kinds of animals that were once living together now found buried in mud and lime layers on either side.

In the creationist understanding, the presence of fossils is a trustworthy indicator of the action of Flood, meaning that a large part of the Flood cataclysm had already unfolded and had generated fossil-bearing sediments on the continental surface *before* any of the present-day ocean floor had appeared. It further implies that all of today's ocean floor formed *since the onset of the Flood*, during roughly the latter half of the cataclysm. It also means that all the pre-Flood ocean floor, plus

122

any ocean floor formed during the earlier portion of the Flood, must have been recycled into the earth's interior during the cataclysm. These considerations indicate in a compelling way that rapid plate tectonics must have been a major aspect of the year-long Flood catastrophe.

Evidence 4: Buckled/Folded Sedimentary Layers

The Genesis Flood laid down tens of millions of cubic miles of sediment like sand and mud all over the globe. It soon hardened into rock. These layers contain most of the fossil record. Some of these massive layers are bent and even folded, proving they were laid down rapidly and then bent before hardening into rock. Otherwise they would have crumbled instead of bending. These folded and bent geological features are found all over the world and most occurred during the latter stages of the Flood when 80% of the world's mountains rapidly formed.

Figure 34. Example of Massive Geologic Folding.[128]

Evidence 5: River Fans

If the evolutionary view about the continents were true (that they moved apart slowly over millions of years), the large rivers on the continents that empty into the Atlantic Ocean would have left a connected trail of mud stretching from one side of the Atlantic to the other. But what the evidence actually shows is that most of the seafloor spreading that formed the Atlantic was *over* before continental runoff and major transport of sediment into the Atlantic basin *began*. Major rivers like the Congo, Mississippi, and Amazon run off the continents and have mud fans with only thousands of years' worth of mud deposits—not millions.

Figure 35. Amazon River Fan (Google Earth)

There are flat sand bottoms on each side of the continents showing they were split apart rapidly—they don't have millions of years' worth of runoff with considerable mud

124

extending into the ocean. The continental shelves exhibit little erosion and still match nearly perfectly when put back together. Millions of years of erosion would have destroyed much of the sharp continental shelfs. These rivers began shaping and eroding only thousands of years ago, not millions.

Evidence 6: Sloss Megasequences

Dr. Tim Clarey has conducted extensive research on the Genesis Flood using over 2,000 stratigraphic columns (bore holes) from across North and South America, Africa, and Europe.[129] These data confirm the existence of six megasequences (called "Sloss-type megasequences"), large-scale sequences of sedimentary deposits that reveal six different stages of global depositions that occurred during the Flood.

The three earliest megasequences (Sauk, Tippecanoe and Kaskaskia) contained mostly marine fossils, indicating that only shallow marine areas were swamped and buried by CPT-caused tsunamis. The 4th megasequence (Absaroka) shows a dramatic rise in ocean level and overall global coverage and volume. This sequence also includes the first major plant (coal) and terrestrial animal fossils. The 5th megasequence (Zuni) was mostly responsible for the demise of the dinosaurs and appears to be the highest water point of the Flood (its zenith) because it shows the highest levels of sediment coverage and volume compared to earlier megasequences. The final megasequence (Tejas) contains fossils from the highest upland areas of the pre-Flood world. Together, these megasequences explain why over 75% of earth is covered by an average of about one mile of sedimentary deposits.

Figure 36. World Sediment Map (showing 75% of earth is covered by an average of about one mile of sedimentary deposits).

Evidence 7: Massive Coal Deposits

One of the highest and most severe stages of the Flood occurred during the 4th Sloss Megasequence, the Absaroka. Land creatures and plants start showing up in the fossil record laid down by this megasequence. This is also the time when the world's ocean floor began to be created anew. In other words, the oldest ocean crust today only goes back to the time of the deposition of the Absaroka Megasequence.

Notice the top bars in the first seven labeled rows in Figure 37. This shows the global animal fossil occurrences from the Paleodatabase.[130] The lower bars in each row represent aquatic animals and the top bars represent land animals. The megasequences are shown on the left. Note that few land animals appear until the end of the Kaskaskia, then land animals begin increasingly showing up in the fossil record as the Flood progressed.

126

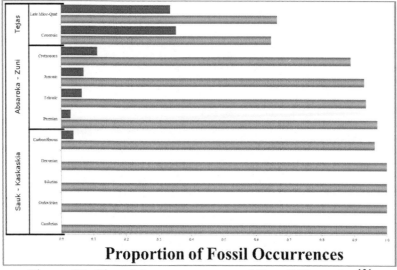

Proportion of Fossil Occurrences

Figure 37. Sloss Megasequences and Fossil Deposits.[131]

Entire ecosystems were buried during this megasequence in enormous deposits that later turned into coal, such as the extensive Appalachian coal beds. Even more coal was formed in the later Zuni and Tejas megasequences as the waters of the Flood rose yet higher. The U.S. has over seven trillion tons of coal reserves. Where did it all come from? While we know that coal is formed by dead plant material being sandwiched between sediment layers, we only have enough vegetation on the earth's surface today to produce just a fraction of the existing coal reserves.[132] This shows that the pre-Flood world was mostly covered by lush vegetation. The rising Flood waters and tsunamis that were necessary to sweep over the land and bury vast amounts of vegetation that turned into coal are best explained by a catastrophe of worldwide proportions.

Figure 38. United States Coal Beds.

In the later run-off stages of the Flood (called the Tejas sequence), plants swept off the pre-Flood lands formed massive coal beds such as in the Powder River Basin of Wyoming and Montana. The Powder River Basin layers are the largest coal deposits in North America, currently supplying over 40% of the coal in the U.S. Some of these stacked coal beds are up to 200 feet thick and cover areas that are 60 miles long by 60 miles wide. The sheer volume of plant material required to form such a massive layer of coal testifies to catastrophic circumstances.

Was Noah's Ark Seaworthy?

Next let's investigate whether the Ark was seaworthy. God gave certain dimensions to Noah for building the Ark: 300 cubits long, 50 cubits wide, and 30 cubits high. Using the Nippur Cubit[133] at 20.4 inches, this works out to a vessel about

128

510 feet long, 85 feet wide, and 51 feet high. Accounting for a 15% reduction in volume due to the hull curvature, the Ark had about 1.88 million cubic feet of space, the equivalent of 450 semi-trailers of cargo space.[134] Twice as long as a Boeing 747 and stretching over one-and-a-half football fields, this was a massive ship.

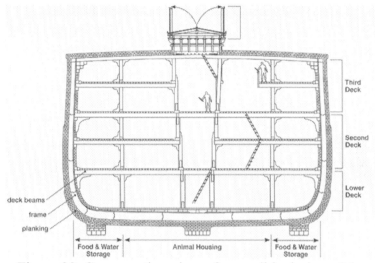

Figure 39. Cross-section view of a possible design of the interior of the ark.[135]

God knew *exactly what He was doing* when He gave Noah the specific dimensions of the Ark. In 1993 Dr. Seon Won Hong conducted a scientific study[136] to investigate the seaworthiness of the Ark at the renowned ship research center KRISO (now called MOERI) in South Korea.[137] After evaluating the seaworthiness of over 10 various ship dimensions, the study showed that the Ark dimensions given in the Bible were ideal for handling everything a highly turbulent sea could throw at it, while balancing the need for inhabitant safety. The study showed that the Ark could handle 100-foot waves.

An earlier study conducted in the 17th Century by Peter Jansen of Holland showed that the length-to-width ratio of the

129

Ark (about 7-to-1) was ideal for such a massive, non-powered sea vessel. Some oil tankers have a 7-to-1 ratio as well. He also demonstrated using replica models of the Ark how tough it was to capsize.[138]

Noah was instructed by God to coat the inside and the outside of the Ark with pitch, a thick gooey substance secreted by trees as a means of protection against infection or insect attack. Isn't it interesting that one of the very first historical references to using pitch for ships is in the Bible? It's also interesting that pitch has been the most effective and widely-used ship waterproofing substance in history. For centuries, tar, which is made from pitch, was among Sweden's most important exports, peaking at over a quarter million barrels per year in the late 1800s. Many of the eastern states in the U.S. were also major tar exporters for ship building purposes until the 1900s.[139]

When heated into a liquid state and applied to ship planking, pitch hardens almost instantly into a protective, waterproof shell, very similar to how epoxy or fiberglass are used in shipbuilding today. The strong outer shell provided by hardened pitch adds both strength and waterproofing beyond the natural capability of the wood. These "divine shipbuilding instructions" given to Noah certainly seem to make realistic sense.

Noah's Ark vs. the Gilgamesh Ark

Now let's compare the Biblical Flood to the leading flood myth, the Epic of Gilgamesh. In 1853, archaeologists found a series of 12 tablets dated to around 650 BC, although parts of the story existed in earlier, fragmentary versions.[140] Because the story had many of the same elements as the Genesis account, skeptics believed that Gilgamesh preceded the Biblical account, negating the Genesis account as just a spin-off. Fortunately for Christians, however, there are major clues that point to the Biblical account as the accurate one, and Gilgamesh as a later work of fiction that incorporated legendary elements of a flood within a cultural fantasy. Here are the reasons why.

First, we have the feasibility of the Gilgamesh version of the Ark, described as a massive, unstable cube that was about 200 feet on each side with six decks that divided it into seven parts. Along with help from the community and craftsmen, he supposedly built this vessel—which was over three times the size of the Biblical Ark, in just a week.

6 DAYS

Comparison between Noah's Ark and Gilgamesh Ark: Length and Ocean Time

TO SCALE COMPARISON

371 DAYS

Figure 40. Noah's Ark vs. Gilgamesh Ark.[141]

How would something like this fare during a catastrophic, worldwide Flood? It would obviously tumble, killing or maiming its passengers. That's obviously quite different than the biblical Ark which had a 7-to-1 length-to-width ratio which is very similar to many of today's ocean barges, making it a feasible design for staying afloat during the Flood. Scripture provides clues that Noah and helpers likely had between 55 and 75 years to build the Ark.[142]

The second key for determining which of these Flood accounts is the original is the *duration* of the Flood provided by each. The Gilgamesh flood lasted a mere six days, whereas the Genesis Flood lasted 371 days. Both accounts claim the Flood was worldwide, but how could water cover earth in just six days? A floating, 200 X 200 X 200-foot cube and six days for worldwide inundation certainly stretch credulity.

The next consideration is the reasons for the Flood given by each of the two accounts. In the Genesis account, God's judgment is *just*—he was patient with utterly wicked mankind for 120 years before sending the Flood and showed mercy to the last righteous family. In the Gilgamesh account, the Flood was ordered by multiple, self-centered squabbling 'gods' that were 'starving' without humans to feed them sacrifices. These two are quite different!

Finally, there are several other parts of the Gilgamesh account that are obviously mythical, such as Gilgamesh being 2/3rds divine and 1/3rd mortal. After oppressing his people, Gilgamesh and others call upon the 'gods' and the sky-god Anu creates a wild man named Enkidu to fight Gilgamesh. The battle is a draw, and they become friends. Gilgamesh apparently also encounters talking monsters and a "Scorpion man" in his journeys.

Scholars rely on their anti-Bible bias, not science, to assert that the Gilgamesh story came first. These stark differences between Genesis and Gilgamesh accounts highlight the feasibility and priority of the biblical one. The Gilgamesh account was written 800 years *after* Genesis and describes a cube-shaped Ark 200 feet on each side tumbling around in the ocean in a 6-day flood put on by the "angry, fighting gods" that sent it. The Bible's Flood was recorded earlier, has an Ark sealed on the inside and out with dimensions that are on par with today's ocean liners, lasted a full year, and was sent to judge an Earth that deserved it.

In fact, it's the similarities between these two accounts that shows the Bible's account to be the historical one. Many myths are based on historical accounts, but they get embellished over time, becoming more and more mythical as the story is repeated over generations. This is exactly what we see with flood myths like Gilgamesh—they take the original, historical account (the Biblical Flood) and grow it into a mythical, interesting story over time.

For example, the earlier version of the Gilgamesh Flood account[143] clearly identifies the flood as a local river flood, with the dead bodies of humans filling the river "like dragonflies" and moving to the edge of the boat "like a raft" and moving to the riverbank "like a raft." Centuries later, this gets exaggerated into a global, worldwide flood where humans killed in the flood "fill the sea" like a "spawn of fish."

Both accounts have a God or "gods" that are sending judgment, describe a worldwide inundation, have an Ark built to specific dimensions that are loaded with surviving humans and animals, and land just a few hundred miles apart from each other after using birds as a test to find dry land. Myths often grow from historical to being more mythical, but they almost never develop in the reverse, becoming more truthful and accurate over time. While these accounts mirror each other in so many ways, which account is the original, historical one? The feasible one of course. While both accounts describe plenty of divine intervention, only the Biblical ark size, shape, function, build time, and flood duration makes sense.

Jesus taught about a real flood and compared it to what the end times will be like. Jesus warned: "But of that day and hour no one knows, not even the angels of heaven, but My Father only. But as the days of Noah were, so also will the coming of the Son of Man be. For as in the days before the flood, they were eating and drinking, marrying and giving in marriage, until the day that Noah entered the ark, and did not know until the flood came and took them all away, so also will the coming of the Son of Man be."

Because Jesus stood firmly on the historicity of the Flood and likened it to end times (Matthew 24:36–44), the two go hand-in-hand. If the Genesis Flood never happened, we have no foundation for believing in the rest of what Jesus said, including His second coming. At least for Christians, Matthew 24 alone should destroy the "Flood as myth" idea. When looking back through history, we observe that some mythical accounts begin with a true event, but then get embellished over time, becoming more and more mythical.

Noah's Flood: How Could All the Animals Fit on the Ark?

Next let's look at one of the most frequently asked questions about the Ark: "How could it fit all the animals?" Two factors help answer this question: (1) the size of the Ark, and (2) the number (and size) of the animals and supplies on board. First, the size. Given the size of the Ark (discussed above), the Ark had a total volume of at least 1,396,000 cubic feet.[144] The inside dimensions of a 40-foot school bus gives about 2,080 cubic feet of space. Therefore, at least 671 school buses without their wheels and axels could fit inside of Noah's Ark. If each bus carried 50 students, then 33,550 kids could easily fit in the Ark.

Next, we have the number of animals. The Genesis Flood account states that God brought two (male/female) of every *kind* of animal (and seven pairs of some) to Noah, who loaded them into the Ark. The Hebrew term for kind is *min*, which occurs only 31 times in the Old Testament. So just what is a biblical kind? Biblically and biologically speaking, a kind is a group of animals that were naturally interfertile at the time of the Flood. Some organisms have complex histories since then, so it's difficult to determine which of them belongs to which kind. Most often, however, plants and animals interbreed within their modern "Family" classification. Thus, each family—give or take—had at least two representatives on Noah's ark. Several creation scientists have spent considerable amount of time studying this very topic (it's called the field of *baraminology*, or the study of "created kinds").[145]

While there are various methods for determining "kinds," (e.g., cognitum and statistical baraminology), hybridization (whether two species can have offspring) is considered the most valuable evidence for inclusion within an Ark *kind*.

Take mammals for example. Some biologists list them in 28 orders that include 146 families and over 4,800 species.[146] Some place the species estimates higher, around 5,400.[147] So how many different mammal pairs would Noah have to take on the Ark to produce all the mammal species we have today? Take the dog (Canine) kind for starters. The World Canine Organization currently recognizes 339 different breeds of dogs—all are or were interfertile. There are 335 horse breeds that are all interfertile. There are eight bear species in the bear (Ursidae) family and all except for one are interfertile. Notice how the high number of species quickly collapses to a much smaller number?

Figure 41. Ursidae Family (Bears).

Some scientists have boiled down this list of mammal species to only 138 created kinds (using extant species, or animals still alive today). Including the extinct mammalian families known from the fossil record, the actual number on the Ark could have exceeded 300.[148] By collapsing the other animal categories in a similar manner, the total estimate of the number of kinds needed on the Ark is fewer than 2,000.[149] Dinosaurs were certainly included on the ark, since Scripture says any animal that walked and had nostrils went in, with many dinosaur count estimates at the species level less than 1,000 and fewer than 80 at the family level.[150] Probably only 160 individual dinosaurs survived the Flood on Noah's Ark. Noah's family could have loaded young behemoths, not the larger older

135

ones. Dinosaur kinds, plus many other animals, went extinct after the Flood.

Noah's Flood: How Did People and Animals Disperse Around the World after the Flood?

After the Flood, God commanded humanity to "increase in number and fill the earth" (Genesis 9:1). As rebellious humans, we did the opposite: "Then they said, 'Come, let us build ourselves a city, with a tower that reaches to the heavens, so that we may make a name for ourselves and not be scattered over the face of the whole earth'" (Genesis 11:4). About 100 years after the Flood, God responded to this disobedience by confusing our language and dispersing us from the Tower of Babel around the globe. This dispersal included between 78 and 100 people groups (and languages).[151]

Assuming the Babel dispersion is a true account, how did people spread across the globe when much of it is presently covered by water? The answer is quite simple: during the (single) Ice Age that began after the Flood and lasted for a few hundred years after, the ocean levels were between 100 and 140 meters lower[152] than they are today. This made *land bridges* and *ice bridges* that melting ice has since submerged. Also, in many cases (e.g., Hawaii, North America, Tahiti, and other locations) both humans and animals arrived by boat. For more about this topic, we recommend Bill Cooper's book, *After the Flood: The Early Post-flood History of Europe Traced Back to Noah (2008)* and other resources by Answers in Genesis.[153]

Worldwide Flood Legends

Looking back through history, there are actually hundreds of flood accounts, and the similarity between these accounts and the Genesis Flood are uncanny.[154] Most of them seem to draw from the same common themes: judgement from God, a family chosen to preserve humanity, and loading animals. The early Chinese certainly seemed to have Genesis

136

and the Flood in mind when they invented the earliest version of written language.[155]

For example, the character for create includes the idea of speaking into dust to create man. "Garden" is symbolized by placing a person who was created by breathing into dust into an enclosure. "Boat" is a "vessel with eight people," and flood is represented by a global watery inundation over the earth and "eight" is included. The character for "forbidden"[156] is "two trees with God," in a way that notifies "God makes a commandment about two trees." The one for "temper" is "devil with trees under cover." Where did the Chinese picture concepts come from? Why do these figures match Genesis history so clearly?

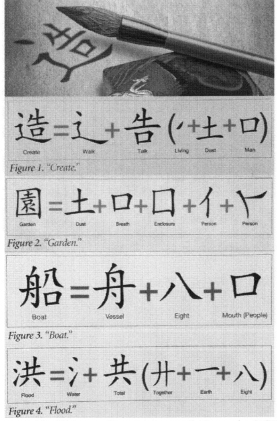

Figure 42. Chinese Language and Genesis (ICR).

Isn't it also interesting that all human history disappears about the same time as the Biblical Flood? Even secular school textbooks admit this, with most placing the earliest human writing between 4,000 and 5,000 years before present. This is exactly what we would expect with civilization starting again after the Flood.

In summary, the Bible clearly lays out a Flood account that, while miraculous, fits into history with much more believability than the mythical accounts. The Ark is the only vessel in the ancient Flood accounts that could have actually survived the Flood. It was seaworthy and watertight, it fits the dimensions of many similar ships today, and could certainly hold the thousands of animal kinds necessary to blossom into the variety of animal life we see today. The obvious scars around the world also coincide well with the Bible's account, matching both the megasequences in the geologic record and the massive, worldwide fossil record consisting of billions upon billions of animals buried in the muddy catastrophe that killed them.

Noah's Flood: Worldwide or Local?

Some Christians believe the earth is 4.5 billion years old and that the Flood described in the book of Genesis 6–9 was a local event limited to where Noah lived in the Mesopotamian Valley region. Why? Primarily because of their perspectives on the fossil record and radiometric dating. They believe the fossil record was laid down over millions of years and do not believe that a global flood could have formed those fossils. By tracing genealogies in the Bible, we know the Flood occurred around ~4,400 years ago. However, according to conventional geologists (who believe in long ages) there is no evidence in the geologic record for a recent global flood. Yet, there is significant evidence that most of the fossil record was created by the Genesis Flood! Let's look at eight reasons for believing the Genesis Flood was a global, catastrophic event.

1. **Massive geologic layers**: The Genesis Flood laid down millions of cubic feet of sediment like sand and mud all over the globe. It soon hardened into rock. These layers contain most of the fossil record. Some of these massive layers are bent and even folded (such as at the Kaibab Upwarp in the Grand Canyon), proving they were laid down rapidly and then bent before hardening into rock. Otherwise they would have crumbled instead of bending.

2. **Fossil record**: The fossil record is world-wide and shows evidence of rapid burial. Specific examples include clam and oyster shells on mountain tops that were fossilized while still closed, fish buried in the process of eating other fish, jellyfish and other soft-bodied organisms which decay rapidly, and ichthyosaurs that were buried while giving birth. The Flood accounts for such widespread watery catastrophe.

3. **The Flood covered the highest mountains**: Scripture says that the "waters rose and increased greatly on the earth, and the ark floated on the surface of the water. They rose greatly on the earth, and **all** the high mountains **under the entire heavens** were covered. The waters rose and covered the mountains to a depth of more than fifteen cubits [about 22 feet]" (Genesis 7:18–20, emphasis added). Of course, the writer refers to the mountains of the pre-Flood world, which were likely much shorter than today's tallest mountains. Since water seeks its own level, it would be impossible for the water to cover the highest mountains and still be only a local event.

4. **Purpose of the Flood**: Due to widespread wickedness and violence, God decided to wipe out all of mankind, the land-dwelling animals and birds (except for those who were on the Ark). God said the

earth "was corrupt and filled with violence" (Genesis 6:11–12), and that He was going to "bring floodwaters to destroy every creature on the face of the earth that has the breath of life in it" (Genesis 6:17). He also specifically mentioned people multiple times: "I will wipe from the face of the earth the human race I have created" (Genesis 6:7). Since it is highly improbable that all of the people on earth lived in the Mesopotamian Valley region, a local flood would not have accomplished God's purpose.

5. **Use of the words "all" and "every" and "everything" in Genesis chapters 6–9**: The words "all," "every" and "everything" are used 66 times in the Genesis Flood account. Many of these verses describe the creatures and people that perished during the flood. It is very clear by the context of these passages that God meant He was going to destroy all living creatures that live on land (except for those on the Ark). For example: "**Every** living thing that moved on land perished—birds, livestock, wild animals, **all the creatures** that swarm over the earth, and **all mankind**. **Everything** on dry land that had the breath of life in its nostrils died. **Every** living thing on the face of the earth was **wiped out**; people and animals and the creatures that move along the ground and the birds were **wiped from the earth**. **Only Noah was left**, and those with him in the ark" (Genesis 7:21–23, emphasis added). If the text doesn't mean what it says, then it means nothing. Jesus and Peter also referred to the universality of Noah's Flood. Who are we (who were not even there) to say that they were wrong?

6. **The Ark: It likely took between 55 and 75 years to build the Ark.**[157] If the Flood was just a local event, why would God tell Noah to build a ship over 400 feet long (Genesis 6:15) and then bring on board

all the different kinds of animals including birds to be saved? (Genesis 6:19–21). If the flood was only a local event, there would be no need for an ark— Noah and the animals that God wanted to save would have had plenty of time to travel to a safer area.

7. **God's covenant**: in Genesis 9:11, God made a promise, "Never again will all life be destroyed by the waters of a flood; never again will there be a flood to destroy the earth." If the flood was local, then every time a local flood happens, God would break His promise.

8. **Jesus believed in a global flood**: "Just as it was in the days of Noah, so also will it be in the days of the Son of Man. People were eating, drinking, marrying and being given in marriage up to the day Noah entered the ark. Then the flood came and destroyed them all" (Luke 17:26–27). Peter also affirmed a worldwide Flood (2 Peter 3:6).

We recommend the following resources for further study:

- *Old Earth Creationism on Trial*, Tim Chaffey and Jason Lisle
- *The Global Flood; Unlocking Earth's Geologic History*, John D. Morris
- *The Fossil Record; Unearthing Nature's History of Life*, John D. Morris
- *The New Answers Book 3*, Andrew Snelling and Ken Ham. Available here: _https://answersingenesis.org/the-flood/global/was-the-flood-of-noah-global-or-local-in-extent/_

Study Questions

1. Read Genesis 6:1–10. What were the reasons for the Flood and why did God preserve Noah and his family?

   _____
   _____
   _____
   _____
   _____
   _____
   _____
   _____

2. What are some of the key evidences of the Flood that we can see on earth today?

   _____
   _____
   _____
   _____
   _____
   _____
   _____
   _____

3. Why does the Biblical Ark seem more like the "real, original" vessel when compared to the some of the other vessels from Ancient Near East writings?

   _____
   _____
   _____
   _____
   _____
   _____

_____

_____

4. Read Matthew 24:36–44. How did Jesus regard the
   Flood and what does this teach us about the time we live
   in today?

   _____

   _____

   _____

   _____

   _____

   _____

   _____

   _____

Myth 6: "Moses actually did not write the first five books of the Bible"[158]

Suggested Videos:

Myth 6: https://genesisapologetics.com/myth-6/

Professors in many colleges today assert that Moses did not produce the Torah, the first five books of the Bible. They allege that "Moses did not have the ability to write…" or, that "the Hebrew language doesn't date back far enough for the events recorded in the Bible." Let's find out why these claims couldn't be further from the truth.

To begin with, keep in mind that Jesus himself supported that Moses produced the Torah, stating in John 5, "For if you believed Moses, you would believe Me; for he wrote about Me. But if you do not believe his writings, how will you believe My words?" When praying to the Father in John 17, Jesus said this: "Sanctify them by Your truth. Your word is truth." Jesus had a high view of Scripture, and He clearly believed in the Mosaic authorship of the Torah.

New Testament authors mention Moses 80 times and always give him credit for producing the Torah. Paul even noted in Romans 3 that God committed His "oracles" and teachings to the Jewish people, and this came through Moses. But wait a minute—Moses wasn't *present* during the six days of creation recorded in the first chapter of Genesis—*no one was*, and Adam wasn't created until the *end* of creation week. Moses also didn't witness the Flood, or the events leading up to it. In fact, Moses didn't even show up until at least 700 years *after* the Flood. So just how did he write or compile the biblical history that came before him?

The answer is quite simple: they were transmitted orally or in writing, or both. Interestingly, the first set of writings referenced in the Bible is the "Book of the generations of Adam" in Genesis 5. This book is actually 1 of 11 *toledotes* (pronounced "Toll-Dotes") which means "histories" or "genealogies" that are included in the Book of Genesis, which is broken into 50 chapters in our Bibles today.

While we don't know for sure, it's likely that these 11 toledotes were memorized, compiled, or both by the generations that are relevant to them, and handed like historical batons between generations. For example, the toledote from Genesis 5:1 to 6:8 includes 13 people listed by name. The next one dealing with the Flood includes nine. The next toledote picks up in Chapter 10 and describes Noah's sons and grandchildren, with over 70 people listed by name. The events of the *toledot* for Terah, Ishmael, Isaac, Esau, and Jacob *even* occurred during the period for which we have evidence of Hebrew writing.

While we don't know for sure just how these histories were transmitted to Moses—whether by oral tradition, writing, or both—the Bible is clear and specific about the histories that pre-date Moses. It's hard to imagine how the birth, death, or lifespan years given for the 87 patriarchs in the first 11 chapters of Genesis were passed down through oral history alone. However, the ancients transmitted stories orally much more frequently than we do today, and they were often quite reliable when they did so. Also, remember that the Holy Spirit had no limitations for guiding Moses through the transmission process, as "men being borne along by the Holy Spirit spoke from God" (2 Peter 1:21).

Another major clue that the early chapters of Genesis were preserved and given to Moses is found in Genesis 2. This chapter describes river systems that encircled certain areas that were rich with precious minerals and gems. Moses was not around to see this landscape, as it was completely reworked by Noah's Flood which occurred long before his day. He knew about these things because they were passed down beforehand and given to him. So, if these accounts were preserved *through* the Flood and preserved *after* the Flood, it is conceivable that they were passed down from one generation to another by oral transmission or writing.

Liberal scholars today promote the "documentary hypothesis," which argues against the Mosaic authorship of the Torah and suggests instead that it was a compilation of four originally independent documents, abbreviated as the "J-E-P-D" sources. This idea originally was promoted by Julius Wellhausen in the 19th Century. Creation Ministries International provides a thorough rebuttal of this hypothesis, showing even how modern scholarship does not support it.[159]

Next we have the many instances in the Bible where Moses recorded the commands or words of God. For example, in Exodus 17:14, The Lord said to Moses, "Write this for a memorial in the book and recount it in the hearing of Joshua." Exodus 24:4 states that "Moses wrote all the words of the Lord," and verse 7 records that Moses "took the Book of the Covenant" and read it to the people. Deuteronomy 6 also indicates the Israelites were collectively using writing, being directed by God to write His commandments "on the doorposts of their houses and gates."

Then there are the 10 commandments, where God instructed Moses: "Come up to Me on the mountain and be there; and I will give you tablets of stone, and the law and commandments which I have written, that you may teach them." Exodus 32:15 even says that these "tablets were written on both sides."

So, it looks like God Himself was writing in a language that the Israelites would understand. Many Christians and Jews alike believe that this interchange occurred in ancient Hebrew. However, for one to compile a work like the Bible, the flexibility of an alphabet is necessary. While opinions vary, many secular scholars today hold that the Phoenicians developed the world's first alphabet around 1050 BC. How can this be when most biblical scholars hold the view that Moses wrote the Torah in the 15th Century BC?

In filmmaker Tim Mahoney's movie, "Patterns of Evidence: The Moses Controversy (2019)," he answers this question thoroughly. In this movie, Mahoney establishes Mosaic authorship by looking at evidence that answers four key

146

questions: (1) Could Moses have written the Torah in a language by the time of the Exodus, (2) in the region of Egypt, (3) using the power of an alphabet, and (4) in a form of writing like Hebrew? This movie documents over two hours of evidence that supports the Biblical case. We'll review some of the highlights here.

First, since at least the last third of the 19th century, we've known of alphabetic inscriptions that pre-date the alphabet-based writings from the Phoenicians that date to about 1,000 BC. Some of these discoveries were made in 1904 by Flinders Petrie, a man who has been called the father of Egyptian archaeology, in the turquoise mines that were controlled by the ancient Egyptians on the Sinai Peninsula. The inscriptions became known as "Proto-Sinaitic" and were dated to the middle of Egypt's 18th Dynasty, which equates to the 15th century BC.

A more recent discovery of two alphabetic inscriptions was made in 1999 at a place called Wadi el-Hol. These inscriptions, which use the same script as the ones from the turquoise mines, also are alphabetic letters that are based on 22 specific hieroglyphic signs from the Egyptian sign list, but they date back to 1834 BC.

An additional tablet, called "Sinai 375a" also dates to the 15th Century BC and has the name *Ahisamach* from Exodus 31:6 written on two horizontal lines. Dr. Doug Petrovich stated that there is no other instance of this name in any other Semitic language than Hebrew. In the Bible, Ahisamach was the father of Oholiab, who along with Bezalel was one of the chief craftsmen appointed for constructing the Tabernacle and its furnishings. Dr. Petrovich points out clear evidence that the Hebrew letters developed continuously, becoming less pictographic over time, until the Hebrew script eventually converted into block letters under the Persian administration (6th and 5th centuries BC).

Leading up to the 7th century BC an excavation of a burial tomb near Jerusalem in 1979 uncovered two small silver scrolls with the "priestly blessing" from the Book of Numbers

147

chapter 6. Today this is regarded as the earliest known copy of the biblical text!

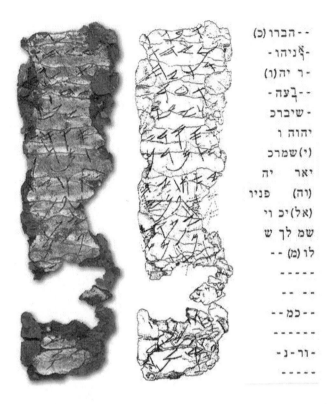

Figure 43. A photograph of the scroll KH2 and a transcription of the letters.[160]

Study Questions

1. Read Numbers 23:19, Titus 1:2, Matthew 24:35, Psalm 12:6–7, Proverbs 30:5, and Psalm 138:2. In summary, these verses collectively show that God's Word is always true (God cannot lie), unchanging, perfect, permanent, and even honored by God above His own name. What does this say about how we should regard God's Word?

_____

_____

_____

_____

_____

_____

_____

_____

_____

2. The further we go back in history, the more history is lost—writings on clay tablets crumble and are found in fragmented pieces and papyrus scrolls fade away. Nevertheless, today we have a reliable set of Scriptures which validate all the way back to the Dead Sea Scrolls. Why do you think God did this?

_____

_____

_____

_____

_____

_____

_____

Myth 7: "Dinosaurs died out millions of years ago, did not walk with man, and are not mentioned in the Bible"

Suggested Videos:

Myth 7: https://genesisapologetics.com/myth-7/
Resources/videos: www.genesisapologetics.com/dinosaurs/

Introduction

The secular viewpoint on dinosaurs directly opposes what the Bible teaches. In a nutshell, the secular idea is that dinosaurs evolved through death of the unfit and survival of the fittest random mutants starting about 220 million years ago and ending at a supposed extinction event about 65 million years ago. This view invokes the trinity of time, chance, and death as the *creators* of dinosaurs.

According to biblical history, however, dinosaurs were intentionally designed by God, each made to reproduce after its own kind, and were spontaneously placed on Earth just thousands of years ago. The following Bible passages outline some dinosaur basics:

1. God created **all living things**. Therefore, God created dinosaurs (Genesis 1; Exodus 20:11; Colossians 1:16; John 1:3).
2. God created all land-dwelling, air-breathing animals on the **6th Day** of Creation, right before He created man (Genesis 1:24–25).
3. Tallying the genealogies in Genesis 1–11, this 6th Day occurred about **6,000 years ago**,[161] so dinosaurs were placed here fully-formed (in several different "kinds") at that time.

4. Adam's first job from God was to name **all** the animals (including dinosaurs) after they were **all** created (Genesis 2:20).
5. After God created all animals, He gave Adam and Eve the charge of **taking dominion over every living creature**: "Be fruitful and multiply; fill the earth and subdue it; have dominion over the fish of the sea, over the birds of the air, and over **every living thing** that moves on the earth" (v. 28). All of God's creatures were present when this dominion order was given.
6. The book of Job describes two dinosaur-like creatures: **Leviathan** and **Behemoth**. Behemoth is given the title of God's "chief" or "first in rank" over all God's creative works (Job 40:19). A plain interpretation of the 13 characteristics that describe this animal match a sauropod dinosaur that was "made along with" man (verse 40:15).
7. All land-dwelling, air-breathing animals **died in a worldwide Flood** (except those on Noah's Ark) about 4,400 years ago (Genesis 6:7, 7:20–23). Part of the reason for this worldwide extinction event was that "all flesh" (including animals) had "corrupted their way on the Earth" (Genesis 6:12).
8. Not all animal "kinds" that got off the Ark after the Flood survived for long in the new, post-Flood world (e.g., many dinosaurs). While we don't know the details, many animal kinds (and probably most of the dinosaurs) **quickly went extinct** after the Flood. Some dinosaurs, however, survived for centuries after the Flood, and contributed to the dragon myths and legends that exist all over the world (see section below on dragons).

Which of these two viewpoints on dinosaurs is correct? Were all varieties of dinosaurs the products of time, chance, and "survival of the fittest" millions of years ago? Or, were they placed here by an intentional, all-powerful God who spoke them into existence, and then later wiped out in the Global Flood described in Genesis?

Next, we'll explore 13 lines of reasoning that provide evidence that the historical view of Genesis is accurate. Rather than dinosaurs being used to "prove" evolution, dinosaur design and the dinosaur fossil record actually fits the "biblical hypothesis" better than the one provided by evolution!

Evidence #1: Clever Design

Some dinosaur design features are just plain astounding. We'll start by looking at the grandest of all God's creatures— one that He calls the "Chief" in Job 40: the sauropod dinosaur. Sauropods are the largest land animals in history, with some of them (such as *Argentinosaurus* and *Patagotitan mayorum*) exceeding 115 feet and weighing over 140,000 pounds.[162]

Figure 44. Sauropod Dinosaur.[163]

Figure 45 shows a sauropod dinosaur leg. Notice how the bone at the top is made of one solid piece, followed by the two bones below the knee, followed by five foot bones, then five toes? This "large and solid" to "smaller and spread out" system allowed these massive creatures to distribute their weight and walk on mobile pillars. What an amazing design plan that allowed these creatures to walk! Unlike other dinosaurs, sauropods could lock their legs straight, conserving energy.

Figure 45. Royal Tyrrell Museum (Author).

Where are all the sauropods that don't have this weight-bearing design? They don't exist. All ~300 that have been found so far are made this way.[164] As we'll soon see, this is just the tip of the iceberg when it comes to the design features that need to be present *at the same time* for these creatures to live.

Job 40 and the Behemoth

It's no wonder that the Book of Job (the oldest book of the Bible, written about 3,500 years ago[165]) refers to Behemoth—a sauropod dinosaur—as the "chief" or "first in rank" of all God's creation. Consider the description of this animal from Job 40:6–24:

> Then the Lord answered Job out of the whirlwind, and said: "Now prepare yourself like a man; I will question you, and you shall answer Me... Look at Behemoth, which I **made along with you** and which feeds on grass like an ox. What **strength it has in its loins**, what **power in the muscles of its belly**! Its **tail sways like a cedar**; the **sinews of its thighs are close-knit**. Its **bones are tubes of bronze**, its **limbs like rods of iron**. It **ranks first among the works of God**, yet its Maker can approach it with his sword. The hills bring it their produce, and all the wild animals play nearby. Under the lotus plants it lies, hidden among the reeds in the marsh. The lotuses conceal it in their shadow; the poplars by the stream surround it. **A raging river does not alarm it; it is secure, though the Jordan should surge against its mouth.** Can anyone capture it by the eyes, or trap it and pierce its nose?

In context, Job and his philosopher friends just finished over 30 chapters of dialogue trying to explain God and why He would allow such hardships into Job's life. Then God shows up in a whirlwind, tells Job to "brace himself like a man" and says that He would be the one asking Job the questions for a while (KJV: "Gird up thy loins now like a man: I will demand of thee, and declare thou unto me"). Then, for four chapters straight, God asks Job 77 rhetorical questions that are all about Creation. After explaining to Job that He is the master designer of space and earth, God describes 13 of His created animals, such as an ostrich, horse, and deer, then caps off the discussion by telling Job about His two grandest creations: Behemoth and Leviathan. God calls Behemoth the "first of all of His ways," using the Hebrew term (re'shiyth), which means *first in a rank*, the *chief*, the *most supreme* of His creative works.

When God says to Job, sit down, brace yourself, and now I will tell you of the chief of all my works—the biggest, most amazing land creature I ever made—he's not talking about a common animal like a hippo or a crocodile. When we scan through all land-dwelling creatures—both living and extinct—which one comes up as the "first in rank," the most colossal or the chief? Clearly the sauropod dinosaur. Pairing God's Word that Behemoth is the grandest creature He ever made with the fact that sauropods are the largest land creatures we've ever found should give us a clue to Behemoth's identity.

Sauropods were huge. The largest one found to date (named *Patagotitan mayorum*) was over 120 feet long—that's 10 freeway lanes across! At a weight of 76 tons, it's a wonder these creatures could even walk! Let's start by looking at one of their unique design features: their long necks.

The necks of the sauropod dinosaurs were by far the longest of any animal, six times longer than that of the world record giraffe and five times longer than those of all other terrestrial animals.[166]

Mamenchisaurus youngi
(Pi et al, 1996)

Figure 46. *Mamenchisaurus* a Type of Sauropod Dinosaur.[167]

The engineering required for a living creature to have such a long neck has perplexed dinosaur researchers for years—the physics just don't seem to work because the necks would be too heavy for their length. Leading sauropod researcher, Dr. Matthew Wedel notes: "They were marvels of biological engineering, and that efficiency of design is especially evident in their vertebrae, the bones that make up the backbone."[168]

After spending years studying the long necks of sauropods, Dr. Wedel made a discovery that was so significant it earned him the Fourth International Award in Paleontology Research. In short, Dr. Wedel revealed that the vertebrae of these massive sauropods were pneumatic—they were *filled with air*![169]

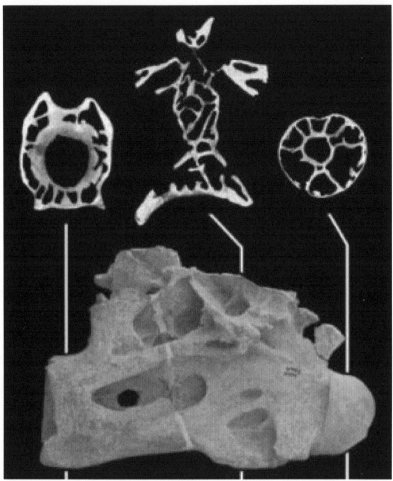

Figure 47. Apatosaurus Vertebra Showing Most of Its Space Filled with Air Cavities.[170]

Dr. Wedel started researching these air-filled vertebrae as an undergraduate researcher in Oklahoma, where he spent his Saturdays running dinosaur bones through the CT scanner at his local hospital. There, he discovered that "one of Sauropod's four and a half foot vertebrae would have been surprisingly light and could reach 90% air by volume!"[171]

Figure 48. A 4-1/2-Foot Sauropod Vertebra That Could Reach
90% Air by Volume.

These big creatures needed *light* vertebrae to enable
them to lift their heads—but these extra-long necks also needed
to be *designed* in such a way that the animal could eat, drink,
and move its head without its neck folding in half or pinching
vital nerves or even the trachea (for breathing) or esophagus
(for eating). Having an extra-light structure was only part of the
solution.

God even describes Behemoth's diet: eating grass like
an ox. In 2005 researchers found grass in sauropod coprolites in
India, and some palaeobotanists are even saying that this will
cause a "rewrite in our understanding of dinosaur evolution,"
because evolution holds that grass didn't evolve until millions
of years after the dinosaurs had gone extinct.[172]

God describes Behemoth's strength in his hips, and
power in his stomach muscles. Again, we have a strong clue
that Behemoth was a sauropod dinosaur because, while many
animals have strong hips and stomach muscles, none were as
strong as the sauropod! The muscular structure around the hips

and stomach that were necessary for sauropods to move, walk, turn, and eat would be incredible!

In fact, for some sauropods, like the Diplodocus, its highest point of its core body was the hips and its whole body balanced on the hips, front-to-back. Diplodocus was able to rear up on its back legs and balance on its tail like a tripod, making use of the hips to support not just the back half of its body, but the front half, too. This required enormous strength in the hip and stomach muscles, considering they lifted tons of its own body into the air. Below the hips was an incredible weight distribution system that went from a massive femur (which in some cases was nearly 8 feet long), to two shin bones, then five foot bones, and then five toes.

Behemoth's tail also closely matched those of sauropods. God describes that he "moves his tail like a cedar tree" and follows this by stating, "the sinews of his thighs are tightly knit." Paleontologists have learned from the muscle attachment locations in their bones that the tightly-knit structure of Behemoth's thighs and hips actually made his tail sway from side-to-side with each step, much as a cedar tree does when it sways in the wind![173] Tail drag marks are only rarely found behind sauropod footprints, indicating their tails were raised while they walked. It's difficult to think of a creature that fits this Biblical description better than a sauropod dinosaur.

God describes his bones "like beams of bronze." Most Bible versions translate this phrase as "tubes of bronze," "conduits of bronze," or "pipes of brass," which conveys both "strength" and being hollow like a channel or a tube. This matches the fact that that sauropods had the largest leg bones of any animal, and they are in fact just like tubes of metal, having a hard outer casing and spongy marrow and veins on the inside.

Then God says that its "ribs are like bars of iron." Unlike much of the sauropod's skeleton that was spongy and filled with air for weight savings, its ribs were *fully ossified*— they were made of solid bone![174] Again, there is a perfect match between God's description of Behemoth and a sauropod dinosaur.

158

God even describes Behemoth's habitat: "He lies under the lotus trees, in a covert of reeds and marsh. The lotus trees cover him with their shade" and "The willows by the brook surround him." This was a creature that had to be near lots of green food—living in a lush, tropical environment. Large sauropods had to eat a half a ton of vegetation every day, and they likely had to eat all day long to consume this amount of food.

Next God says: "Indeed the river may rage, yet he is not disturbed; He is confident, though the Jordan gushes into his mouth." Why would God point out that this animal can stand in a rushing river? Lots of animals can do this, depending on the size of the rushing river. In this case, God said, "the river may *rage*, yet he is *not disturbed*" and that Behemoth is confident even though this raging river should gush into his mouth. The Jordan river is the largest river in Palestine and it currently flows at only 15% of the rate it flowed in the past.[175] Even so, in the winter this river would be incredibly difficult to cross, and it would take a *very* sizable animal to stand *undisturbed* in the rushing current and, even more, let the current gush into its mouth! Some of the larger sauropods stood over 20 feet at the shoulders and weighed over 70 tons. Creatures of this size and mass could withstand a raging river better than any others.

Even with all this evidence, some say that Behemoth was a just a mythical creature. Why would God try to display His awesome creative power by describing something that never existed? Anyone can do that. And why would God say that Behemoth was the "chief" of all His creations after describing 13 real, still-living animals in the same passage? Why go through all the trouble to describe Behemoth as a grass-eating animal that lies peacefully in the shadow of the river plants along with his physical description, diet, and habitat—all of which happen to fit a known creature: a sauropod dinosaur?

Certain Bible footnotes[176] state that Behemoth was a hippo, elephant, or crocodile but these do not come close to matching all 14 characteristics God used to describe Behemoth. They certainly are not the "first in rank" or "chief" of God's creations. Would God tell Job to "gird up his loins" to behold the "chief of His creations" just to show off a hippo? An elephant? These creatures were plentiful! They also don't have tails that sway like cedar trees, and both these animals have been captured and killed by man throughout history.

Table 6 lists 14 characteristics of this creature that are provided in Job 40, and a sauropod dinosaur seems to fit the description better than any other creature, alive or extinct.

Table 6. Behemoth Description from Job 40.

Behemoth Description (Job 40)	Sauropod	Hippo	Crocodile
1 - "made along with" man	YES	YES	YES
2 - eats grass like an ox	YES	YES	NO
3 - strength in hips/stomach muscles	YES	NO	NO
4 - he moves his tail like a cedar	YES	NO	NO
5 - sinews of his thighs are tightly knit	YES	YES	YES
6 - bones are like beams of bronze	YES	NO	NO
7 - ribs like bars of iron	YES	MAYBE	MAYBE
8 - "chief/first" in rank of all God's creations	YES	NO	NO
9 - mountains yield food for him, and all the beasts of the field play there	YES	MAYBE	NO
10 - lies under lotus trees, in reeds/marsh	YES	YES	YES
11 - lotus trees cover him with their shade; willows by the brook surround him	YES	YES	YES
12 - The river may rage, yet he is not disturbed	YES	NO	NO
13 - He is confident, though the Jordan gushes into his mouth	YES	MAYBE	MAYBE
14 - unapproachable by anyone but its maker	YES	NO	NO

God says that only Behemoth's Creator can approach him, that he cannot be captured by humans when he is on watch, and that no one can use barbs to pierce his nose. These impossibilities fit sauropod dinosaurs better than other animals because of their towering heads and huge size. With a head that reached over 40 feet high, it could see people coming from far away. Its massive tail also makes him unapproachable. Based on what we know from fossils, some sauropods could cover a 200-foot circle with deadly force using their tails which could be over 50-feet long and weigh over 13,000 pounds.[177] Studies have shown that some sauropods could probably create sonic booms with their tails—just like a whip.[178]

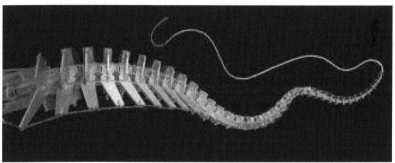

Figure 49. Sauropod Tails Could Create Sonic Booms[179]

Figure 50. Behemoth's Tail Was One Reason Behemoth Was Unapproachable by Anyone but God, His Creator.[180]

161

It's not by chance that God says to Job that Behemoth can *only be approached by his creator*. Good luck even getting near this creature to put a snare in its nose. To this day, elephants and hippos are surrounded by hunters and killed, but sauropods better fit this passage because they are simply unapproachable.

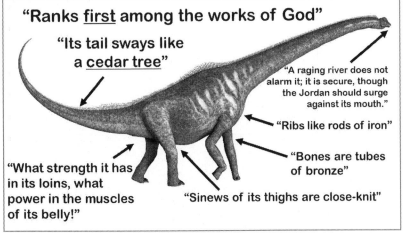

"Ranks **first** among the works of God"

"Its tail sways like a **cedar tree**"

"A raging river does not alarm it; it is secure, though the Jordan should surge against its mouth."

"Ribs like rods of iron"

"Bones are tubes of bronze"

"What strength it has in its loins, what power in the muscles of its belly!"

"Sinews of its thighs are close-knit"

Figure 51. Behemoth in Job Chapter 40.

This section has reviewed the incredible design features that all need to be present for these creatures to live. And the fact that these features—weight-bearing hips, legs, feet, and toes, incredible air-filled vertebrae, and others—show up already formed in the ~300 sauropods that have been found! Yes, there is variability within the sauropod kind, but these animals have been grouped by these (and other) common design characteristics. If God Himself created these animals and placed them on the Earth, then no wonder they had every aspect of their essential design features already in place and fully integrated from the start. The next dinosaur evidence that fits the Bible reviews the fossils.

Evidence #2: Lack of Dinosaur Ancestors and Transitions

The fact that secular dinosaur researchers cannot find the *ancestors* (from which the dinosaurs supposedly evolved) and the *transitions* between the different dinosaurs confirms the Biblical account that they were spontaneously placed here by God (each after their own *kind*—see Genesis 1:25). Figure 52 shows a reconstructed graphic from a leading dinosaur reference book: *The Encyclopedia of Dinosaurs.*[181]

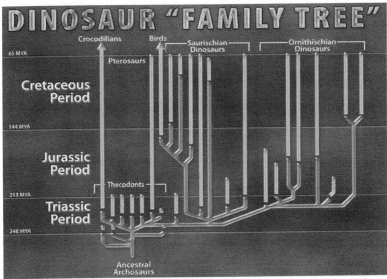

Figure 52. Dinosaur Ancestors and Transitions from *The Encyclopedia of Dinosaurs.*

In small print at the bottom of the chart in the *Encyclopedia of Dinosaurs* it states: "**Tinted areas indicate solid fossil evidence**" (these "tinted areas" are shown in Figure 52 by the broken lines above the tree that starts from the bottom, starting with "Ancestral Archosaurs"). Notice that fossil evidence only exists for the various kinds of dinosaurs themselves, with **no** precursors and **no** transitions! Indeed, the tree that starts at the bottom of the chart is a **theoretical** one because the "real data" based on actual dinosaur fossils only

163

shows the different kinds of dinosaurs, that are always found after their own kind—just like the Bible says in Genesis 1:25: "God made the beasts of the Earth *after their kind...*"

Medical Doctor Carl Werner has done extensive research that confirms there are no ancestors or transitions for the dinosaurs. Dr. Werner spent 17 years traveling to the best museums and dig sites around the globe photographing thousands of original fossils and the actual fossil layers where they were found, and interviewing museum staff about this very question.

One of the examples of this is found in Dr. Werner's book, *Evolution: The Grand Experiment* where he provides a photo taken at the famous Chicago Field Museum. This museum display shows the theoretical evolution of dinosaurs, starting with the "common ancestor" and moving through the "transitions" covering a supposed time span of about 155 million years. There's just one major problem with this museum display—when inserting the number of dinosaur ancestors (at the beginning of the display) and the number of transitions at each of the branches, the display actually proves the *opposite* of what's intended. See Figure 53 that shows the display with these counts added.

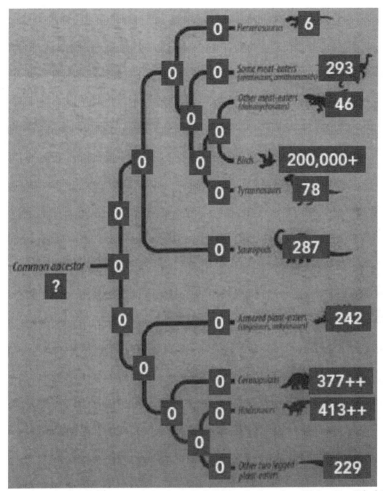

Figure 53. Dinosaur Evolution Display from the Chicago Field
Museum (Counts Added).

After spending 17 years cataloging fossils at museums
and interviewing hundreds of secular scientists about the fossil
evidence of evolution, Dr. Werner found that they could not
agree on a single common ancestor for all dinosaurs or any of
the key supposed transitions between dinosaur kinds. Instead,
each basic kind suddenly appeared on Earth. Notice that all the
supposed transitions between the various dinosaur kinds have a
0 next to them. Dr. Werner could not find a *single* in-between

165

transition that evolutionists can agree on. It's almost like someone just miraculously put dinosaurs here on Earth, each to reproduce after its own kind, just like the Bible says.

Dr. Werner explains the significance of Figure 53 by stating, "Over 30 million dinosaur bones have been discovered. Of these, thousands of individual dinosaur skeletons have been collected by museums representing over 700 dinosaur species. Yet, not a single direct ancestor has been found for any dinosaur. Also, the proposed theoretical common ancestor for all dinosaurs has not been found."[182]

For example, Dr. Viohl, Curator of the Famous Jura Museum in Germany states the following about pterosaurs: "We know only little about the evolution of pterosaurs. The ancestors are not known... When the pterosaurs first appear in the geologic record, they were *completely perfect*. They were *perfect pterosaurs*"[183] (emphasis added). The same is true for every dinosaur group reflected on the chart.

If the theory of evolution is true, and one type of dinosaur evolved into another over millions of years, dinosaur evolution charts in textbooks around the world should be filled with numerous examples of dinosaur kinds evolving into others over the supposed 155 million years they were on Earth. But actual data shows the *exact* opposite.

Now that museums around the world have collected over 100,000 dinosaurs,[184] the number of "transitional" dinosaurs going between the various categories should be evenly distributed if evolution were true. But this is not the case. Even when interviewing numerous leading, evolution-believing scientists at these museums, Dr. Werner could not find a single scientist to offer any transitions. Instead, Dr. Werner found secular scientists stating the opposite.

For example, Dr. David Weishampel, Editor of the encyclopedic reference book *The Dinosauria* wrote, "From my reading of the fossil record of dinosaurs, **no direct ancestors have been discovered for any dinosaur species**. Alas, my list of dinosaurian ancestors is an **empty** one." It appears that dinosaur evolution finds no basis in fossils.

166

Evidence #3: Dinosaur Anatomy Shows They Were Better-suited for the Pre-Flood World

Biblical creationists and evolutionists both agree that the world in which dinosaurs lived was *different* than the world we live in today.[185] While we may not agree on *how* it was different and *when* it was created and changed, we at least agree that Earth has not always been like it is today.

Volumes of evolutionary science papers and books have been written on the atmospheric conditions in which these massive and unusual dinosaurs existed. Some books, such as Peter Ward's *Out of Thin Air: Dinosaurs, Birds, and Earth's Ancient Atmosphere,*[186] have attempted to describe what this ancient world must have been like.

Ward, speaking from the evolutionary viewpoint, believes that changes in oxygen and carbon dioxide levels in the atmosphere over millions of years led to significant changes that allowed the expansion of different types of plants and animals. The basic idea is that the types of plants and animals that were suited for each period of Earth's changing condition survived, and those that were not died off.

Biblical Creation holds that God created a perfect initial world with no death, no carnivory, and no "survival of the fittest."[187] Further, animals were created to reproduce—just as we observe today—after their "own kind." Creationists also believe that this perfect world held out until it was marred by the sin of Adam and Eve, which brought death, suffering, bloodshed, and disease.[188] Geographically, this pre-Flood world had only a single landmass (Rodinia) until the Flood broke the continents apart less than 1,700 years after Creation.[189]

Biblical creationists have presented many pre-Flood climate models over the years, with many of them falling under the heading of "Canopy Models." While several variants exist, all canopy models interpret the "waters above" (firmament) in Genesis 1:7 to be some type of water-based canopy encircling the Earth that existed from the beginning of creation until the Flood. As scientific models, these ideas held promise to explain the pre-Flood climate, but they also produce many conditions (e.g., extreme surface temperatures) that make them problematic. While these models and others exist, we ultimately don't know what the pre-Flood world was like because we weren't there. Further, the Bible only gives a few insights to what the pre-Flood world was like:

- Before the Fall, the atmosphere was *perfect* for sustaining life in all ways (Genesis 1:31) and there was no death (Genesis 2:17; Romans 5:12; 1 Corinthians 15:22).
- Earth's atmosphere likely had sunlight and temperature variations within the days and nights (Genesis 3:8).
- Given that Adam and Eve were told to be "fruitful and multiply and fill the earth" (Genesis 1:27; 3:21) and they were "naked and unashamed" before the Fall (Genesis 2:25), it appears they had no need of clothing before the Fall.
- The Flood ruptured Rodinia and rearranged continents, creating extreme weather on the high mountains that were pushed up that the Flood elevated (Psalm 104:8).
- Genesis 2:5–6 states, "For the Lord God had not caused it to rain on the earth, and there was no man to till the ground; but a mist went up from the earth and watered the whole face of the ground." While some interpret this passage to mean that there was no rain until the Flood (a possibility), this passage is at least clear that before the Sixth Day of Creation Week, God had watered the plants with a mist and had not yet caused rain or created a man to till the ground.
- Because the rainbow was given to mark a new covenant between God and the Earth (to never again Flood the entire earth) (Genesis 9:13), there is the possibility that Earth's climate was changed after (and by) the Flood to allow rainbows.[190] However, God may have used an existing phenomena as a sign of His covenant.

168

These insights point to the idea that the pre-Flood world was quite different than the post-Flood world of today. The New Testament also acknowledges this distinction (2 Peter 3:6: "by which the world that then existed perished, being flooded with water"). Next let's turn to some clues in the fossil record that may also indicate that the pre-Flood world wasn't like today's world.

- Giant land beasts, such as sauropod dinosaurs that grew as large as 115 feet and 140,000 pounds (estimates vary).
- Giant flying reptiles, pterosaurs, with over 50-foot wingspans (e.g., *Quetzalcoatlus*).
- Giant dragonflies with 2-1/2 foot wingspans and 17-inch bodies (*Meganeura*).
- Mushrooms that grew over 20-feet high (*Prototaxites*).[191]
- Giant millipedes that grew over eight feet long (*Arthropleura*).

The above list could be much longer; these are just a few examples. Biblical creationists and evolutionists agree that these giant creatures and plants existed. Indeed, they are in the fossil record for everyone to evaluate, regardless of the worldview lens through which they are viewed. We also agree that these giant creatures and plants existed in a *different version of the Earth*, with evolutionists placing this version millions of years ago and Biblical creationists placing it before the Flood, about 4,400 years ago. Let's briefly review each of these examples.

Giant Land Beasts (Sauropods)

In the previous section, we looked at the massive, unmatched size of the sauropod dinosaurs, but we left out one important feature of this magnificent animal until now—*how they breathed*. Many who have studied this issue would agree

169

that these creatures would have a difficult time staying alive very long in today's current atmosphere with only 21% oxygen levels. This is, at least in part, due to this animal's extremely small nasal passages compared to its enormous body size. See Figure 54.

"**An 80-foot-long brontosaurus had a set of nostrils about the same size as a horse's... There were some serious problems with trying to get air into that animal.**"
– Richard Hengst, Purdue University Physiologist

Figure 54. Giant Sauropod.

Notice the immense size of the sauropod's body compared to its nasal passages? While the nasal structures of the different sauropods vary, one consistent trait is the extremely small nasal passages compared to their body size. The explanation given by some evolutionists is simply that the ancient Earth had higher oxygen levels (35%),[192] and when the oxygen level dropped, the dinosaurs died out (one of many dinosaur extinction theories offered by evolutionists).[193]

Scientists that have studied sauropod anatomy have recognized this challenge, stating: "An 80-foot-long brontosaurus had a set of nostrils about the same size as a horse's ... there were some serious problems with trying to get air into that animal. Dinosaurs could not have existed without having more oxygen in the air to start with."[194]

So just what were the oxygen levels of the pre-Flood world? To be fair, we really don't know. Some Biblical

170

creationists have theorized, at least when it comes to giant insects that are in the fossil record that grew to enormous sizes, that oxygen levels might have played a part. For example, when discussing the fact that pre-Flood insects grew much larger than today and the possibility that higher oxygen levels may be one possible explanation, Drs. Carl Wieland and Jonathan Sarfati stated, "This may be because the pre-Flood world carried more oxygen-producing vegetation."[195]

Giant Flying Reptiles (Pterosaurs)

One of the largest flying reptiles is *Quetzalcoatlus*, which was named after the Mesoamerican feathered serpent god, Quetzalcoatl. Many studies have attempted to estimate this creature's wingspan, with most estimates coming in over 36 feet.[196]

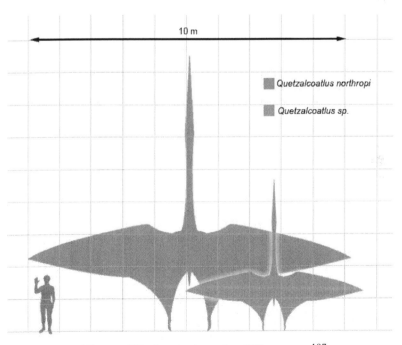

Figure 55. Quetzalcoatlus Wingspan.[197]

The wingspan, however, is not what puzzles scientists about this giant—it's the *large wingspan given its weight*. While estimates vary, some studies estimate the weight of the larger specimens discovered to exceed 500 pounds.[198] That's likely too much weight for a flying creature to bear and still be able to fly. Several studies have investigated how these massive creatures could fly, with some reports even titled, "This Pterodactyl was so big it couldn't fly" and opening sentences such as "Bad news dragon riders: Your dragon can't take off."[199]

Scientists who have studied and published on this extensively have even admitted: "…it is now generally agreed that even the largest pterosaurs could not have flown in today's skies" and have offered explanations such as "warmer climate" or "higher levels of atmospheric oxygen" as reasons it could have flown only during the era in which it lived.[200]

Some secular studies that have investigated air bubbles trapped in amber that was dated to the "ancient world in which dinosaurs lived," have found *both* increased pressure as well as greater oxygen levels: "'One implication is that the atmospheric pressure of the Earth would have been much greater during the Cretaceous era, when the bubbles formed in the resin. A dense atmosphere could also explain how the ungainly pterosaur, with its stubby body and wingspan of up to 11 meters, could have stayed airborne,' he said. 'The spread of angiosperms, flowering plants, during the Cretaceous era could have caused the high oxygen levels[201] reported by Berner and Landis.'"[202]

Interesting—giant sauropods couldn't likely breathe in today's world, giant flying reptiles that could not have flown in today's atmosphere—what's next? Giant dragonflies.

Giant Dragonflies (Meganeura)

The largest dragonfly species alive today (*Megaloprepus caerulatus*) has a wingspan of up to seven inches and a body up to five inches long. Based on the fossil record, the largest pre-

Flood dragonflies (*Meganeura*) had wingspans up to 2-1/2 feet and a 17-inch body. See Figure 56.

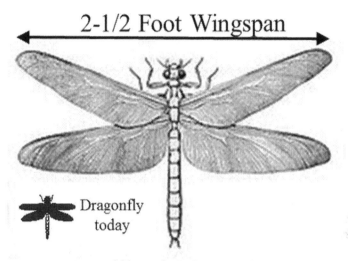

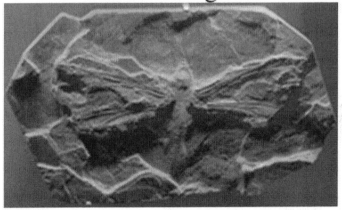

Figure 56. Giant Pre-Flood Dragonfly (*Meganeura*).[203]

In October 2006, *Science Daily* publicized a study led by Arizona State University staff titled "Giant Insects Might Reign if Only There Was More Oxygen in the Air."[204] The article claims:

The delicate lady bug in your garden could be frighteningly large if only there was a greater concentration of oxygen in the air, a new study concludes. The study adds support to the theory that some insects were much larger during the late Paleozoic period because they had a much richer oxygen supply, said the study's lead author Alexander Kaiser. The Paleozoic period...was a time of huge and abundant plant life and rather large insects—dragonflies had two-and-a-half-foot wing spans, for example. The air's oxygen content was 35% during this period, compared to the 21% we breathe now, Kaiser said.

This research lends evidence to the fact that the pre-Flood world was different than the one we live in today. One study conducted in 2010 by researchers at Arizona State University tested this "more oxygen = bigger insects" theory directly by raising 12 different types of insects in simulated atmospheres with various oxygen levels. Their study included three sets of 75 dragonflies in atmospheres containing 12%, 21%, and 31% oxygen levels and their experiment confirmed that dragonflies grow bigger with more oxygen.[205] While there are likely a host of reasons why the pre-Flood dragonflies grew much larger than those today, especially genetic bottlenecking at the Genesis Flood, it is quite interesting to see the clear dichotomy between larger creatures of many types before the Flood compared to the animals alive today.

Giant Millipedes (Arthropleura)

Giant millipedes (called *Arthropleura*) that grew to be over eight feet long[206] used to crawl around before the Flood in what became northeastern America and Scotland. While evolutionists assign "millions of years" to these creatures, all we can know for total certainty is that they died. The larger

174

species of this group are the largest known land invertebrates of all time. Evolutionists attribute their grand size to different pressures and/or oxygen levels of Earth's ancient past.[207]

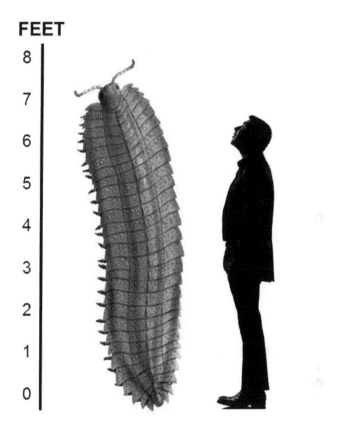

FEET

Figure 57. Giant Pre-Flood Millipedes (*Arthropleura*).

Evidence #4: The Vast Extent of the Fossil Record

President of Answers in Genesis, Ken Ham, has become well-known for making this statement: "If there really was a Global Flood, what would the evidence be? Billions of dead things, buried in rock layers, laid down by water all over the Earth." This is exactly what we see.

For example, the Paleobiology Database (PaleoBioDB) is a free, searchable database that is designed to "provide global, collection-based occurrence and taxonomic data for organisms of all geological ages."[208] This database includes 183,739 fossil *collections* totaling 1,323,009 *occurrences* (with each "occurrence" ranging from a few fossils to numerous). From a Biblical Creation standpoint, the Genesis Flood deposited the vast majority of these fossils. The circles in Figure 58 shows the extent of the known fossil record.

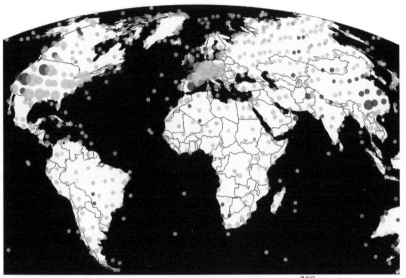

Figure 58. Paleobiology Database.[209]

If the untestable assumptions that hold up the ideas of radiometric dating are not true (and we believe they are not[210]), then Figure 58 displays a massive, watery graveyard, most of which was filled during the year-long Genesis Flood.

The number of dinosaur "mass graves" around the world is astounding. These fossil graveyards contain a mixture of many different kinds of fossils that have been *transported by large volumes of water* (see Figure 59). Modern, small-scale debris flows offer examples of what likely entrained in some cases millions of animals. Like a giant water wing, a debris flow carries its load largely undisturbed inside, as it rides upon a watery cushion either underwater or over land. As soon as the flow slows to a certain speed, turbulence overwhelms the load and it drops in place.

Figure 59. Fossil Graveyard Example.

Bone fossils typically occur as broken fragments. They were violently carried along with enormous mounds of mud and shifting sediments. By studying some of these fossil graveyards, we can gather clues that will demonstrate that the Flood was in fact catastrophic and worldwide, as stated in Genesis 7:20–23:

> The waters rose and covered the mountains to a depth of more than fifteen cubits [at least 22 feet]. *Every living thing* that moved on land perished—birds, livestock, wild animals, *all the creatures* that swarm over the earth, and *all mankind. Everything* on dry land that had the breath of life in its nostrils died. *Every living thing* on the face of the earth was wiped out; people and animals and the creatures that move

along the ground and the birds were wiped from the earth. *Only Noah was left,* and those with him in the ark. (emphasis added)

If this passage in Genesis is true, we would expect to find *billions of dead things buried in rock layers laid down by water all over the earth.*[211] And this is exactly what we find *all over the world.*

Another profound example is Dinosaur National Monument in Utah, which is only a part of the 700,000-square mile Morrison Formation, a geologic unit that has spawned excavations of more than a hundred dinosaur quarries.[212]

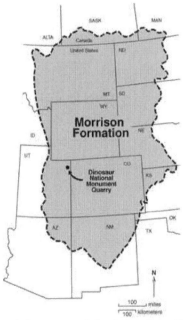

Figure 60. Aerial extent of the Morrison Formation.[213]

What type of catastrophe could possibly bury hundreds of massive bone beds in this 700,000-square mile area, all at once? It could represent an enormous, ancient debris flow that only a worldwide watery catastrophe could reasonably explain.

178

Evidence #5: Dinosaurs Were Buried Furiously (Disarticulated)

Only about 3,000 of the dinosaur fossils that have been collected represent "articulated"[214] (bones still in place) animals. Because over 100,000 dinosaurs have been found, this represents only about 3% of the dinosaur fossil record.[215] So these animals did not die peacefully. Whatever wiped them out was *sudden* and *violent*. A good example is Dinosaur Provincial Park in Canada, which is one of the largest mass dinosaur graves in the world. In just this one area, over 32,000 fossil specimens have been found, representing 35 species, 34 genera, and 12 families of dinosaurs. Astonishingly, dinosaur fossils intermingle with fish, turtles, marsupial and other mammals, and amphibians. Also, only 300 complete animals have been found! The large majority were scrambled, pulverized, and blended together, as if the world became an enormous washing machine.

Evidence #6: Dinosaurs Were Quickly Buried in Mud

The very fact that we have so many preserved dinosaur fossils shows that they were buried quickly because fossilization requires rapid burial in muddy ground. The fossil record is full of dinosaurs that suddenly died in watery graves around the world, with many of them found in the famous death pose" with their necks arched back, as if drowning in mud.[216]

Figure 61. Dinosaurs in the Common "Death Pose," Indicating Rapid Burial and Suffocation (Royal Tyrrell Museum, Author).

Evidence #7: Dinosaurs Were Buried Simultaneously, Fleeing in Groups

Sauropod and Triceratops Graveyards

From a Biblical viewpoint, the Paleobiology Database is useful for finding where extinct animal groups (like dinosaurs) may have lived before they were wiped out by the Flood. For example, Figure 62 plots both the sauropod and triceratops dinosaur fossils that have been found in the Midwestern United States. Isn't it interesting that these totally different dinosaur types were simultaneously wiped out and buried in the *same areas*? Something stopped these two very large dinosaur types dead in their tracks and buried them in mud, preserving their fossils for us to find today.

Sauropod Fossils in the Midwest

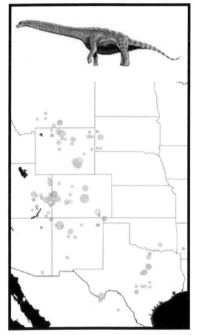

Triceratops Fossils in the Midwest

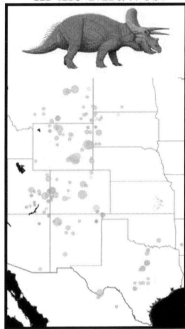

Figure 62. Sauropod and Triceratops Graveyards.

Sauropods and Triceratops are some of the largest dinosaurs to ever live. What type of event would it take to bury these massive creatures in mud so quickly that they would be disarticulated and preserved for us to find today—locked in mud that hardened into rock before getting scavenged? Slow, gradually-rising creeks or rivers? A sudden worldwide Flood explains more.

Thousands of Buried Centrosaurs in Hilda, Canada

The famous Hilda bone beds in Canada, briefly discussed above, actually include 14 dinosaur "bone beds" that contain thousands of buried Centrosaurs *found in the same*

181

stratigraphic column (a term used in geology to describe the vertical location of rocks in a particular area). The authors who completed the most extensive study of the area described the sediment in which these dinosaurs are buried as "mudstone rich in organic matter deposited on the tract of land separating two ancient rivers."[217] They also concluded that each of the 14 bone beds was actually part of a single, massive "mega-bone bed" that occupied 2.3 square kilometers—almost a square mile! Stop and think about this for a minute. How did thousands of dinosaurs—of the same species—get herded up and simultaneously buried in mud?

These authors even concluded that the massive bone beds were formed when a herd of Centrosaurs *drowned during a flood.* These bone beds are also found with aquatic vertebrates such as fish, turtles, and crocodiles, showing that water was definitely involved in their transport and burial. In addition, almost no teeth marks indicated any scavenging after these animals died, probably because most of them died at the same time.[218]

Massive Dinosaur Graveyard Found in China

An online article on Discovery.com describes the dinosaur graveyard in China as the largest in the world, writing, "Researchers say they can't understand why so many animals gathered in what is today the city of Zhucheng to die." Thousands of dinosaur bones stack on top of each other in "incredible density," then they "suddenly vanished from the face of the earth."[219] Most of the bones are found within a single 980-foot-long ravine in the Chinese countryside, about 415 miles southeast of Beijing. Clearly, processes were going on in the past that were so violent they are hardly imaginable.

10,000+ Duck-billed Dinosaurs Buried Alive in Montana

In his article titled, "The Extinction of the Dinosaurs," Creation researcher and career meteorologist Michael Oard describes some of the numerous dinosaur graveyards that are found all over the world.[220] He believes this is solid evidence of Noah's worldwide Flood. Oard reported that one of the largest bone beds in the world is located in north-central Montana:

> Based on outcrops, an extrapolated estimate was made for 10,000 duckbill dinosaurs entombed in a thin layer measuring 2 km east-west and 0.5 km north-south. The bones are disarticulated and disassociated, and are orientated east-west. However, a few bones were standing upright, indicating some type of debris flow. Moreover, there are no young juveniles or babies in this bone-bed, and the bones are all from one species of dinosaur.

Two other scientists, Horner and Gorman, also described the bone bed: "How could any mud slide, no matter how catastrophic, have the force to take a two- or three-ton animal that had just died and smash it around so much that its femur—still embedded in the flesh of its thigh—split lengthwise?"[221] Oard concluded that a cataclysmic event is the best explanation for the arrangement of the bones.

Figure 63 shows the text from museum displays or articles about the particular dinosaur graveyard shown. Isn't it incredible that everyone admits that some type of watery catastrophe was responsible for piling up the dinosaurs into these mass graves?

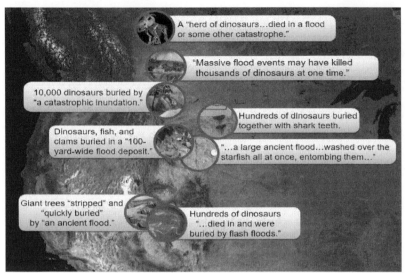

Figure 63. Dinosaur Graveyards in Midwestern U.S. with "Flood Catastrophe" Explanations from Secular Sources.[222]

Evidence #8: Dinosaur Fossils Are Frequently Mixed with Marine Fossils

Mainstream scientists who deny that dinosaurs were buried in the Global Flood seem to closely clutch a "trade secret"—that dinosaur fossils are commonly found with marine fossils.[223] This is especially true of the Hell Creek Formation in Montana, where five shark species and 14 species of fish fossils have been found alongside dinosaurs.[224]

What in the world are shark and fish doing with massive land dinosaurs? Did a tropical storm pick up the sharks and fish and bury them with the dinosaurs? It seems that the Flood provides just about the only logical explanation. The Bible states in Genesis 7:11: "In the six hundredth year of Noah's life, in the second month, the seventeenth day of the month, the same day were *all the fountains of the great deep broken up, and the windows of heaven were opened.*" This describes a catastrophe of incomprehensible proportions. Breaking up *all the fountains of the deep* describes a mechanism that could cause massive, worldwide tsunamis that could carry ocean

184

water far onto the continents, especially if the fountains of the deep included magma, and that magma repaved and elevated the world's ocean floors as geophysicist John Baumgardner has modeled.[225]

In addition to the Hell Creek area, this "mixing" of marine and land creatures is also evident in the Dinosaur Provincial Park in Canada where 12 families of dinosaurs are found mixed together with fish, turtles, marsupials, and amphibians. In Morocco, they've discovered sharks, sawfish, ray-finned fishes, and coelocanths in the same rock layers as a Spinosaurus dinosaur.[226]

Evidence #9: Dinosaurs Are Frequently Buried without Juveniles

Jack Horner, secular paleontologist, has spent a lifetime in the field hunting dinosaur fossils. In his book, *Digging Dinosaurs*, Horner reported one of the oddest findings of his career: The discovery of a huge dinosaur graveyard—over 10,000 adult Maiasaura in a small area, and yet no young were mixed in with them.[227]

What could have caused this odd sorting? If one adopts the Biblical Creation view, the Flood provides a very practical explanation. As Dr. Tim Clarey explains: "The adult dinosaurs were likely stampeding away from the imminent danger of raging floodwaters; their young could not keep up and became engulfed in some lower part of the peninsula."[228] This would explain Horner's maiasaurs, as well as the age-sorted deposits described above.

Evidence #10: Fresh Dinosaur Biomaterials[229]

Next, we'll look at 14 short-lived dinosaur biomaterials that remain in dinosaur bones and other body parts like skin and horns. Decay experiments have placed outer limits on how long they should last before completely decaying. For each of these materials, their "expiration date" is well before 65 million years, which is when dinosaurs supposedly went extinct. So, rather than being 65 million years old, these materials are just thousands of years old. The science of protein decay fits the Bible's timeline of dinosaurs recently buried in Noah's Flood. Secular scientists have published each of these dinosaur-era fresh biomaterials in peer-reviewed evolution-based science journals. One of most frequently used "rescuing devices" that's given by evolutionists to try to explain some of these findings is "bacterial contamination." However, microbes do not produce *any* of the biomaterials covered below, ruling out recent contamination.

For readers who would like to dive deeper into this line of research, we recommend the Spring 2015 issue of the *Creation Research Society Quarterly Journal*,[230] which includes a technical review of what's covered in summary form below.

Fresh Dinosaur Biomaterial #1: Blood Vessels

Blood vessels transport blood throughout the body. They include the tiny capillaries, through which water and chemicals pass between blood and the tissue. Bones include capillaries and larger vessels. Small, pancake-shaped cells loaded with long-lasting collagen protein comprise blood vessels.

The blood vessels shown in Figure 64 were discovered when Dr. Mary Schweitzer's team was attempting to move a gigantic *Tyrannosaurus rex* fossil by helicopter that turned out to be too heavy. They were forced to break apart the leg bone. When looking at the inside of the leg bone at the lab, they discovered that the inside of the bone was partially hollow (not mineralized), revealing the soft tissue shown in Figure 64 that was extracted after treatments to remove the minerals.[231]

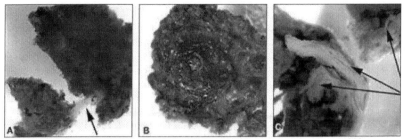

Figure 64. Tissue Fragments from a *T-rex* Femur.[232]

The tissues that are shown on the left of Figure 64 show that it is flexible and resilient. When stretched, it returned to its original shape. The middle photo shows the bone after it was air dried. The photo at right shows regions of bone showing fibrous tissue, not normally seen in fossil bone.

Since this publication in 2005, blood vessels from several other dinosaurs and other extinct reptiles have been described and published in numerous leading scientific journals, including the *Annals of Anatomy, Science* (the leading journal of the American Association for the Advancement of Science), *Public Library of Sciences ONE*, and the *Proceedings from the Royal Society B*, which focuses on the biological sciences.[233]

Fresh Dinosaur Biomaterial #2: Red Blood Cells

Red blood cells carry oxygen and collect carbon dioxide using hemoglobin protein—also found in dinosaur and other fossils. Dr. Mary Schweitzer was one of the first to discover and publish the discovery of red blood cells, which she shares in her own words: "The lab filled with murmurs of amazement, for I had focused on something inside the vessels that none of us had ever noticed before: tiny round objects, translucent red with a dark center. Then a colleague took one look at them and shouted, 'You've got red blood cells. You've got red blood cells!'"[234]

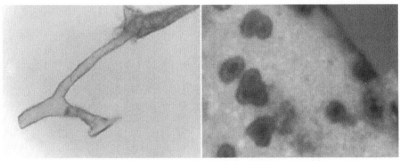

Figure 65. Red Blood Vessels and Cells from a *T-rex* Bone.

These two photos in Figure 65 are from a 2005 discovery from Dr. Schweitzer that clearly show blood vessels from a *T. rex* bone (left) and red blood cells (right). How could these cells last for 65 million years? At least five peer-reviewed scientific journals have published accounts of red blood cells in dinosaur and other fossil bones.[235]

Regarding this discovery, Dr. Schweitzer remarked, "If you take a blood sample, and you stick it on a shelf, you have nothing recognizable in about a week. So why would there be anything left in dinosaurs?"[236] That's certainly a good question, and one that has an easier answer if dinosaurs are only thousands of years old!

After this discovery, Dr. Schweitzer ran into challenges when trying to publish her work in the scientific literature. Dr. Schweitzer remarks, "I had one reviewer tell me that he didn't care what the data said, he knew that what I was finding wasn't possible." Dr. Schweitzer wrote him back and asked, "Well, what type of data would convince you." The reviewer replied, "None."

Fresh Dinosaur Biomaterial #3: Hemoglobin

Hemoglobin protein contains iron and transports oxygen in red blood cells of most vertebrates. Some invertebrates, including certain insects and some worms, also use hemoglobin. In vertebrates, this amazing protein picks up oxygen from lungs or gills and carries it to the rest of the body's cells. There, oxygen fuels aerobic respiration by which cells produce energy. Scientific studies have reported "striking evidence for the presence of hemoglobin derived peptides in the (T-rex) bone extract"[237] and several other dinosaur "era" bones.[238]

Fresh Dinosaur Biomaterial #4: Bone Cells (Osteocytes)

Secular scientists have described dinosaur proteins like hemoglobin, even though no experimental evidence supports the possibility that they can last for even a million years. But dinosaur bones hold more than just individual proteins. They sometimes retain whole cells and tissue remnants. An osteocyte is a bone cell that can live as long as the organism itself. Osteocytes constantly rebuild bones and regulate bone mass.

Figure 66 shows highly magnified blood vessels, blood products, and osteocytes that were found on the inside of a brow horn of a Triceratops.

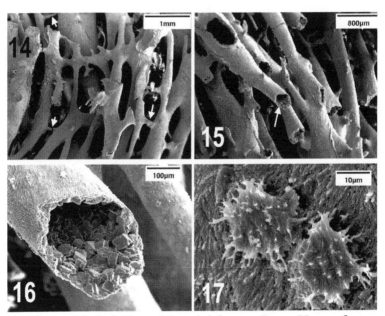

Figure 66. Soft Bone Material from a Brow Horn of a *Triceratops horridus* from Montana.[239]

Figure 66 shows blood vessels linked together (white arrows in frame 14). Frame 15 shows possible blood products lining inner wall of hardened vessel (white arrow). Frame 16 is enlarged from frame 15 and shows crystallized nature of possible blood products lining inner wall of hardened vessel. Frame 17 shows two large oblate osteocytes lying on fibrillar bone matrix.

At least four scientific studies have established osteocytes in dinosaur bones. One study even found nucleic acid signatures consistent with ancient DNA right where the nucleus would have been in dinosaur osteocytes.[240]

Fresh Dinosaur Biomaterial #5: Ovalbumin (Proteins)

Another protein found in fossils that microbes don't make is called ovalbumin. It makes up 60–65% of the total protein in egg whites. Ovalbumin has been found in exceptionally preserved sauropod eggs discovered in Patagonia, Argentina, a dig site that included skeletal remains and soft tissues of embryonic titanosaurid dinosaurs. These findings were reported in a peer-reviewed scientific journal.[241]

Fresh Dinosaur Biomaterial #6: Chitin

Chitin is a biochemical found in squid beaks and pens, arthropod exoskeletons, and certain fungi. If chitin was meant to last for millions of years, then it might have filled Earth's surface as dead insects, krill, and fungi left their remains over eons. Chitin is tough, but no known experiment supplies any reason to so much as suspect that it could last a million years, let alone hundreds of millions, as at least two scientific studies report finding in fossils.[242] Our Creator equipped many microbes with unique enzymes that digest chitin, so what could have kept those microbes away from all that chitin for millions of years?

Fresh Dinosaur Biomaterial #7: Unmineralized Bone

Fresh-looking, un-mineralized dinosaur bones pop up in dig sites around the world. In Alaska, for example, a petroleum geologist working for Shell Oil Company discovered well-preserved bones in Alaska along the Colville River. The bones looked so fresh that he assumed these were recently deposited, perhaps belonging to a mammoth or bison. Twenty years later scientists recognized them as Edmontosaurus bones—a duck-billed dinosaur.[243]

Figure 67. Unfossilized Hadrosaur Bone from the Liscomb Bone Bed.[244]

Mineralized bones can look darker than bone and typically feel quite heavy. Un-mineralized bones retain their original structure, often including the tiny pore spaces in spongy bone, as shown in Figure 67. One study includes an interesting section that states:

191

Finally, a two-part mechanism, involving first cross-linking of molecular components and subsequent mineralization, is proposed to explain the surprising presence of still-soft elements in fossil bone. These results suggest that present models of fossilization processes may be incomplete and that *soft tissue elements may be more commonly preserved, even in older specimens, than previously thought.*[245] Additionally, in many cases, osteocytes with defined nuclei are preserved, and may represent an important source for informative molecular data (emphasis added).

Numerous other studies published in scientific journals have described these un-mineralized dinosaur bone findings.[246] Sometimes evolutionists are surprised by the fact that many dinosaur bones contain "fresh," original bone. It seems that decades of conditioning that "dinosaur bones become solid rocks" and ideas of "millions of years" have framed assumptions that are frequently being broken today. However, researchers out in the field—actually digging up bones—oftentimes have a different viewpoint. Take Dr. Mary Schweitzer's testimony for example, where she notes that many "fresh" dinosaur bones still have the stench of death:

> This shifting perspective clicked with Schweitzer's intuitions that dinosaur remains were more than chunks of stone. Once, when she was working with a *T. rex* skeleton harvested from Hell Creek, she noticed that the fossil exuded a distinctly organic odor. "It smelled just like one of the cadavers we had in the lab who had been treated with chemotherapy before he died," she says. Given the conventional wisdom that such fossils were made up entirely of minerals, Schweitzer was anxious when mentioning this to Horner [a leading paleontologist]. "But he said, 'Oh, yeah, all Hell Creek bones smell,'" she says. To most old-line paleontologists, the smell of death didn't even

register. To Schweitzer, it meant that traces of life might still cling to those bones.[247]

Experienced dinosaur fossil collectors have developed similar opinions. Take experienced dinosaur hunter and wholesaler, Alan Stout, for example. Alan Stout is a long-time fossil collector and has collected and sold millions of dollars' worth of dinosaur specimens to collectors, researchers, and museums worldwide.[248] After collecting in the Montana Hell Creek formation (and surrounding areas) for over a decade Alan states that many of the dinosaur bones he finds in the Cretaceous layers are only 40% mineralized, with as much as 60% of the bone being original material. He even notes that some of the fossils "look just like they were buried yesterday after scraping off just the outside layer of mineralization."[249]

Fresh Dinosaur Biomaterial #8: Collagen

Collagen is the main structural protein found in animal connective tissue. When boiled, collagen turns into gelatin, showing its sensitivity to temperature. In 2007, scientists discovered collagen amino acid sequences from a *T. rex* fossil that supposedly dated at 68 million years. Met with controversy, some suggested these proteins came from lab workers who accidentally contaminated the samples being studied. Or perhaps traces of ostrich bone proteins lingered in the equipment used in the study. Some even said, well perhaps "a bird died on top of the *T. rex* excavation site."[250] However, three separate labs verified collagen in dinosaurs in 2009[251] and again in January 2017.[252] The 2017 study even confirmed the collagen at the *molecular level*, and stated, "We are confident that the results we obtained are not contamination and that this collagen is original to the specimen."[253]

193

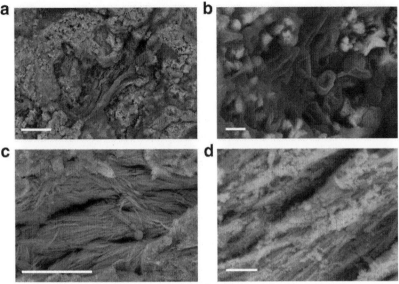

Figure 68. Fibers and Cellular Structures in Dinosaur
Specimens.[254]

Experiments have projected that the absolute theoretical
maximum life of collagen ranges from 300,000 to 900,000 years
under the best possible conditions.[255] This shows that collagen
proteins should not last one million years, but could (in the
absence of microbes) last for thousands of years. This confronts
millions-of-years age assignments for dinosaur remains, but is
consistent with the biblical time frame.

But the "rescuing devices" being offered by
evolutionists are not far behind. For example, in a recent article
published in *Science*, Dr. Schweitzer tried to explain how the
collagen sequences supposedly survived tens of millions of
years: "... as red blood cells decay after an animal dies, iron
liberated from their hemoglobin may react with nearby proteins,
linking them together. This crosslinking, she says, causes
proteins to precipitate out of solution, drying them out in a way
that helps preserve them." Critical of this idea, however, Dr.
Matthew Collins, a paleoproteomics expert at the University of
York in the United Kingdom, stated that he doesn't think that

the process described by Dr. Schweitzer could "arrest protein degradation for tens of millions of years, so he, for one, remains skeptical of Schweitzer's claim: 'Proteins decay in an orderly fashion. We can slow it down, but not by a lot.'"[256]

Fresh Dinosaur Biomaterial #9: DNA (Limited)

One measured decay rate of DNA, extracted from recently deposited fossil bird bones, showed a half-life of 521 years. DNA decays quickly. It should have spontaneously decayed into smaller chemicals after several tens of thousands of years—and it could only last that long if kept cool. A few brave secular scientists have reported DNA structures from dinosaur bones, although they did not directly address the question of its age.[257]

Fresh Dinosaur Biomaterial #10: Skin Pigments

In 2008, a group of paleontologists found exceptionally well-preserved Psittacosaurus remains in China and published images of dinosaur collagen fiber bundles. Other scientists published stunning skin color images from a separate Psittacosaurus, also from China, and found evidence of original, unaltered pigments including carotenoids and melanins. Nobody has performed an experiment that so much as suggests these pigments could last a million years. Still other studies have reported scale skin and hemoglobin decay products—still colored red as were some of Dr. Mary Schweitzer's *T. rex* and hadrosaurine samples—in a Kansas mosasaur.[258]

Fresh Dinosaur Biomaterial #11: PHEX (Proteins)

PHEX is a protein involved in bone mineralization in mammals. In 2013, Dr. Mary Schweitzer published detailed findings of the soft, transparent microstructures her team found in dinosaur bones. Because this discovery was so controversial, her team used advanced mass spectrometry techniques to sequence the collagen. Other methods demonstrated that proteins such as Actin, Tubulin, and PHEX found in osteocytes from two different dinosaurs were not from some form of contamination, but came from the creatures' remains.[259]

Fresh Dinosaur Biomaterial #12: Histone H4 (Proteins)

Bacteria do not make histone H4, but animals do. DNA wraps around it like a spool. Dr. Mary Schweitzer and her team found this protein inside a hadrosaur femur found in the Hell Creek Formation in Montana, which bears an assigned age of 67 million years. It might last for thousands of years if kept sterile, but no evidence so much as hints that it could last for a million years.[260]

Fresh Dinosaur Biomaterial #13: Keratin (Structural Protein)

Keratin forms the main structural constituent of hair, feathers, hoofs, claws, and horns. Some modern lizard skins contain tiny disks of keratin embedded in their scales. Researchers identified keratin protein in fossilized lizard skin scales from the Green River Formation that supposedly date to 50 million years ago. They explained its presence with a story about clay minerals attaching to the keratin to hold it in place for all that time. However, water would have to deposit the clay, and water helps rapidly degrade keratin. The most scientifically responsible explanation should be the simplest one—that this fossil is thousands, not millions of years old.[261] Other fossils with original keratin include Archaeopteryx[262] bird feather residue and stegosaur spikes.[263]

Fresh Dinosaur Biomaterial #14: Elastin

Elastin is a highly elastic protein found in connective tissue, skin, and bones. It helps body parts resume their shape after stretching or contracting, like when skin gets poked or pinched. Bacteria don't need it or make it, and elastin should not last a million years, even under the best preservation environment. Scientists reported finding this protein in a hadrosaur femur found in the Hell Creek Formation in Montana.[264]

Biomaterial Summary

Because these findings are game-changers, they are not without challenge by those who hold strongly to evolutionary ideas. Some of the "rescuing devices" that have been offered to attempt to explain these findings include iron in the blood acting as a preservative, the material being mistaken from a bird carcass mixed with the fossil, laboratory contamination, and even microbial biofilm (from bacteria in the bones). These explanations show an eagerness to attempt to dismiss the findings while clinging to the belief in millions of years. Rather than questioning the supposed long ages needed to prop up the evolutionary view, they seek other explanations to explain the presence of these materials.

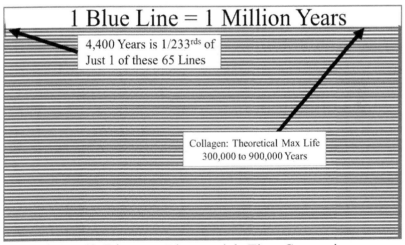

Figure 69. Dinosaur Biomaterials Time Comparison.

Figure 69 shows a simulated timeline to attempt to put these findings into perspective. Each of these 65 lines represents

1 million years. Showing 4,400 years on this chart is difficult, but is represented by a tiny dot in the upper left, which is 1/233rds of just one of these lines, or less than one-half of 1 percent of one of these lines. While this assumption can never be tested, some studies have measured an absolute theoretical maximum life of between 300,000 and 900,000 years.[265] If these dinosaur bones are really 65 million years old (and older), this collagen lasted for *72 to 217 times longer than these measured and extrapolated maximum collagen shelf lives.* Does this require strong faith?

Is it really possible that all 14 of these biomaterials lasted for 65 million years? If they represent more recent deposits and were quickly sealed in Noah's Flood only thousands of years ago, then these finds fit fine. The fact that these materials lasted even this long is remarkable, but within measured age estimates. These 14 fresh biomaterials—along with carbon-14 as we'll see next—clearly fit a timescale of just thousands of years more accurately than millions of years.

Evidence #11: Carbon-14 Found in Dinosaur Bones

Secular scientists typically don't look for carbon-14 in dinosaur bones because evolutionary deep time does not allow the possibility of recently-deposited dinosaurs. Carbon-14 decays so fast that all of it would spontaneously turn into nitrogen 14 in fewer than 100,000 years. According to evolutionists, why even look for it in samples that are supposed to be much older than this?

The Spring 2015 issue of the *Creation Research Society Quarterly Journal*[266] carried a study that tested seven dinosaur bones from Montana, Canada, and Oklahoma that five different laboratories detected carbon-14 in all samples from Cenozoic, Mesozoic, and Paleozoic source rocks. How did radiocarbon get there if it supposedly has a maximum shelf life of 100,000 years?

Several carbon-14 dating studies have shown the presence of carbon-14 in dinosaur bones and other fossils and

Earth materials. If dinosaur bones are 100,000 years—let alone 65 million years—old, not one atom of carbon-14 should remain in them. But both secular and creation scientists have now published findings of small amounts of carbon-14 from ancient wood, coal, fish bones, lizard bones, ammonites, clams, diamonds, oil, marble, and dinosaur bone. It's as if the whole Earth's surface is thousands, not millions, of years old. But that means the Bible's history is correct and that evolutionary history leans more on imagination than observation.

Evidence #12: Dinosaur Mummies

Charles Sternberg discovered the first dinosaur mummy in Wyoming in 1908. This duck-billed dinosaur (*Edmontosaurus annectens*) was one of the finest dinosaur specimens discovered (until replaced by "Leonardo"—see below). It was the first dinosaur find on record that included a skeleton encased in skin impressions from large parts of the body (see Figure 70).

Figure 70. The Trachodon Mummy on Exhibit in the American Museum of Natural History (2008).[267]

Dan Stephenson discovered "Leonardo" in 2000. This dinosaur mummy is one of the best-preserved dinosaur fossil in the world, which is about 90 percent covered in soft tissue, including skin, muscle, nail material, and a beak. Skin impressions have even been found on the underside of the skull and all along the neck, ribcage, legs, and left arm.[268] This finding was so well preserved it even made the *Guinness Book of World Records*!

Figure 71. Leonardo's Certificate.

They even found the "fresh" content of Leonardo's last meal in his stomach! More than 40 different kinds of plants were found in his stomach and intestines, including tree leaves, flowers, ferns, shrubs and even algae that he likely swallowed getting a drink of water.[269] One must ask: How in the world did these soft tissues, leaves, flowers, and ferns last for over 77 million years? Seems very unlikely. Biblical creationists would place this animal about 4,400 years old, quickly buried by the Genesis Flood and sealed beneath sand for us to find today in "fresh" condition. Comparing the two worldviews, 77 million years is about *18,000 times longer* than 4,400 years.

These types of finds do not surprise Biblical creationists. Rapidly-sealed animals can stay intact for thousands of years. But millions upon millions of years is another story! Our discussion on collagen (above) provides some estimates on how soft tissues can possibly last thousands of years, but certainly not millions. Recently even a fossilized heart was found that supposedly dates to over 113 million old.[270] A fossilized dinosaur brain was also recently discovered, dating to 133 million years old using the evolutionary timescale.[271]

Figure 72. Fossilized Dinosaur Brain.[272]

Soft tissues disintegrate. They go back to the dust. Seeing how some soft tissues can in fact be preserved and last for thousands of years testifies to both the *recent* and *catastrophic nature* of the Flood.

Evidence #13: Dragons

There are numerous ancient drawings and carvings of dinosaur-like creatures in almost every continent around the world. Dragon legends also exist in almost every culture around the world. Many of these describe creatures that are similar in size, shape, and features.

From a Creationist perspective, *some* of the dragon legends are based on real accounts of dinosaurs living after the

Flood. While many of these are likely fictional stories or exaggerations, it's quite surprising how many of these "dragon tales" are told by credible historians—historians that we trust for framing history as we know it today. Why do so many accept historical facts from these famous historians, but readily dismiss their accounts of dragon/dinosaur creatures? Are we selectively choosing only the parts of their accounts that fit our worldviews?

For example, in 1271 Marco Polo authored the *Travels of Marco Polo*. Marco was the first European (on record) to visit China and Asia and record it in *detail*. His work and maps popularized the 4,000-mile "Silk Road" trade route. Maps of Asia were based on his descriptions until the sixteenth century, and Christopher Columbus relied on these maps for finding a sea route to China (1492).

Marco recorded dragons living with man. Regarding the Province named Karajan, he wrote, "Here are found snakes and huge serpents, ten paces in length and ten spans in girth (that is, 50 feet long and 100 inches [about eight feet] in girth). At the fore part, near the head, they have two short legs, each with three claws, as well as eyes larger than a loaf and very glaring. The jaws are wide enough to swallow a man, the teeth are large and sharp, and their whole appearance is so formidable that neither man, nor any kind of animal can approach them without terror. Others are of smaller size, being eight, six, or five paces long (1961, pp. 158–159)." He continues by explaining how the "local citizens of the area hunted and killed the creatures."

In 330 BC, Alexander the Great invaded India and brought back reports of seeing a great hissing dragon living in a cave, which people were worshiping as a god.[273] Later Greek rulers supposedly brought dragons alive from Ethiopia.

Athanasius Kircher (lived AD 1601–1680) was a German Jesuit Scholar who published 40 major works and taught at Roman College for over 40 years. In his chapter on dragons in *Mundus Subterraneus*, Kircher records: "Of winged dragons, dispute has only arisen between authors, most of whom declare them to be fanciful, but these authors are

202

contradicted by histories and eyewitnesses. Winged dragons—small, great, and greatest—have been produced in all times in every land." These could well refer to pterosaurs alive after the Flood.

Pliny the Elder (lived from AD 23–79), a well-known Roman scholar and historian was the author of *Naturalis Historia* ("Pliny's Natural History"). In this famous work, Pliny writes: "Africa produces elephants, but it is India that produces the largest, as well as the dragon." Less than two centuries later, Greek historian and philosopher Lucius Flavius Philostratus (AD 170– 247) wrote: "The whole of India is girt with dragons of enormous size; for not only the marshes are full of them, but the mountains as well, and there is not a single ridge without one. Now the marsh kind are sluggish in their habits and are thirty cubits long, and they have no crest standing up on their heads."[274]

Herodotus was a famous Greek historian who lived between 484 and 425 BC. He was the first Greek writer who succeeded in writing a large-scale historical narrative that has survived the passage of time, which contributed to Herodotus being known as the "father of history." Herodotus records: "Winged serpents are said to fly from Arabia at the beginning of spring, making for Egypt: but the ibis birds encounter the invaders in this pass and kill them...the serpents are like water snakes. Their wings are not feathered but very like the wings of a bat."

The above is only a selection of examples. Several more exist. The reader is encouraged to draw from the resources at *www.answersingenesis.org* for books that discuss this topic thoroughly. The book by Vance Nelson titled, "Untold Secrets of Planet Earth: Dire Dragons" give the clearest evidence that dragons were dinosaurs.

Conclusion

We've reviewed 13 lines of evidence that seem to align more with biblical history than evolution-based theories. We started with how dinosaurs seem to be "cleverly designed" with features that shout "intention" and "intelligent design." Dinosaur fossil evidence shows that when these creatures are found in the crust of the earth, they always show up completely formed, with incredible design. Transitional forms that are "leading" to dinosaurs are simply not found. The evidence points to a magnificent designer placing the creatures here, fully-formed, and ready to live and thrive in a pre-Flood paradise.

The vast fossil record indicates catastrophic burial, with the animals furiously buried in mud—found fleeing in groups—and sometimes without juveniles. The fact that many dinosaur mass graves are found mixed together with marine fossils points to only one logical conclusion: the oceans came quickly onto dry land, burying both land- and sea-creatures simultaneously. Some dinosaurs are even buried so fast that they are mummified and found complete with their last meals still in their stomachs.

Finally, we have at least 14 "fresh" biomaterials found in dinosaur bones, horns, and claws that—according to even secular science—cannot last for millions of years. Finding detectable levels of carbon-14 in their bones also confirms a timescale of thousands of years, not millions.

Reading this book was not an academic exercise—these evidences beg a conclusion for each reader. If the biblical narrative is correct about dinosaurs, and we believe that it is, then it's also likely correct about *everything else*.[275] After diving into this research years ago, this is exactly what I learned. It became clear to me that the dinosaur data fit the biblical framework better than the evolutionary one, and it fueled my faith even more, solidifying my understanding that the Bible is true both theologically *and* historically.

Study Questions

1. The Bible takes the position that the earth and creation are only thousands of years old and that dinosaurs were wiped out in Noah's Flood (save those on the Ark), but the world holds to millions of years and extinction by any one of a variety of theories. How does believing in either one of these two different views impact our daily life regarding what we believe? The decisions we make?

    _____

    _____

    _____

    _____

    _____

    _____

    _____

    _____

2. Job 40 describes "Behemoth" which was the "Chief" of all God's creations. We advocate in this chapter that Behemoth was a sauropod dinosaur. What does this creature say about God's nature?

    _____

    _____

    _____

    _____

    _____

    _____

    _____

    _____

3. The recent discoveries of soft tissue in dinosaur bones seems to point to their demise occurring only thousands of years ago, not millions. Why do you think secular

scientists are not likely to change their minds about the millions-of-years narrative?

_____

_____

_____

_____

_____

_____

_____

_____

_____

Helpful Resources

Genesis Apologetics

Mobile App:
Search for "Genesis Apologetics" in the iTunes or Google Play stores.

Free Books and Videos:
www.debunkevolution.com
https://genesisapologetics.com/store/

YouTube Channel:
Channel Name: Genesis Apologetics

Dinosaurs:
http://genesisapologetics.com/dinosaurs

Theistic Evolution
http://genesisapologetics.com/theistic

"Lucy" (leading human evolution icon):
http://genesisapologetics.com/lucy

Answers in Genesis
www.answersingenesis.org

Institute for Creation Research
www.ICR.org

Evolution Grand Experiment
www.thegrandexperiment.com

Creation Website Search Tool
www.searchcreation.org

Prayer of Salvation

You're not here by accident—God *loves* you and He *knows* who you are like no one else. His Word says:

Lord, You have searched me and known me.
You know my sitting down and my rising up;
you understand my thought afar off. You
comprehend my path and my lying down, and
are acquainted with all my ways. For there is not
a word on my tongue, but behold, O Lord, You
know it altogether. You have hedged me behind
and before, and laid Your hand upon me. Such
knowledge is too wonderful for me; It is high, I
cannot attain it. (Psalm 139:1–6)

God loves you with an everlasting love, and with a love
that can cover all of your transgressions—all that you have ever
done wrong. But you have to repent of those sins and trust the
Lord Jesus Christ for forgiveness. Your past is in the past. He
wants to give you a new future and new hope.

But starting this new journey requires a step—a step of
faith. God has already reached out to you as far as He can. By
giving His Son to die for your sins on the Cross, He's done
everything He can to reach out to you. The next step is yours to
take, and this step requires faith to receive His son into your
heart. It also requires repentance (turning away) from sin–a
surrendered heart that is willing to reject a sinful lifestyle. Many
believers have a much easier time leaving sinful lifestyles after
they fully trust Jesus and nobody else and nothing else. Along
with forgiveness, the Holy Spirit enters your life when you
receive Jesus, and He will lead you into a different lifestyle and
way—a way that will lead to blessing, joy, patient endurance
under trials, and eternal life with Him.

If you are ready to receive Him, then consider four key
Biblical truths.

1. Acknowledge that your sin separates you from God. Most simply, sin is our failure to measure up to God's holiness and His righteous standards. We sin by things we do, choices we make, attitudes we show, and thoughts we entertain. We also sin when we fail to do right things or even think right thoughts. The Bible also says that all people are sinners: "there is none righteous, not even one." No matter how good we try to be, none of us does right things all the time. The Bible is clear, "For all have sinned and come short of the glory of God" (Romans 3:23). Admit it. Agree with God on this one.

2. Our sins demand punishment—the punishment of death and separation from God. However, because of His great love, God sent His only Son Jesus to die for our sins: "God demonstrates His own love for us in this: While we were still sinners, Christ died for us" (Romans 5:8). For you to come to God you have to get rid of your sin problem. But, in our own strength, not one of us can do this! You can't make yourself right with God by being a better person. Only God can rescue us from our sins. He is willing to do this not because of anything you can offer Him, but **just because He loves you!** "He saved us, not because of righteous things we had done, but because of His mercy" (Titus 3:5).

3. It's only God's grace that allows you to come to Him— not your efforts to "clean up your life" or work your way to Heaven. You can't earn it. It's a free gift: "For it is by grace you have been saved, through faith—and this not from yourselves, it is the gift of God—not by works, so that no one can boast" (Ephesians 2:8–9). Will you accept this gift?

4. For you to come to God, the penalty for your sin must be paid. God's gift to you is His son, Jesus, who paid the debt for you when He died on the Cross. "For the wages of sin is death, but the gift of God is eternal life in Jesus

209

Christ our Lord" (Romans 6:23). God brought Jesus back from the dead. He provided the way for you to have a personal relationship with Him through Jesus. Trust Him. Pursue Him.

When we realize how deeply our sin grieves the heart of God and how desperately we need a Savior, we are ready to receive God's offer of salvation. To admit we are sinners means turning away from our sin and selfishness and turning to follow Jesus. The Bible word for this is "repentance"—to change our thinking to acknowledge how grievous sin is, so our thinking is in line with God's.

All that's left for you to do is to accept the gift that Jesus is holding out for you right now: "If you confess with your mouth, 'Jesus is Lord,' and believe in your heart that God raised him from the dead, you will be saved. For it is with your heart that you believe and are justified, and it is with your mouth that you confess and are saved" (Romans 10:9–10). God says that if you believe in His son, Jesus, you can live forever with Him in glory: "For God so loved the world that He gave his one and only Son, that whoever believes in him shall not perish, but have eternal life" (John 3:16).

Are you ready to accept the gift of eternal life that Jesus is offering you right now? Let's review what this commitment involves:

- I acknowledge I am a sinner in need of a Savior. I repent or turn away from my sin.
- I believe in my heart that God raised Jesus from the dead. I trust that Jesus paid the full penalty for my sins.
- I confess Jesus as my Lord and my God. I surrender control of my life to Jesus.
- I trust Jesus as my Savior forever. I accept that God has done for me what I could never do for myself when He forgives my sins.

If it is your sincere desire to receive Jesus into your heart as your personal Lord and Savior, then talk to God from your heart. Here's a suggested prayer:

Lord Jesus, I know that I am a sinner and I do not deserve eternal life. But, I believe You died and rose from the grave to make me a new creation and to prepare me to dwell in your presence forever. Jesus, come into my life, take control of my life, forgive my sins and save me. I am now placing my trust in You alone for my salvation and I accept your free gift of eternal life.

If you've prayed this prayer, it's important that you take these three next steps: First, go tell another Christian! Second, get plugged into a local church. Third, begin reading your Bible every day (we suggest starting with the book of John). Welcome to God's forever family!

Technical Appendix

Wait a Minute: Doesn't Radiometric Dating Show that the Earth is 4.5 Billion Years Old?

Suggested Videos:

Radiometric Dating: https://youtu.be/fg6MfnmxPB4
Six Days: https://youtu.be/pjx88K8JTY8
Young/Old Earth: https://youtu.be/QzEzkrMdgIs
The Bible and History: https://youtu.be/6okZJlw84lo

Secular scientists date the Earth to about 4.5 billion years old by using selected radiometric dating results. Ultimately, what they call "deep time" serves as the very *foundation* of evolution theory. High school biology books openly acknowledge this necessary connection:

> Evolution takes a long time. If life has evolved, then Earth must be very old. Geologists now use radioactivity to establish the age of certain rocks and fossils. This kind of data could have shown that the Earth is young. If that had happened, Darwin's ideas would have been refuted and abandoned. Instead, radioactive dating indicates that Earth is about 4.5 billion years old—plenty of time for evolution and natural selection to take place.[276]

But as we show here, geologists do not use radioactivity to establish the age of certain rocks. They instead use selected radioactivity results to confirm what they need to see. As discussed in previous chapters, this viewpoint, being secular, contradicts God's stated Word in Genesis and even the Ten Commandments, where He wrote with His own hand that He created the heavens, Earth, sea, and all that is in them in six days (Exodus 20:11).

Belief in deep time rests upon evolution's required time. That's sure putting a lot of faith in something that can't be tested through direct observation. After all, plenty of assumptions go into the calculations, as we'll discuss in this section. While this section reviews the details behind radiometric dating, keep in mind that only two key "fatal flaws" are necessary to debunk the inferences made by radiometric dating.

The **first fatal flaw** is that it relies upon *untestable assumptions*. The entire practice of radiometric dating stands or falls on the veracity of four *untestable* assumptions. The assumptions are untestable because we cannot go back millions of years to verify the findings done today in a laboratory, and we cannot go back in time to test the original conditions in which the rocks were formed. If these assumptions that underlie radiometric dating are not true, then the entire theory falls flat, like a chair without its four legs.

The **second fatal flaw** clearly reveals that at least one of those assumptions must actually be wrong because radiometric dating *fails to correctly date rocks of known ages*. For example, in the case of Mount St. Helens, we watched rocks being formed in the 1980s, but when sent to a laboratory 10 years later for dating, the 10-year-old rocks returned ages of hundreds of thousands to millions of years. Similarly, some rocks return radiometric "ages" twice as old as the accepted age for earth. Most rocks return conflicting radiometric "ages." In these cases, researchers select results that match what they already believe about earth's age (see the section **Brand New Rocks Give Old "Ages"** for details of this study and several others like it).

Overview of Radiometric Dating[277]

Fossil remains are found in sedimentary rock layers. Layers of sediment form when various size particles (e.g., dirt, rocks, and vegetation) accumulate in places such as deserts, rivers, lakes, and the ocean. Most texts teach that it takes a long time for these sediments to build up, with older layers buried beneath younger layers. Fossils found in lower layers are deemed to be older than those in the upper layers, older on the bottom younger on the top. This is called *relative* age dating, the first step.

Next, evolutionary scientists then use *index fossils* to help establish the relative ages of rock layers that are not directly related to one another and their fossils. Index fossils are distinct fossils, usually of an extinct organism found in only one or a few layers, though that layer or layers outcrops in many places—at least that's the theory. They help establish and correlate the relative ages of rock layers. Index fossils typically have a short stratigraphic or vertical range. In reality, many index fossils occur above or below their expected ranges. In some cases, they turn up still alive today, but these can go unreported. Evolutionists assume that the creature evolved somehow, lived for a certain time period, and then died out. Textbooks are correct when they state that relative dating provides no information whatsoever about a fossil's absolute age. Nevertheless, most textbook writers and the scientists they rely on grew up with a belief in uniformitarian geologic processes. The principle of uniformity is a philosophy and an assumption that the slow geologic processes going on today must explain the deposits of the past. They teach the motto, "the present is the key to the past." It's not. As any judge in court will attest, eyewitness records record the past more accurately. Also, keen observations in the field testify that the sediments comprising the ancient rock layers were laid down *catastrophically*, not slowly over millions of years.

Today, the geologic time scale shows ages based on radiometric age dating. Many textbook authors consider radiometric ages as absolute ages. However, as you will soon learn, these techniques stray far from absolute dates, though they may reveal relative ages of some rocks.

214

The Age of the Earth

Today's evolutionists base their age of the Earth on their interpretation of radioactive elements. They assign 4.5 billion years to earth based on the belief that earth itself evolved, so to speak, from a molten mass. But they cannot directly date the earth using selected isotopes because they believe all rocks have cycled over imagined eons, leaving no original rocks to test. They assume meteorites formed when earth did. Researchers age-dated a meteorite to sometime around the age they would accept. Thus, the earth itself has no direct evidence for its vast evolutionary age assignment.

The various rock layers are given names with assigned ages (Figure 1). Those who believe these ever-changing but always unimaginably old age assignments call each rock System a "Period." The names help, but their age assignments derive from results chosen to agree with evolutionary time. To understand exactly why, we must first learn the basics of radioactive elements and of the techniques used when treating these systems of elements as clocks.

Many elements on the periodic table have radioactive forms. Stable atoms have a set number of protons, neutrons, and orbital electrons. Isotopes are atoms of the same elements with the same number of protons but different numbers of neutrons. Some isotopes are radioactive and others are stable. A radioactive nucleus is not stable. It changes into another element by emitting particles and/or radiation.

EON	ERA	PERIOD	EPOCH	Alleged Age Years	Young Earth Evidences
Phanerozoic — This is where most fossils occur	Cenozoic	Quaternary	Holocene	10,000	
			Pleistocene	2,600,000	Soft Frog with bloody bone marrow
		Tertiary	Pliocene	5,300,000	
			Miocene	23,000,000 ⇐	Salamander muscle
			Oligocene	30,900,000 ⇐	Young coal, Penguin feathers, Lizard skin
			Eocene	55,800,000	
			Paleocene	65,500,000	
	Mesozoic	Cretaceous		145,500,000	⇐ Young Diamonds, Young Coal
		Jurassic		201,600,000	Dinosaur DNA, blood, blood vessels and protein
		Triassic		251,000,000	
	Paleozoic	Permian		299,000,000	
		Pennsylvanian		318,000,000	⇐ Young Coal
		Mississippian		359,000,000	
		Devonian		416,000,000	
		Silurian		444,000,000	
		Ordovician		488,000,000	
		Cambrian		542,000,000	
Precambrian	Proterozoic Eon				⇐ Helium in zircon crystals
				2,500,000,000	
	Archean Eon			3,850,000,000	

Figure 1. Uniformitarian Geologic Time Scale with problems noted under "Young Earth Evidence." The time scale is placed vertically because older sedimentary deposits are buried beneath younger sedimentary deposits. The assumption of slow geologic processes and radiometric age dating has drastically inflated the age of the Earth and its strata.

A basic way to express the rate of radioactive decay is called the half-life. This equals the length of time needed for 50% of a quantity of radioactive material to decay. Unstable radioactive isotopes called parent elements become stable elements called daughter elements. Each radioactive element has its own specific half-life (see Table 1).

216

Table 1: Radiometric Isotopes and Half-Lives.

Examples of Radioactive Isotopes that Change into Stable Elements		
Radioactive Parent Element	Stable Daughter Element	Half-Life
Carbon-14 (^{14}C)	Nitrogen-14 (^{14}N)	5,730 Years
Potassium-40 (^{40}K)	Argon-40 (^{40}Ar)	1.3 Billion Years
Uranium-238 (^{238}U)	Lead-206 (^{206}Pb)	4.5 Billion Years
Rubidium-87 (^{87}Rb)	Strontium-87 (^{87}Sr)	48.6 Billion Years

Note: Carbon-14 is not used to date minerals or rocks, but is used for organic remains that contain carbon, such as wood, bone, or shells.

To estimate a radioisotope age of a crystalline rock, geologists measure the ratio between radioactive parent and stable daughter products in the rock. They can even isolate isotopes from specific, crystallized minerals within a rock. They then use a model to convert the measured ratio into an age estimate. The models incorporate key assumptions, like the ratio of parent to daughter isotopes in the originally formed rock. How can anyone know this information? We can't. We must assume some starting condition. Evolutionists assume that as soon as a crystalline rock cooled from melt, it inherited no daughter product from the melt. This way, they can have their clock start at zero. However, when they find isotope ratios that contradict other measurements or evolution, they often invoke inherited daughter product. This saves the desired age assignments.

Igneous (crystalline) rocks—those that have formed from molten magma or lava—are the primary rock types analyzed to determine radiometric ages. For example, let's assume that when an igneous rock solidified, a certain mineral in it contained 1,000 atoms of radioactive potassium (^{40}K) and zero atoms of argon (^{40}Ar). After one half-life of 1.3 billion years, the rock would contain 500 ^{40}K and 500 ^{40}Ar atoms, since 50% has decayed. This is a 500:500 or 500-parent:500-daughter ratio, which reduces to a 1:1 ratio. If the sample contained this ratio, then the rock would be declared 1.3 billion years old. If the ratio is greater than 1:1, then not even one half-life has expired, so the rock would be younger. However, if the ratio is less than 1:1, then the rock is considered older than the half-life for that system.

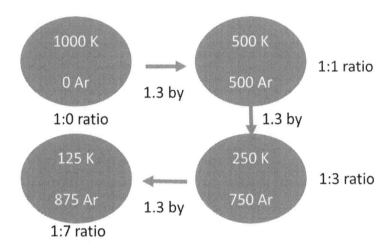

Figure 2. Decay of Radioactive potassium-40 to argon-40. "by" means "billions of years," K is potassium, Ar is argon. After three half-lives of this system, totaling 3.9 billion years, only 125 of the original 1000 radioactive potassium-40 atoms remain, assuming even decay for all that time.

Age-dating a rock requires at least these four basic assumptions:

1. Laboratory measurements that have no human error or misjudgments,
2. The rock began with zero daughter element isotopes,
3. The rock maintained a "closed system" (defined below), and
4. The decay rate remained constant.

Each of these deserves further description.

1. Measuring the radioactive parent and stable daughter elements to obtain the ratio between them must be accurate, and it usually is. Keep in mind that most laboratory technicians believe in deep time. This sets the time periods they expect. They all memorized the geologic time scale long before they approached their research, and thus may not even consider that processes other than radioisotope decay may have produced the accurately measured isotope ratios.

2. Next, this technician assumes that all the radioactive parent isotopes began decaying right when the mineral crystallized from a melt. He also assumes none of the stable daughter element was present at this time. How can anyone really know the mineral began with 100% radioactive parent and 0% daughter elements? What if some stable daughter element was already present when the rock formed? After all, these experts often explain away unexpected radioisotope age results using the excuse that daughter or parent isotopes must have been present when the rock formed. Without knowledge of the starting condition, the use of isotopes as clocks means nothing.

3. A closed system means that no extra parent or daughter elements have been added or removed throughout the history of the rock. Have you ever seen an atom? Of course not. It is too small, but we must think about this on an atomic level. Decay byproducts like argon and helium are both gases. Neither gas tends to attach to any other atom, meaning they rarely do chemistry. Instead of reacting with atoms in rock crystals, they build up in rock systems and can move in and out of the rocks. One leading expert in isotope geology states that most minerals do not even form in closed systems. A closed system would retain all the argon that radioactive potassium produces. He emphasizes that for a radioactive-determined date to be true, the mineral must

be in a closed system.[278] Is there any such thing as a closed system when speaking of rocks?

4. The constant-decay rate assumption assumes the decay rate remained the same throughout the history of the rock. Lab experiments have shown that most changes in temperature, pressure, and the chemical environment have very little effect on decay rates. These experiments have led researchers to have great confidence that this is a reasonable assumption, but it may not hold true. Is the following quote an overstatement of known science? "Radioactive transmutations must have gone on at the present rates under all the conditions that have existed on Earth in the geologic past."[279] Some scientists have found evidence that zircon crystals endured high levels of radioactive decay in the past, as discussed below. This evidence challenges assumption #4.

To illustrate how much radioisotope dating hinges on assumptions, imagine you encounter a burning candle sitting on a table. How long has that candle been burning? We can calculate the answer if we know the candle's *burn rate history* and *original length*. However, if the original length is not known, or if it cannot be verified that the burning rate has been constant, it is impossible to tell for sure how long the candle was burning. A similar problem occurs with radiometric dating of rocks. Since the initial physical state of the rock is unknowable, workers must assume it."[280]

Brand New Rocks Give Old "Ages"

Scientific literature omitted from public school textbooks reveal radioisotope age assignments much older than the known ages of many rocks. These results first arrived in the 1960s and 1970s, but most of the scientific community still pays no attention. Argon and helium isotopes were measured from recent basalt lava erupted on the deep ocean floor from the Kilauea volcano in Hawaii. Researchers calculated up to

220

22,000,000 years for brand new rocks![281] The problem is common. Table 2 gives six examples among many more.

Table 2: Young Volcanic Rocks with Really Old Whole-Rock K-Ar Model Ages.[282]

Lava Flow, Rock Type, and Location	Year Formed or Known Age	^{40}K-^{40}Ar "Age"
Kilauea Iki basalt, Hawaii	AD 1959	8,500,000 years
Volcanic bomb, Mt. Stromboli, Italy	AD 1963	2,400,000 years
Mt. Etna basalt, Sicily	AD 1964	700,000 years
Medicine Lake Highlands obsidian, Glass Mountains, California	<500 years	12,600,000 years
Hualalai basalt, Hawaii	AD 1800–1801	22,800,000 years
Mt. St. Helens dacite lava dome, Washington	AD 1986	350,000 years

The oldest real age of these recent volcanic rocks is less than 500 years. People witnessed and described the molten lava solidify into most of these rocks just decades ago. Many of these were only about 10 years old. And yet ^{40}K-^{40}Ar dating gives ages from 350,000 to >22,800,000 years.

Potassium-Argon (^{40}K-^{40}Ar) has been the most widespread method of radioactive age-dating for the Phanerozoic rocks, where most fossils occur. The misdated rocks shown above violate the initial condition assumption of no radiogenic argon (^{40}Ar) present when the igneous rock formed. There is too much ^{40}Ar present in recent lava flows. Thus, the method gives excessively old ages for recent rocks. The amounts of argon in these rocks indicate they carry isotope "ages" much, much older than their known ages. Could the argon they measured have come from a source other than radioactive potassium decay? If so, then geologists have been trusting a faulty method. If they can't obtain correct values for rocks of known ages, then why should we trust the values they obtain for rocks of unknown ages?

These wrong radioisotope ages violate the initial condition assumption of zero (0%) parent argon present when the rock formed. Furthermore, the slow radioactive decay of ^{40}K shows that there was insufficient time since cooling for measurable amounts of ^{40}Ar to have accumulated in the rock. Therefore, radiogenic argon (^{40}Ar) was *already present* in the rocks as they formed.

Radiometric age dating should no longer be sold to the public as providing reliable, absolute ages. Excess argon invalidates the initial condition assumption for potassium dating, and excess helium invalidates the closed-system assumption for uranium dating. The ages shown on the uniformitarian geologic time scale should be removed.

"Young" Fossils in "Old" Mud

Researchers have scoured the Ono Formation near Redding in northern California. They described it in scientific publications for more than 140 years. Because the area has millions of fossils (including the valuable ammonites) and fossilized wood trapped in the same mudflow layers, it provides a unique opportunity for carbon dating. If the wood still has relatively short-lived radiocarbon inside it, then the age of the supposedly ancient fossils would need revision.

Geologist Andrew Snelling gathered four samples of ammonites and wood buried and fossilized together in this solidified mudstone and sent them to the IsoTrace Radiocarbon Laboratory at the University of Toronto, Canada for dating analysis.[283] Table 3 summarizes the results.

222

Table 3. Ono Formation Radiocarbon Dating Results.

Dating Results from Ammonites and Wood Fossils in the Ono Formation (Snelling, 2008)			
Specimen	Rock layers	Ammonites	Wood
Dating	112 to 120 Million (conventional age)	36,400 to 48,710 carbon years	32,780 to 42,390 carbon years

Because the ammonites and wood fossils came from a rock unit conventionally regarded as 112 to 120 million years old, the fossils should share that same age. Such an age far exceeds the limit of the radioactive carbon (^{14}C) method, which in theory extends to artifacts less than 100,000 carbon years old. In other words, if these fossils are really over 100 million years old, then there should have been absolutely no measurable ^{14}C in them—but there was—enough to produce easily measurable ages of 32,000 to 48,000 years!

Scientists who believe in long ages assert that the ammonites and wood samples were contaminated with modern carbon in the ground, during sampling, or even in the laboratory. But this study took extensive steps to guard against such contamination. So how can 36,000 carbon-year-old ammonites and 32,000 carbon-year-old wood be stuck in a mudflow of 112 million or more conventional years? Two logical options present themselves:

1. One of the three dates is correct and the other two are wrong.
2. All three of the dates are wrong.

If Biblical history is accurate as we believe it is, then the second option is the correct choice—*none of the dates are correct.* The fact that measurable ^{14}C existed in the ammonites and wood fossils shows that they are very young–certainly not 112–120 million years old. But how can they still outdate the Biblical age of Creation of about 6,000 years? A number of factors help explain this. First, the Earth's stronger magnetic field in the recent past would have reduced the atmospheric ^{14}C production rate. Second, "because the recent Genesis Flood removed so much carbon from the biosphere and buried it, the measured apparent radiocarbon ages are still much higher than the true ages of the fossil ammonites and wood."[284]

Therefore, the true ages of the ammonites and wood are consistent with their burial during the Genesis Flood about 4,400 years ago.[285] Back then, muddy waters washed sediments and ammonites onto land.

Figure 3. Fossil Ammonites in Rock Concretions in the Ono Formation, California.

Human and Chimp DNA: Is It Really 98% Similar?[286]

Suggested Video:

Human Chimp DNA Similarity
https://youtu.be/Rav8sfuJFYc

One of the great trophies that evolutionists parade to prove human evolution from some common ape ancestor is the assertion that human and chimp DNA are 98 to 99% similar.[287] People quote this statistic in hundreds of textbooks, blogs, videos, and even scientific journals. Yet any high school student can debunk the "Human and Chimp DNA is 98% similar" mantra that this chapter covers.

Why does this matter? We know that genes determine body features from gender to hair color. If we are genetically related to chimps, some may conclude that humans should behave like animals, with no fear of divine justice. But if we all descended from Adam, not from animals, then common animal behavior such as sexual promiscuity cannot be justified on these grounds.[288] This has been a primary foundation for the mistreatment of humans worldwide by genocidal political leaders and governments over the past 150 or so years. One highly reputable study showed that the leading cause of death in the 20th century was "Democide"—or "murder by government," which has claimed well over 260 million lives.[289] All of the totalitarian murderous tyrannies the world over, despite their different political variations, maintained the same Darwinian evolutionary philosophy that humans are higher animals to be herded and culled in wars, death-camps, abortions, mass starvations, and outright slaughter.[290] Does this issue matter? Well, it's a matter of life and death. It needs to be refuted if it's not true.

We should evaluate the major evidences that exposes the 98% myth and supports the current conclusion that the actual similarity is 84.4%, or a difference of 15%, which translates to over 360 million base pairs' difference.[291] That is an enormous difference that produces an unbridgeable chasm between humans and chimpanzees. The chimp genome is much longer than the human genome. Humans have forty-six chromosomes, while chimps have forty-eight. According to the latest data, there are 3,096,649,726 base pairs in the human genome and 3,309,577,922 base pairs in the chimpanzee genome. This amounts to a 6.4% difference.[292] The 98% similarity claim fails on this basis alone.

If human and chimp DNA is nearly identical, why can't humans interbreed with chimps?[293] Furthermore, such an apparently minor difference in DNA (only 1%) does not account for the many obvious major differences between humans and chimps.

If humans and chimps are so similar, then why can't we interchange body parts with chimps? Over 30,000 organ transplants are made every year in the U.S. alone, and currently there are over 120,000 candidates on organ transplant lists—but *zero* of those transplants will be made using chimp organs.

Table 4. Organ Transplants.[294]

Organ Transplants (2016)			
Organs	# Currently Waiting	% of Transplants Made Using	
		Human Organs	Chimp Organs
All Organs	121,520	100%	0%
Kidney	100,623	100%	0%
Liver	14,792	100%	0%
Pancreas	1,048	100%	0%
Kid./Panc.	1,953	100%	0%
Heart	4,167	100%	0%
Lung	1,495	100%	0%
Heart/Lung	47	100%	0%
Intestine	280	100%	0%

A Basic Overview

The living populations of the chimp kind include four species that can interbreed. From the beginning, they were *spirit-less* animals created on Day 6 of creation. Later that Day, God made a single man in His own image, and He gave him an everlasting *spirit* or *soul* (Genesis 2:7). Then God commanded man to "rule over the fish in the sea and the birds in the sky, over the livestock and all the animals," including chimps (Genesis 1:26).

If the creation narrative from the Bible is true, we would expect *exactly* what we see in today's ape-kinds. First, all varieties of chimps have no concept of eternity. For example, they do not bury their dead nor do they conduct funeral rituals. Secondly, apes use very limited verbal communication—they cannot write articles or even sentences. Thirdly, they do not display *spiritual or religious practices* as humans do. In other words, they show no capacity for knowing their creator through worship or prayer. This fits the Biblical creation account that God created humans as spiritual beings with an everlasting *spirit* or *soul* (Genesis 2:7).

It stands to reason that God, in His desire to create diverse life forms on Earth, would begin with the same building materials, such as DNA, carbohydrates, fats, and protein, when making various animal kinds. Research has revealed that He used similar building blocks for all the various physical life forms that He created. Genetic information in all living creatures is encoded as a sequence of principally 4 nucleotides (guanine, adenine, thymine, and cytosine, shown by the letters G, A, T, and C). We also see this principle in nature—such as many plants and animals sharing Fibonacci or similar spirals with clear algorithms and sequences as building patterns.

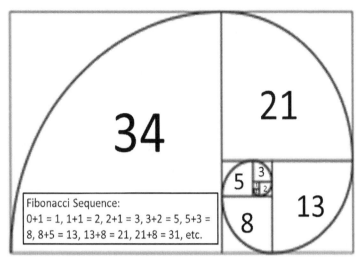

Fibonacci Sequence:
0+1 = 1, 1+1 = 2, 2+1 = 3, 3+2 = 5, 5+3 = 8, 8+5 = 13, 13+8 = 21, 21+8 = 31, etc.

Figure 4. Fibonacci Number Sequence. A Fibonacci spiral approximates the golden spiral using quarter-circle arcs inscribed in squares of integer Fibonacci-number side, shown for square sizes 1, 1, 2, 3, 5, 8, 13, 21, 34 etc.

Figure 5. Examples of the Fibonacci Sequence in Nature.[295]

Chimp and human DNA use the same chemicals and share many sequence similarities. However, these likenesses do not prove that those similarities came from shared ancestors, since similar design can also explain them. After all, design constraints require an engineer to use many of the same raw materials and building plans to produce different types of biological machines—especially if those machines need to interact with the same building blocks for growth and life. For example, an automotive engineer could make a Volkswagen bug and a Porsche Carrera framework out of steel, glass, and plastic but not oxygen, carbon dioxide, and sulfuric acid. When experts talk about DNA similarity, they refer to a variety of different features. Sometimes they talk about humans and chimpanzees having the same genes. At other times, they talk about certain DNA sequences being 98 to 99% similar. First, let's consider why human and chimpanzee DNA sequences are actually closer to 84.4% than 98% similar.[296] Then, describing the concepts of genes and gene similarity will reveal much insight into human and chimp DNA dissimilarity.

Comparisons of Chimps and Humans

Once you understand that the new DNA evidence debunks the alleged human evolution paradigm, you will appreciate that you are a unique creation whom the Creator made in His own image. You are special and unique compared to all of creation.

A child that sees a chimpanzee can immediately tell that it is radically different from a human. Compared to chimps, humans are about 38% taller, are 80% heavier, live 50% longer, and have brains that are about 400% larger (1330 ccs compared to 330 ccs).[297] Look at someone next to you and roll your eyes at them. Chimps can't do that because their sclera, like most other animals, is hidden behind their eyelids. Now tap your fingertips with your thumb. Chimps can't do that either—their fingers are curved, their thumbs are both tiny and set further back on their wrists than humans, and they are missing the flexor pollicis longus—the major muscle that controls thumb dexterity in humans. Additionally, their knees point out, whereas ours point forward. Humans can build space shuttles and write songs. Chimps don't do anything close.

Scientists now know that chimpanzees are radically different than humans in many different ways besides their outward appearance. Humans and chimpanzees have differences in bone structures, in brain types, and in other major parts of their physiology. Humans also have the ability to express their thoughts abstractly in speech, writing, and music, as well as develop other complicated systems of expression and communication. This is why humans stand above all other types of creatures. **The claimed small genetic differences between human and chimp DNA (1 to 2%) must account for these and many other major differences!** The difference between humans and chimpanzees is major and includes about 350 million different DNA bases. In fact, it is hard to compare the two genomes because of radical differences in arrangement.

Telomeres in Chimps and other apes are about 23 kilobases (a kilobase is 1,000 base pairs of DNA) long. Humans stand out from primates with much shorter telomeres only 10 kilobases long.[298] The human Y chromosome almost completely misaligns with chimpanzees.[299] Even if human and chimpanzee DNA sequences are as similar as some evolutionists claim, the DNA coding makes two entirely different creatures!

The chromosome fusion theory claims that two smaller chimpanzee chromosomes fused to form human chromosome 2. Geneticists have refuted the claim. Sadly, this false claim has been used as proof of human evolution, even in textbooks.

Research by Dr. David A. DeWitt has revealed new stunning insights regarding the major differences between human and chimp DNA: There exist 40–45 million bases [DNA "letters"] in humans missing from chimps and about the same number present in chimps that are absent from man. These extra DNA nucleotides are termed "insertions" and "deletions" because they are assumed to have been added or lost from the original common ancestor sequence. These differences alone put the total number of DNA differences at about 125 million. However, since the insertions can be more than one nucleotide long, about 40 million total separate mutation events would be required to separate the two species. To put this number into perspective, a typical 8½ x 11-inch page of text has about 4,000

230

letters and spaces. It would require 10,000 such pages of text equaling 40 million letters or 20 full-sized novels.

The difference between humans and chimpanzees includes about 45 million human base pairs that chimps don't have and about 45 million base pairs in the chimp absent from the human.[300] More research has left no doubt that a specific set of genetic programming exists for humans and another specific set exists for chimps. If chimps run on Microsoft, then humans run on Apple software. Both use binary code, and they have overlapping functions, but each has unique features.

Biology textbooks typically explain that humans descended from some common ancestor related to the great apes. This animal group consists of orangutans, gorillas, and chimpanzees. Of these apes, evolutionists claim that humans are most closely related to chimpanzees based on comparisons of human DNA to chimp DNA. The real-world consequences of this ideology involve concluding that humans are not special creations, but that they are evolved animals.

Reality of DNA and Genome Similarity

Let's review some basics to get a more accurate picture of genomes. Human, plant, and animal DNA is packaged into separate packages called chromosomes. Each one contains millions of the four different DNA bases (T, A, C, G), stacked like rungs on a ladder. Their specific order forms a complex set of instructions called the "genetic code." Humans have two copies of each chromosome: one set of 23 from the mother and one set of 23 from the father. Each chromosome set contains over 3 billion base pairs. The information they encode builds whole organisms from single egg cells and maintains each creature throughout its life. Our 46 chromosomes have a total of 6 billion DNA bases. Nearly every cell in our body has all of them. When scientists talk about a creature's genome, they refer to one set of chromosomes. Thus, the reference genome in humans is the sum total of one complete set of 23 chromosomes.

The "initial draft" of DNA sequences in the human genome was published in 2001. In 2004, scientists published a more complete version, but there were still small parts that remained to be sequenced, so researchers kept updating the human genome as DNA sequencing technologies improved and more data were acquired. The human genome is now one of the most complete of all known genome sequences–mostly because considerably more research money has been spent on it compared to other life forms.

To organize 3 billion bases, researchers use unique DNA sequences as reference markers. Then they determine where these short sequences are located on each chromosome. They assumed that comparing sequences between related creatures would help locate them. Scientists initially chose chimpanzees as the closest creature to humans because they knew that their proteins and DNA fragments had similar biochemical properties.[301] However, some curious researchers chose gorillas and orangutans for comparison. A recent research paper made the claim that orangutans' DNAs were more similar to humans' DNA in structure and appearance than chimpanzee, and thus orangutans should be considered our closest ancestor. Evolutionary scientists disregard this to maintain a consensus that chimpanzees are closest to humans on the hypothetical evolutionary tree. For this reason, most genetics studies assume this relationship before they even begin analyzing DNA.

In the early days of DNA sequencing, in the 1970s, scientists could sequence only very short segments of DNA. For this reason, they focused on DNA segments that they knew would be highly similar between animals, such as blood globin proteins and mitochondrial DNA (DNA which is inherited from the mother). They selected similar regions for comparison, because you cannot glean any meaningful comparisons between two DNA sequences that exist only in one and not the other. Researchers discovered that many of the short stretches of DNA genetic sequences that code for common proteins were not only highly similar in many types of animals, but that they were nearly identical between certain creatures including humans and apes.[302]

A basic understanding of what DNA sequencing actually entails helps us understand human and chimp genome accuracy. While the basic DNA sequencing techniques have not changed much since they were developed, the use of small-scale robotics and automation now enable researchers to sequence massive amounts of small DNA fragments. The DNA of an entire organism is too long to sequence all at once, thus they sequence millions of pieces, each hundreds of bases long. Workers then use computers to digitally assemble the small individual pieces into larger fragments based on overlapping sections.[303] DNA regions that have hundreds of repeating sequences are, for this reason, very difficult to reconstruct, yet we now know that they are important for cell function.

Enter New Technology

Despite the early, crude indications of apparently high DNA similarity between humans and chimps, precise DNA sequences began to present a very different picture. In 2002, a DNA sequencing lab produced over 3 million bases of chimp DNA sequence in small 50 to 900 base fragments that it obtained randomly across the entire chimp genome.[304] They then assembled the short sequences—get this—onto the human genomic framework.[305] Talk about circular reasoning. This turned out to be only one of many problems. When the chimp DNA sequences were matched with the human genome by computers, only two-thirds of the DNA sequences could be lined up with human DNA. While many short stretches of DNA existed that were very similar to human DNA, more than 30% of the chimp DNA sequence was not even close enough to attempt an alignment.

In 2005, a collaboration of different labs completed the first rough draft of the chimpanzee genome.[306] As a rough draft, even after the computational assembly based on the human genome, it still consisted of thousands of small chunks of DNA sequences. The researchers then assembled all the small sequences of chimp DNA together to estimate the complete genome. By assuming that humans evolved from a chimp-like ancestor, they used the human genome as the framework to assemble the chimp DNA sequences.[307] At least one lab that helped to assemble the chimp sequence admitted that they inserted chimp DNA sequences into the human genome layout based on evolution. They assumed that many human-like sequences were missing from the chimp DNA, so they added them electronically. That published chimp genome is thus partly based on the human genome. Because it contains human sequences, it appears more human than the chimp genome in fact is. The newest chimp genome, published in 2018, did not use human digital scaffolds and confirms a 15% dissimilarity between humans and chimps. How long will it take this correction to reach museums and textbooks that need bad science to prop up human evolution?

A large 2013 research project sequenced the genomes of chimpanzees, gorillas, and orangutans to determine their genetic variation. They again assembled all these genomes using the human genome as a framework![308]

Unfortunately, the research paper describing the 2005 chimp draft genome avoided the problem of overall average genome similarity with humans by analyzing the regions of the genomes that were already known to be highly similar. This cherry-picking deceptively reinforced the mythical 98% similarity notion. However, enough data were in the 2005 report to allow several independent researchers to calculate overall human-chimp genome similarities. They came up with estimates of 70 to 80% DNA sequence similarity.[309]

This result is important because evolutionary theory has a difficult enough time explaining how only 2% of 3 billion bases could have evolved in the 3–6 million years since they believe chimps and humans shared a common ancestor. They want to avoid the task of explaining how 15 or 20% of three billion bases evolved in such a short time! Natural processes cannot create 369 million letters of precisely coded information

234

in a billion years, let alone a few million years.[310] Instead, as shown in the above section on genetics, more time produces more mutations, which lead to more extinctions.

Thus, the ever so popular high levels of human-chimp DNA similarity rely on highly similar, selected regions and exclude vastly different regions of these separately created genomes. Cherry-picking of data is bad science. Other published research studies completed between 2002 and 2006 compared certain isolated regions of the chimp genome to human DNA. These also seemed to add support to the evolutionary paradigm, but reinserted dissimilar DNA sequence data where it could be determined that evolutionists had omitted it from their analyses. This significantly changed the results, which showed that the actual DNA similarities for the analyzed regions varied between about 66% to 86%.[311] Again, this showed at least a 14% difference—not the fake 1%.

One of the main problems with comparing DNA segments between different organisms that contain regions of strong dissimilarity is that the computer program commonly used (called BLASTN) stops matching DNA when it hits regions that are markedly different. These unmatched sections consequently are not included in the final results, raising significantly the overall similarity between human and chimp DNA. In other words, the human-coded software automatically cherry picks the data. The computer settings can be changed to reject DNA sequences that are not similar enough for the research needs. The common default setting used by most evolutionary researchers kicks out anything less than 95% to 98% in similarity. In 2011, Dr. Tompkins compared 40,000 chimp DNA sequences (after removing them from the human-genome scaffold bias) that were about 740 bases long and already known to be highly similar to human.[312] The longest matches showed a DNA similarity of only 86%. A secular report independently found the same level of dissimilarity, again nailing the coffin on top of the false 98% claims.[313]

If chimp DNA is so dissimilar to human, and the computer software stops matching after only a few hundred bases, how can we find the actual similarity of the human and chimp genomes? A 2013 study resolved this problem by digitally slicing up chimp DNA into the small fragments that the software's algorithm could optimally match.[314] Using a powerful computer dedicated to this massive computation, all 24 chimp chromosomes were compared to humans' 23 chromosomes. The results showed that, depending on the chromosome, the chimp chromosomes were between 43% and 78% similar to humans. Overall, the chimp genome was only about 70%[315] similar to human. These data confirmed results published in secular evolutionary journals, but not popularized by the media or evolutionists.

Although textbooks still contain the 98% DNA similarity claim, many scientists in the human-chimp research community now recognize the 96% to 98% similarity was derived from isolated areas and biased assemblies. However, while the 98% similarity is crumbling, geneticists rarely make public statements about overall estimates because they know it would debunk human evolution. Although the human and chimpanzee genomes overall are only about 84.4% similar, some regions have high similarity, mostly due to protein-coding genes. Even these high similarity areas actually have only about 86% of matching sequences overall when the algorithm used to analyze them is set to produce a very long sequence match.[316]

The regions of high similarity can be explained by the fact that common genetic code elements are often found between different organisms because they code for genes that produce proteins with similar functions. For the same reason that different kinds of craftworkers all use hammers to drive or pry nails, different kinds of creatures use many of the same biochemical tools to perform common cellular functions. The genome is a very complex system of genetic codes, many of which are repeated in organisms with similar functions. This concept is easier to explain to computer programmers and engineers than biologists who are steeped in the evolutionary worldview.

Gene Similarities—the Big Picture

If two different kinds of creatures have the same basic gene sequence, they usually share only a certain part of that sequence. The entire gene could be only 88% similar, while a small part of it may be 98% similar. Protein-coding gene regions called "exons" in humans are on average only about 86% to 87% similar to chimps. Often, a matching chimp gene completely misses the exon sequences inside the human version of that gene.

The original definition of a gene describes it as a DNA section that produces a messenger RNA which in turn codes for a protein. Early estimates projected that humans contained about 22,000 of these protein-coding genes, and the most recent estimates suggest 28,000 to 30,000.[317] We now know that each of these protein-coding genes can produce many different individual messenger RNA variants due to gene regulation strategies. Cellular machinery cuts and splices gene sections to generate sometimes dozens of useful products from just one of those 28,000 or so traditional genes. Consequently, over a million RNA varieties can be made from 30,000 or fewer genes! Nevertheless, less than 5% of the human genome contains actual "exon" protein-coding sequences.

Humans have a high level of DNA/gene similarity with creatures other than chimps

The human body has many molecular similarities with other living things. After all, they all use the same basic molecules. They share the same water, oxygen, and food sources. Their metabolism and therefore their genetic makeup resemble one another in order to occupy the same world. However, these similarities do not mean they evolved from a common ancestor any more than all buildings constructed using brick, iron, cement, glass, etc. means that they share origins.

DNA contains much of the information necessary for an organism to develop. If two organisms look similar, we would expect DNA similarity between them. The DNA of a cow and a whale should be more alike than the DNA of a cow and a bacterium. Likewise, humans and apes have many body similarities like bones, hair, and the ability to produce milk, so we would expect DNA sequences to match that. Of all known animals, the great apes are most like humans, so we would expect that their DNA would be most like human DNA.[318]

This is not always the case, though. Some comparisons between human DNA/genes and other animals in the literature including cats have 90% of homologous genes with humans, dogs 82%, cows 80%,[319] chimpanzees 79%, rats 69%, and mice 67%.[320] Other comparisons found include fruit fly (Drosophila) with about 60%[321] and chickens with about 60% of genes corresponding to a similar human gene.[322] These estimates suffer from the same problems that humans-chimp comparisons do, but they illustrate the patterns of similarity that one would expect from a single divine designer.

The Human-Chimp Evolution Magic Act

Stage magicians, otherwise known as illusionists, practice their trade by getting you to focus on some aspect of the magician's act to divert your focus from what the other hand is doing. This way, they get you to believe something that isn't true—a fake reality. The human-chimp DNA similarity "research" works almost the same way.

The evolutionist who promotes the human-chimp fake paradigm of DNA similarity accomplishes the magic act by getting you to focus on a small set of data representing bits and pieces of hand-picked evidence. In this way, you don't see the mountains of hard data that utterly defy evolution. While some parts of the human and chimpanzee genomes are very similar— those that the evolutionists focus on—the genomes overall are vastly different, and the hard scientific evidence now proves it. The magic act isn't working any longer, and more and more open-minded scientists are beginning to realize it.

Confronting Human-Chimp Propaganda

To close this section, let's discuss a hypothetical exchange. How can you use the information in this section in conversation? First, the person makes the claim that "human and chimp DNA are genetically 98–99% identical or similar." When such a person does not wish to listen, starting with a question, not a counter, almost always helps. If you have memorized the genome lengths, you can ask, "Do you know roughly how many bases are in the chimp and human genomes?" If they do, great. If not, then offer the fact that the chimp genome has 3.3 billion, and the human genome 3.1 billion bases. Then ask, "Do you think the percent difference between these numbers is 1, 2, or more?" You can then calculate it together. Use $((3.1/3.3) - 1) \times 100$. Ignore the negative sign (take the absolute value). When you both see that it equals about a 6% difference, then just ask, "How can the two be only 1% different if their total lengths are already 6% different?"

At this point in the conversation, you will rapidly find out if the person is really interested in learning more about the issue of human origins, or if they are so zealous about evolutionary beliefs that they refuse to listen to challenging evidence. If at that point they begin making up an answer, rest assured that they have no desire to learn anything from you. If, on the other hand, their confidence in the 1% assertion fades, then you may have just earned the right to offer more information.

When the other person shows interest in what you might have to say, you could mention, "The 99% similarity only applies to the highly similar regions. It ignores the many differences in the already dissimilar regions." You can then clarify this response by noting that "2018 research has shown that, overall, the entire genome is no more than 85% similar on average when you include all the DNA that researchers decoupled from the human genome in 2018. This equal to 15 percent difference demands hundreds of millions of precise base

239

pair changes in just 3–6 million years. Can you help me explain how mutations could accomplish that?"

You can also add, "Several thousand genes unique to humans are completely missing in chimps, and scientists have found many genes that are unique to chimps are missing in humans." Then ask, "How can evolutionary processes explain these massive differences?" Take care to ask open-ended and genuine questions. Avoid using "you." We don't want to accuse anybody, just lead them to convince themselves that their own ideas have problems. Another useful question asks, "How could only 1–2% DNA difference account for such major body differences between humans and chimps, like thousands of new genes, different hand, muscle and brain architecture, and the 40 facial muscles that humans use to communicate, compared with the dozen or so in chimp faces?"

In reality, the whole modern research field of genetics and genomics is the worst enemy of evolution. As new genomes of different kinds of organisms are being sequenced, they consistently show unique sets of DNA containing many genes and other sequences that specify that type of creature. Evolutionists call these new creature-specific genes "orphan genes" because they are not found in any other type of known creature.[323] Orphan genes appear suddenly in the pattern of life as unique sections of genetic code with no hint of evolutionary history. Of course, believers in an omnipotent Creator know that each different genome, such as that for humans and that of chimpanzees, was separately, uniquely, and masterfully engineered at the beginning of creation. God created and embedded each creature's orphan genes to network with all the rest of that creature's genetic coding instructions. The scientific data overwhelmingly show that God deserves the credit and evolution deserves none.

Conclusion

With so much at stake, like the answer to life's largest question, "Where did I come from?" do we want to trust in extremely biased answers? Every high school student can refute 98% similarity dogma by tracking the main points above as outlined below.

1. Overall, the entire genome is only about 84.4% similar on average when you include all the DNA. This is equal to a 15% difference, or 360 million+ base pair differences. (Slight differences exist between using the 2004 assembly, which made the data look more human than the unbiased 2018 assembly). Either assembly reveals a genetic chasm between our supposed closest evolutionary relative.

2. The "Junk" DNA claim has long been refuted and most of it has been found to have clear functions which are regulatory in nature.

3. The Chromosome Fusion claim is false for four reasons. First, telomeres are designed not to fuse. Telomere to telomere fusion is unknown in the natural world. This makes the evolutionary assertion hard for them to defend. Second, telomeres contain repeats of the DNA sequence TTAGGG over and over for thousands of bases. Human telomeres are from 5,000 to 15,000 bases long. If these actually fused, then they should have over ten thousand TTAGGG bases, but the alleged fusion site actually has about 800 bases. Third, the "fusion site" sequence shares only 70% similarity to what expectations would dictate. Last, the claimed fusion site contains a gene, proof that it is not a genetic scar at all.

4. The Beta-globin Pseudogene is not a pseudogene! Without this status, its use to argue for human-chimp common ancestry crumbles. It is actually a functional gene in the middle of a cluster of five other genes.

5. The GULO Pseudogene does not show common decent, but simply shows an area of both genomes that is prone to mutate.

Human Fossils: Why Don't We Find Humans Buried with Dinosaurs?

Our ministry receives this question frequently, but few seem to see that inherent assumption upon which the question is based: the *assumption that we should in fact find human fossils with dinosaur fossils because they were living in proximity at the time of the Flood.* Once that's exposed, possible answers become clearer. Science writer Brian Thomas explains:

> Many assume that dinosaur layers should also contain human fossils. Not at all. Dinosaur fossil layers contain sea, swamp, and lake plants and animals, and mostly water birds. They have virtually no remains of land-dwellers like dogs, deer, bears, or bunnies. Humans live on solid ground, not in swamps [wetlands]—and definitely not in pre-Flood swamps where dinosaurs might treat them as light snacks. The best places to look for fossils of pre-Flood humans would be in deposits that contain land-dwellers like pre-Flood dogs and deer.[324]

As a case in point, one of the largest mass dinosaur bonebeds in the world is at Dinosaur Provincial Park in Canada. This massive Flood deposit has 49 different species of dinosaurs buried along with turtles, crocodiles, fish, flying reptiles, birds, and small mammals.[325] This is not exactly a place where humans would want to live—not then; not today. Four other important factors help answer this question:

1. While we don't know the pre-flood human population, most researchers would say that it was much smaller than the 7+ billion people on earth today. Also consider that humans had also not likely spread outside of the area that it currently called Mesopotamia yet.

2. Consider God's promise to wipe humans off the face of the earth: "I will destroy man whom I have created from the face of the earth, both man and beast, creeping thing and birds of the air…" (Genesis 6:7). The Flood mechanisms that He used (see **Noah's Flood: Catastrophic Plate Tectonics**) were the best possible way to scrub humans from existence. Rapidly spreading sea floor sunk beneath the continents. This produced cycles of tsunamis that catastrophically wiped out vast populations of life. This caused, for example, the Morrison Formation, filled with dead dinosaurs mixed with marine life, to cover a 13-state region in the middle of the U.S. This process resulted in an average sediment thickness of about one mile around the globe and 75% of earth being covered with sedimentary layers.

3. When looking at the fossil record as a whole, humans (and even apes) are extremely rare. In fact, the entire primate order represents a mere **0.3%** of the fossil occurrences in the currently known fossil population on record.[326] This is because about 95% of all fossils are marine invertebrates, mostly shellfish like clams. Of the remaining 5%, 95% are algae and plant fossils (5% x 95% or 4.75% of the total) and 5% (5% X 5%, or 0.25% of the total) are insects and other non-marine invertebrates and vertebrates. Of the remaining 0.25% of the total, 95% are insects and other non-marine invertebrates and only 5% (5% x 0.25%, or 1.25% of the total) are vertebrate fossils (mostly fish, and finally, amphibians, reptiles, birds, and mammals).[327]

4. Fossilization requires quick and complete burial. During the onset of the Flood, humans may have tried to save themselves any way possible. It is probable that during the months of rising Flood waters, humans moved to higher ground. Then, as the humans and other animals died, many might have been washed away at the end of the Flood when the mountains rose and the waters rushed off of the earth (Psalm 104:8).[328] Geologist Dr.

Tim Clarey's new research on continent-wide rock layers (based on drill core and seismic data) reveals that many Cenozoic deposits lie offshore since Flood waters washed off of continents and into today's oceans.[329] If many of the fossils are in layers trapped beneath the sea, they would of course be difficult to find.

Endnotes

[1] See: "Does the Bible (Job 40) Describe a Sauropod Dinosaur (Behemoth)?" (Genesis Apologetics) (Available: *https://youtu.be/mEJENaCgq70*); and web resources: *www.genesisapologetics.com/dinosaurs*

[2] It would be a far cry from the intent of this author to say that this is in any way favoring the male role of raising children. When it comes to grounding children, I actually believe that mothers play a bigger role, but in different ways and in different seasons. However, there are certain grounding elements that a father can bring that are unique, and this concept is throughout Scripture.

[3] See college list by Answers in Genesis: *https://answersingenesis.org/colleges/*

[4] See for example: *https://en.wikipedia.org/wiki/Red_pill_and_blue_pill*

[5] See: Ken Ham on Importance of Scripture, Starting with Genesis *https://youtu.be/fynpRNn7ewU*. See also: Answers in Genesis: *https://www.facebook.com/AnswersInGenesis/videos/340396066597121/*

[6] Hugh Ross, "Species Development: Natural Process or Divine Action," Creation and Time Audiotape, Tape 2, Side 1 (Pasadena, CA: Reasons to Believe, 1990).

[7] Overview Eric Hovind and Paul Taylor welcome special guest Dr. G. Charles Jackson in the August 18, 2011 episode of Creation Today.

[8] John MacArthur, "Creation: Believe It or Not, Part 2 (90–209)": *www.gty.org/resources/sermons/90-209/creation-believe-it-or-not-part-2* (March 28, 1999) (January 27, 2017).

[9] Verse 15 and 17 respectively. Also acts 28:25.

[10] For example, in 1946 the Dead Sea Scrolls were discovered, which included over 900 manuscripts dating from 408 BC to AD 318. These manuscripts were written mostly on parchment (made of animal hide) but with some written on papyrus. Because these materials are fragile, they have to be kept behind special glass in climate controlled areas.

[11] Josh McDowell, *The New Evidence that Demands a Verdict*. Nashville: Thomas Nelson Publishers, 1999, 38.

[12] The number is actually higher now, at about 5,801 manuscripts (see: John Piper, *A Peculiar Glory: How the Christian Scriptures Reveal Their Complete Truthfulness*. Wheaton, IL: Crossway, 2016).

[13] McDowell, *The New Evidence that Demands a Verdict*, 38.

[14] Most of the 11 verses come from 3 John: Geisler & Nix, *A General Introduction to the Bible*. Chicago: Moody Press, 1986, 430.

[15] Theophilus ben Ananus was the High Priest in Jerusalem from AD 37 to 41 and was one of the wealthiest and most influential Jewish families in Iudaea Province during the 1st century. He was also the brother-in-law of Joseph Caiaphas, the High Priest before whom Jesus appeared. See Wikipedia and Cooper, B. *The Authenticity of the Book of Genesis*. Portsmouth, UK: Creation Science Movement, 2012.

[16] The Digital Dead Sea Scrolls Online, Directory of Qumran Dead Sea Scroll: *http://dss.collections.imj.org.il/isaiah* (September 1, 2019).

[17] Source for DSS: Fred Mille, "Qumran Great Isaiah Scroll," Great Isaiah Scroll: *http://www.moellerhaus.com/qumdir.htm*; Source for Aleppo Codes JPS: "Mechon Mamre" (Hebrew for Mamre Institute): *http://www.mechon-mamre.org/p/pt/pt1053.htm*. (December 10, 2013).

[18] Geisler & Nix. *A General Introduction to the Bible*.

[19] Samuel Davidson, *Hebrew Text of the Old Testament,* 2d ed. (London: Samuel Bagster & Sons, 1859), 89.

[20] Mary Fairchild, "44 Prophecies of the Messiah Fulfilled in Jesus Christ," About.com: *www.christianity.about.com/od/biblefactsandlists/a/Prophecies-Jesus.htm.* (December 18, 2013).

[21] See website: *https://defendinginerrancy.com/*

[22] See 2 Peter 1:31; 2 Timothy 3:16; Numbers 23:19; Titus 1:2; Matthew 24:35; Psalm 12:6–7; Proverbs 30:5; and Psalm 138:2.

[23] Linking from the present to Abraham's day is well established historically based on correlations between inscriptions and the biblical chronology of the Kings.

[24] The Biblical timelines that rely on the 17th-century chronology formulated by Bishop James Ussher place Creation at 4,004 BC and the Flood at 2,348 BC. Some recent research into the copyist differences in the early Masoretic and early Septuagint texts place the Flood around 2,518 BC based on the Masoretic text and between 3,168 BC and 3,298 BC based on the Septuagint (and other early texts), with Creation as early as 5,554 BC. These differences, however, can be settled by comparing multiple texts to reveal the perfect nature of the original writings which were "written through man by God" without error. These issues have been discussed in papers from three leading creation ministries. See, for example: Brian Thomas, "Two date range options for Noah's Flood," *Journal of Creation* 31(1) (2017); Henry B. Smith Jr., "Methuselah's Begetting Age in Genesis 5:25 and the Primeval Chronology of the Septuagint: A Closer Look at the Textual and Historical Evidence," *Answers Research Journal* 10 (2017): 169–179. Answers in Genesis: *www.answersingenesis.org/arj/v10/methuselah-primeval-chronology-septuagint.pdf* (November 5, 2018); and Lita Cosner and Robert Carter, "Textual Traditions and Biblical Chronology," *Journal of Creation* 29 (2) 2015. Journal of Creation: *https://creation.com/images/pdfs/tj/j29_2/j29_2_99-105.pdf* (November 5, 2018).

[25] Ewald Plass. *What Martin Luther Says: A Practical In-Home Anthology for the Active Christian,* 1523.

[26] See: *https://genesisapologetics.com/faqs/lifespans-before-the-flood-how-did-people-live-to-be-900-years-old-before-the-flood/*

[27] Progressive Creationist, Dr. Hugh Ross, places the emergence of the human race via Adam and Eve about 50,000 years ago: Fazale Rana with Hugh Ross, *Who Was Adam?* (Colorado Springs, CO: NavPress, 2005), 45. See also: *www.reasons.org/articles/new-date-for-first-aussies* (January 26, 2017). While this is the view of Dr. Ross, the time period in which *Homo sapiens* supposedly branched off varies widely in the secular literature, but is typically represented as going back even further (see for example: *http://humanorigins.si.edu/evidence/human-fossils/species/homo-sapiens*).

[28] Kenneth R. Miller and Joseph S. Levine, *Biology.* (Boston, MA.: Pearson, 2006), p. 466.

[29] Tim Chaffey, "Planting Confusion: Were plants created on Day Three or Day Six? (April 10, 2012). Available: *https://answersingenesis.org/biology/plants/planting-confusion/.* See also: Mark Futato, "Because It Had Rained: A Study of Gen 2:5–7 With Implications for Gen 2:4–25 and Gen 1:1–2:3." Westminster Theological Journal, 60:1–21, (Spring 1998), 4. It may not be the best practice to identify something as "wild" prior to the Fall, but the definition given here is based on how the term is commonly understood—not just before sin.

[30] Jason Lisle, "Two Creation Accounts?" (August 31, 2015). *https://www.icr.org/article/two-creation-accounts/*
[31] See also 1 Corinthians 15:45 and Romans 5.
[32] Romans 5:12–19; 1 Corinthians 15:21–22 and 1 Corinthians 15:45.
[33] See 1 Timothy 2:14.
[34] "The Amazing Hearing System" *https://youtu.be/3Lsegdfj2TE*
[35] Image credit: Ossicle Hearing Clinic – Kelowna: *http://kelownahearingclinic.ossiclehearing.com/hearing-services/hearing-tests/*
[36] Jeffrey P. Tomkins, Ph.D. contributed the majority of this section. The complete work can be found in *Debunking Human Evolution Taught in our Public Schools* (Genesis Apologetics).
[37] Dan Biddle, *Creation v. Evolution: What They Won't Tell You in Biology Class* (Maitland, FL: Xulon Press); H. Morris, et al., *Creation Basics & Beyond: An In-Depth Look at Science, Origins, and Evolution* (Dallas, TX: Institute for Creation Research, 2013).
[38] Estimates on the total weight of human DNA in a single body vary greatly, but certainly do not exceed this amount. See for example: Molecular Facts and Figures (Integrated DNA Technologies): *http://sfvideo.blob.core.windows.net/sitefinity/docs/default-source/biotech-basics/molecular-facts-and-figures.pdf?sfvrsn=4563407_4* (September 1, 2019).
[39] See the reference section in this video for references and resources used and cited in this section: Human Chimp DNA Similarity: *https://youtu.be/Rav8sfuJFYc*
[40] See the Genesis Apologetics Human-Chimp DNA video and citations here: *https://youtu.be/Rav8sfuJFYc*
[41] T.J. Parsons, et al., "A High Observed Substitution Rate in the Human Mitochondrial DNA Control Region," Nature Genetics 15 (1997): 363–368.
[42] A. Gibbons, "Calibrating the Mitochondrial Clock," Science 279 (1998): 28–29. (*http://www.dnai.org/teacherguide/pdf/reference_romanovs.pdf*). (Sept. 1, 2019).
[43] Charles Darwin, *On the Origin of Species by Means of Natural Selection, or the Preservation of Favoured Races in the Struggle for Life* (London: John Murray, 1859).
[44] Ibid.
[45] Bill Bryson, *A Short History of Nearly Everything* (London: Black Swan Publishing, 2004), 529.
[46] W.L. Jungers, "Lucy's length: Stature reconstruction in Australopithecus afarensis (A.L. 288-1) with implications for other small-bodied hominids." *American Journal of Physical Anthropology*. 76 (2) (1988): 227–231.
[47] Some of these fatal flaws pertain to Lucy's actual fossil, some are in regards to how her fossil is represented, and some involve both.
[48] NOVA, *In Search of Human Origins (Part I)* (Airdate: June 3, 1997): *www.pbs.org/wgbh/nova/transcripts/2106hum1.html* (September 2, 2015).
[49] Time magazine reported in 1977 that Lucy had a tiny skull, a head like an ape, a braincase size the same as that of a chimp—450 cc. and "was surprisingly short legged" (*Time*, November 7, 1979, pp. 68–69). See also: Smithsonian National Museum of Natural History, "Australopithecus afarensis": *www.humanorigins.si.edu/evidence/human-fossils/species/australopithecus-afarensis* (September 2, 2015).
[50] Solly Zuckerman, *Beyond the Ivory Tower* (London: Taplinger Publishing Company, 1970), 78.

[51] Skull from: www.skullsunlimited.com.

[52] William H. Kimbel and Yoel Rak. "The Cranial Base of Australopithecus Afarensis: New Insights from the Female Skull." *Philosophical Transactions of the Royal Society B: Biological Sciences* 365.1556 (2010): 3365–3376.

[53] Upper Image Credit: M. H. Wolpoff, J. Hawks, B. Senut, M. Pickford, J. Ahern, "An Ape or the Ape: Is the Toumaï Cranium TM 266 a Hominid?" PaleoAnthropology. 2006: 36–50 (upper two images, arrows added). Lower Image Credit: Evolution Facts, Inc. *Evolution Encyclopedia Volume 2, Chapter 18 Ancient Man* (www.godrules.net/evolutioncruncher/2evlch18a.htm). (January 27, 2017). FM differences discussed in: William H. Kimbel and Rak Yoel. "The Cranial Base of Australopithecus Afarensis: New Insights from the Female Skull." *Philosophical Transactions of the Royal Society B: Biological Sciences* 365.1556 (2010): 3365–3376.

[54] Ibid., 3369–3370

[55] Image Credit: Wikipedia.

[56] Fred Spoor, Bernard Wood, Frans Zonneveld, "Implications of Early Hominid Labyrinthine Morphology for Evolution of Human Bipedal Locomotion," *Nature* 369 (June 23, 1994): 645–648.

[57] Smithsonian: www.humanorigins.si.edu/evidence/human-fossils/species/australopithecus-africanus (January 27, 2017).

[58] Bernard Wood, "A precious little bundle," *Nature* 443, 278–281 (Sept. 21, 2006).

[59] Kate Wong, "Special Report: Lucy's Baby An extraordinary new human fossil comes to light," *Scientific American*: www.scientificamerican.com/article/special-report-lucys-baby/ (September 20, 2006) (January 27, 2017).

[60] Healthline Bodymaps: www.healthline.com/human-body-maps/semicircular-canals. Medically Reviewed on January 26, 2015 by Healthline Medical Team (January 27, 2017).

[61] F. Spoor and F. Zonneveld. "Comparative review of the human bony labyrinth," *Am J Phys Anthropology*, Supplement 27 (1998): 211–51. P. Gunz, et al., "The Mammalian Bony Labyrinth Reconsidered: Introducing a Comprehensive Geometric Morphometric Approach," *Journal of Anatomy* 220, 6 (2012): 529–543.

[62] Fred Spoor, Bernard Wood, Frans Zonneveld, "Implications of Early Hominid Labyrinthine Morphology for Evolution of Human Bipedal Locomotion," *Nature* 369 (June 23, 1994): 645–648.

[63] Brian L. Day, et al. "The vestibular system," *Current Biology*, 15 (15), R583-R586.

[64] Adam Summers, "Born to Run: Humans will Never Win a Sprint against your Average Quadruped. But our Species is well-adapted for the Marathon," *Biomechanics:* www.naturalhistorymag.com/biomechanics/112078/born-to-run (September 1, 2015).

[65] Marc R. Meyer, Scott A. Williams, Michael P. Smith, Gary J. Sawyer, "Lucy's back: Reassessment of fossils associated with the A.L. 288-1 vertebral column," *Journal of Human Evolution*, 85 (August 2015): 174–180.

[66] Personal communication: "All [Lucy's bones were] found in an area covering about 3 square meters." Donald Johanson (May 28, 2014).

[67] *Atlas of Science*, "Archaeological surprise! Lucy has company," *https://atlasofscience.org/archaeological-surprise-lucy/* (November 30, 2015) (January 27, 2017).

[68] PBS Evolution, "Finding Lucy": *www.pbs.org/wgbh/evolution/library/07/1/l_071_01.html* (September 2, 2015).

[69] Ibid.

[70] F. Marchal, "A new morphometric analysis of the hominid pelvic bone," *Journal of Human Evolution*, 38(3) (March 2000): 347–65.

[71] Jack Stern & Randall L. Susman, "The Locomotor Anatomy of Australopithecus afarensis," *Journal of Physical Anthropology* 60 (1983): 291–292.

[72] Charles Oxnard, *The Order of Man: A Biomathematical Anatomy of the Primates* (Yale University Press and Hong Kong University Press, 1984): 3.

[73] Image Credit: *Australopithecus afarensis* (*History Alive! The Ancient World* (Palo Alto, CA: Teachers Curriculum Institute, 2004).

[74] Brian G. Richmond and David S. Strait, "Evidence That Humans Evolved From a Knuckle-Walking Ancestor," *Nature*, 404 (2000): 382–385.

[75] Maggie Fox, "Man's Early Ancestors Were Knuckle Walkers," *San Diego Union Tribune* (Quest Section, March 29, 2000).

[76] Richmond & Strait, *Evidence That Humans Evolved From a Knuckle-Walking Ancestor*, 382–385.

[77] Guy Gugliotta, "It's All in the Wrist Early Human Ancestors Were 'Knuckle-Walkers,' Research Indicates," Washington Post (March 23, 2000), A03.

[78] Richmond & Strait, *Evidence That Humans Evolved From a Knuckle-Walking Ancestor*, 382–385.

[79] Ibid.

[80] Manuel Domínguez-Rodrigo, Travis Rayne Pickering, Sergio Almécija, Jason L. Heaton, Enrique Baquedano, Audax Mabulla & David Uribelarrea, "Earliest modern human-like hand bone from a new >1.84-million-year-old site at Olduvai in Tanzania," *Nature Communications* 6, 7987 (2015); Jack Stern & Randall L. Susman, "The Locomotor Anatomy of Australopithecus afarensis," *Journal of Physical Anthropology* 60 (1983): 280.

[81] Ibid.

[82] Ibid.

[83] J. Stern & R. Susman, "The Locomotor Anatomy of Australopithecus afarensis," *Journal of Physical Anthropology* 60 (1983): 280.

[84] W. L. Jungers, "Lucy's limbs: skeletal allometry and locomotion in Australopithecus afarensis." *Nature* 297 (1982): 676–678.

[85] Stern & Susman, 1983.

[86] K.D. Hunt, "The evolution of human bipedality: ecology and functional morphology." *Journal of Human Evolution*, 26 (1994): 183–202.

[87] PBS Evolution, "Finding Lucy": *www.pbs.org/wgbh/evolution/library/07/1/l_071_01.html* (September 2, 2015); National Geographic, "What was 'Lucy'? Fast Facts on an Early Human Ancestor" (September 20, 2006). *National Geographic News: http://news.nationalgeographic.com/news/2006/09/060920-lucy.html* (September 2, 2015).

[88] Donald Johanson & Edgar Blake. *From Lucy to Language* (New York: Simon & Schuster, 1996).

[89] Image Credit: Answers in Genesis (left); Brian Thomas (right).

[90] Personal communication: "All [Lucy's bones were] found in an area covering about 3 square meters." Professor Donald Johanson (May 28, 2014).

[91] Licensed through Alamy. Photo Credit Franck Robichon/epa/Corbis.

[92] M. Häusler & P. Schmid, "Comparison of the Pelves of Sts 14 and AL 288-1: Implications for Birth and Sexual Dimorphism in Australopithecines." *Journal of Human Evolution* 29 (1995): 363–383.

[93] Alan Boyle, "Lucy or Brucey? It Can Be Tricky to Tell the Sex of Fossil Ancestors," *Science* (April 29, 2015).

[94] Image Credit: Wikipedia.

[95] Source: *http://news.utexas.edu/2016/08/29/ut-study-cracks-coldest-case-how-lucy-died* (January 27, 2017).

[96] J. Kappelman, R.A. Ketcham, S. Pearce, L. Todd, W. Akins, M.W. Colbert, et al, "Perimortem fractures in Lucy suggest mortality from fall out of tall tree." *Nature*, 537 (September 22, 2016): 503–507. *www.nature.com/nature/journal/v537/n7621/full/nature19332.html*

[97] Oxnard, *The Order of Man: A Biomathematical Anatomy of the Primates*, p. 332.

[98] Roger Lewin, *Bones of Contention* (Chicago: Univ. of Chicago Press, 1987), 164.

[99] Wray Herbert, "Lucy's Uncommon Forbear," *Science News* 123 (Feb. 5, 1983), 89.

[100] Albert W. Mehlert, "Lucy—Evolution's Solitary Claim for an Ape/Man: Her Position is Slipping Away," *Creation Research Society Quarterly*, 22 (3) (December, 1985), 145.

[101] Marvin Lubenow, *Bones of Contention* (Grand Rapids, MI: Baker Books, 1992), 179.

[102] DeWitt Steele & Gregory Parker, *Science of the Physical Creation*, 2d ed. (Pensacola, FL: A Beka Book, 1996), p. 299.

[103] "Before humans left Babel, it appears that apes had already spread over much of the Old World and had diversified into a large array of species... Paleontologists are still discovering species of post-Flood apes. If we are correct about post-Flood rocks, apes were at their highest point of diversity and were buried in local catastrophes just before humans spread out from Babel." Kurt Wise, "Lucy Was Buried First Babel Helps Explain the Sequence of Ape and Human Fossils," (August 20, 2008), *Answers in Genesis: www.answersingenesis.org/human-evolution/lucy/lucy-was-buried-first/* (September 2, 2015).

[104] American Atheists, "You KNOW it's a Myth: This Season, Celebrate REASON!," quoted in "I Agree with the Atheists!,"Around the World with Ken Ham (blog), June 1, 2011, *https://answersingenesis.org/blogs/ken-ham/2011/06/01/i-agree-with-the-atheists/*.

[105] We are grateful to the contributions and review of this chapter made by Drs. John Baumgardner (Liberty University) and Tim Clarey (ICR).

[106] Image Credit: Dr. John Baumgardner.

[107] Answers in Depth, Vol. 5 (2010). *www.answersingenesis.org/doc/articles/aid/v5/catastrophic_plate_tectonics.pdf* (November 5, 2018).

[108] See: "Noah's Flood and Catastrophic Plate Tectonics (from Pangea to Today)" (Genesis Apologetics) (Available: *https://youtu.be/zd5-dHxOQhg*).

[109] Continental Sprint: A Global Flood Model for Earth History
https://youtu.be/0RLlbUBpzr0
[110] Chandler Burr, "The Geophysics of God: A scientist embraces plate tectonics—and Noah's flood." U.S. News & World Report. pp. 55–8. Archived from the original on August 10, 2007 (Original published June 8, 1997).
[111] Thanks to Dr. John Baumgardner for contributing this section (personal communication, May 21, 2018).
[112] Plate Tectonics Theory, National Park Service: for Teachers Scalera, Giancarlo (December 2, 2009). "Roberto Mantovani (1854–1933) and his ideas on the expanding Earth, as revealed by his correspondence and manuscripts." Annals of Geophysics. 52 (6): 617.
[113] AlteredQualia: *https://alteredqualia.com/xg/examples/earth_bathymetry.html*
[114] Image Credit: National Geographic
[115] "Ring of Fire." USGS. 2012-07-24. Retrieved 2013-06-13; "Where do earthquakes occur?" USGS. 2013-05-13. Archived from the original on 2014-08-05. Retrieved June 13, 2013.
[116] Wikiedia.
[117] S. H. Kirby (1983) "Rheology of the lithosphere," Reviews of Geophysics and Space Physics 25, 1219–1244.
[118] J. R. Baumgardner (2003) "Catastrophic plate tectonics: the physics behind the Genesis Flood," in Proceedings of the Fifth International Conference on Creationism, R. L. Ivey, Jr., Editor, Creation Science Fellowship, Pittsburgh, PA, 113-126.
[119] J. R. Baumgardner (2018). Understanding how the Flood sediment record was formed: The role of large tsunamis. In Proceedings of the Eighth International Conference on Creationism, ed. J.H. Whitmore, 287–305. Pittsburgh, Pennsylvania: Creation Science Fellowship.
[120] Ibid.
[121] Ibid.
[122] J. R. Baumgardner (2018). "The Importance of the Genesis Flood to a Correct Understanding of the Earth's Past" (PowerPoint Presentation).
[123] Image Credit: John D. Morris, 2012. The Global Flood: Unlocking Earth's Geologic History. Dallas, TX: Institute for Creation Research.
[124] Carl Werner, "Evolution the Grand Experiment," The Grand Experiment: *www.thegrandexperiment.com/index.html* (January 1, 2014).
[125] There is disagreement in the paleontology field as to whether the "dinosaur death pose" is due to choking while dying from drowning, or due to strong water currents arching the neck back after death. See: Reisdorf, Achim G. & Wuttke, Michael. "Re-evaluating Moodie's Opisthotonic-Posture Hypothesis in Fossil Vertebrates Part I: Reptiles—the taphonomy of the bipedal dinosaurs Compsognathus longipes and Juravenator starki from the Solnhofen Archipelago (Jurassic, Germany)," Palaeobiodiversity and Palaeoenvironments 92 (2012):119-168. Their findings stated, "From what has been presented above, it can be concluded that the formation of the 'opisthotonic posture' in subaquatically deposited carcasses of long-necked and longtailed reptiles is the result of a postmortem process…this posture must be seen as a normal phenomenon that occurs during subaquatic gradual embedding of these sorts of carcasses." See discussion: Drwile.com, "Arched Necks In Dinosaur Fossils: Is Water to Blame?" *www.blog.drwile.com/?p=7118* (February 16, 2016).
[126] Liu, L., S. Spasojevi & M. Gurnis (2008), Reconstructing Farallon Plate Subduction Beneath North America back to the Late Cretaceous, *Science*,

251

322, 934-938; Spasojevi, S., L. Liu & M. Gurnis (2009), Adjoint Convection Models of North America Incorporating Tomographic, Plate motion and Stratigraphic Constraints, Geochem., Geophy., Geosys. 10, Q05W02; G. A. Bond, Geology 4, 557 (1976); Timothy A. Cross & Rex H. Pilger Jr, "Tectonic controls of late Cretaceous sedimentation, western interior, USA," Nature, Volume 274, 653–657 (1978).

[127] Thanks to Dr. John Baumgardner for contributing this section (personal communication, May 21, 2018).

[128] Image Credit: *https://www.canyonministries.org/bent-rock-layers/*

[129] T.L. Clarey and D.J. Werner (2018). Use of sedimentary megasequences to re-create pre-Flood geography. In Proceedings of the Eighth International Conference on Creationism, ed. J.H. Whitmore, pp. 351–372. Pittsburgh, Pennsylvania: Creation Science Fellowship. Note: the literature on this topic reports 1,500 bore holes, but this has since increased to 2,000.

[130] Courtesy of Dr. Nathaniel Jeanson.

[131] Image Credit: Clarey and D.J. Werner (2018).

[132] Andrew A. Snelling, "How Did We Get All This Coal?" (April 1, 2013; last featured April 1, 2014): *https://answersingenesis.org/biology/plants/how-did-we-get-all-this-coal/*

[133] Answers in Genesis: "Putting the Ark into Perspective" (January 23, 2014): *https://answersingenesis.org/noahs-ark/putting-the-ark-into-perspective/*

[134] Michael Belknap and Tim Chaffey, "How Could All the Animals Fit on the Ark?" (April 2, 2019): *https://answersingenesis.org/noahs-ark/how-could-all-animals-fit-ark/*

[135] John Woodmorappe, "Chapter 5: How Could Noah Fit the Animals on the Ark and Care for Them? (October 15, 2013; last featured March 2, 2014): *https://answersingenesis.org/noahs-ark/how-could-noah-fit-the-animals-on-the-ark-and-care-for-them/*

[136] Dr. Hong earned his Ph.D. degree in applied mechanics from the University of Michigan, Ann Arbor.

[137] S.W. Hong, S. S. Na, B.S. Hyun, S.Y. Hong, D.S. Gong, K.J. Kang, S.H. Suh, K.H. Lee, & Y.G. Je, "Safety investigation of Noah's Ark in a seaway," Creation.com: *www.creation.com/safety-investigation-of-noahs-ark-in-a-seaway* (January 1, 2014).

[138] John Whitcomb, *The World that Perished* (Grand Rapids, Michigan: Baker Book House, 1988): 24.

[139] Y. Eyüp Özveren Shipbuilding, 1590–1790, Vol. 23, No. 1, Commodity Chains in the World-Economy, 1590–1790 (2000), 15–86.

[140] Frank Lorey, The Flood of Noah and the Flood of Gilgamesh (March 1, 1997): *https://www.icr.org/article/noah-flood-gilgamesh/*

[141] Tim Lovett, "Comparing Gilgamesh," (October, 2004) *(http://worldwideflood.com/ark/gilgamesh/gilgamesh.htm#gilgamesh)*.

[142] Gotquestions.org: *https://www.gotquestions.org/Noahs-ark-questions.html*; Ark Encounter, "How Long for Noah to Build the Ark?" (November 18, 2011): *https://arkencounter.com/blog/2011/11/18/how-long-for-noah-to-build-the-ark/*;

Verse by Verse Ministry:
https://www.versebyverseministry.org/bible-answers/how-long-did-noah-take-to-build-the-ark; Bodie Hodge, "How Long Did It Take for Noah to Build the Ark?" (June 1, 2010; last featured May 23, 2018): *https://answersingenesis.org/bible-timeline/how-long-did-it-take-for-noah-to-build-the-ark/*

[143] Jeffrey H. Tigay, "The Evolution of the Gilgamesh Epic," University of Pennsylvania Press, Philadelphia, 1982, 220, 225.

[144] These estimates are based on the smaller cubit size.

[145] Answers in Genesis: Created Kinds (Baraminology): *https://answersingenesis.org/creation-science/baraminology/*

[146] R. M. Nowak, *Walker's Mammals of the World* (6th ed. 2 Vols, Baltimore, Maryland: The Johns Hopkins University Press (1999).

[147] Wilson & Reeder, *Mammal Species of the World* (3rd ed. 2005).

[148] Jean K. Lightner, "Mammalian Ark Kinds," *Answers Research Journal* 5 (2012):151–204. *Answers in Genesis: www.answersingenesis.org/arj/v5/mammalian-ark-kinds.pdf* (November 5, 2018).

[149] Dr. Nathaniel T. Jeanson, "Which Animals Were on the Ark with Noah? Stepping Back in Time." (May 28, 2016) Answers in Genesis: *https://answersingenesis.org/creation-science/baraminology/which-animals-were-on-the-ark-with-noah/* (November 5, 2018).

[150] Ronald J. Litwin, Robert E. Weems, and Thomas R. Holtz, Jr. *Dinosaurs Fact and Fiction (https://pubs.usgs.gov/gip/dinosaurs/types.html* and *https://pubs.usgs.gov/gip/dinosaurs/* (November 5, 2018).

[151] Genesis 10 provides a listing of most of these families. Since not all the family lines are listed in Genesis 10 and a few more are listed in Genesis 11, it's likely that between 78 and 100 language groups were involved.

[152] Australian Institute of Marine Science (2001) & Lambeck, et al., (2002).

[153] Paul F. Taylor, "Chapter 11: How Did Animals Spread All Over the World from Where the Ark Landed?" October 18, 2007; last featured February 17, 2014. Answers in Genesis: *https://answersingenesis.org/animal-behavior/migration/how-did-animals-spread-from-where-ark-landed/* (October 24, 2018).

[154] Returning to Genesis: Why are there so many Flood Legends? (June 8, 2012). *http://www.rtgmin.org/2012/06/08/flood-legends/*

[155] Creation Ministries International: Chinese Characters and Genesis (*https://creation.com/chinese-characters-and-genesis*); *https://creationtoday.org/chinese-language-goes-back-to-genesis/*

[156] James Johnson, Genesis in Chinese Pictographs, Acts and Facts, February 27, 2015): *https://www.icr.org/article/genesis-chinese-pictographs/*

[157] See Gotquestions.org: *https://www.gotquestions.org/Noahs-ark-questions.html*; *https://arkencounter.com/blog/2011/11/18/how-long-for-noah-to-build-the-ark/*; *https://www.versebyverseministry.org/bible-answers/how-long-did-noah-take-to-build-the-ark*; *https://answersingenesis.org/bible-timeline/how-long-did-it-take-for-noah-to-build-the-ark/*

[158] We are grateful for the review work on this chapter by Dr. Doug Petrovich.

[159] Creation Ministries International: Who wrote Genesis? (December 18, 2013): *https://www.youtube.com/watch?v=KLzRDKDcJ_E*

[160] Image Credit: Tamar Hayardeni (Wikimedia).

[161] See previous endnote regarding the differences between the Masoretic and Septuagint Creation and Flood dates.

[162] An early reconstruction by Gregory S. Paul estimated Argentinosaurus at between 30–35 meters (98–115 ft.) in length and with a weight of up to 80–100 tonnes (88–110 short tons). The length of the skeletal restoration mounted in Museo Carmen Funes is 39.7 meters (130 ft.) long and 7.3 meters (24 ft.) high. This is the longest reconstruction in a museum and contains the original material, including a mostly complete fibula. Other estimates place the creature at 115 feet long and between 165,000 and 220,000 pounds (*www.bbc.co.uk/nature/life/Argentinosaurus*) (January 26, 2017).

[163] Image credit: Wikipedia.

[164] Carl Werner, *Living Fossils, Evolution: The Grand Experiment*, vol 1. (Green Forest, AR: New Leaf Press, 2009).

[165] "Fast Facts about the Bible." Bibleresources.org: *http://bibleresources.org/bibleresources/bible-facts/* (January 26, 2017)

[166] M. P. Taylor and M. J. Wedel. "Why sauropods had long necks; and why giraffes have short necks." *PeerJ* 1: (2013), e36.

[167] Image Credit: Wikipedia (*https://en.wikipedia.org/wiki/Mamenchisaurus*) (January 26, 2017).

[168] M.J. Wedel, "Aligerando a los gigantes (Lightening the giants)." *¡Fundamental!* 2007, 12:1–84. [in Spanish, with English translation]

[169] See also: "Mechanical implications of pneumatic neck vertebrae in sauropod dinosaurs." Daniela Schwarz-Wings, Christian A. Meyer, Eberhard Frey, Hans-Rudolf Manz-Steiner, Ralf Schumacher *Proc. R. Soc. B* 2010 277 11–17.

[170] Wedel, 2007.

[171] University of California Museum of Paleontology, Matt Wedel: Hunting the inflatable dinosaur: *https://ucmp.berkeley.edu/science/profiles/wedel_0609.php* (January 26, 2017).

[172] David Catchpoole, Grass-eating dinos: A 'time-travel' problem for evolution (*www.creation.com/grass-eating-dinos*) (August 22, 2017); Brian Thomas, Dinosaurs Ate Rice, *www.icr.org/article/6428/* (August 22, 2017).

[173] Nicole Klein, Kristian Remes, Carole T. Gee, and P. Martin Sander, Biology of the Sauropod Dinosaurs Understanding the Life of Giants (Indiana University Press, 2011).

[174] M. Hallett & M. Wedel, *The Sauropod Dinosaurs: Life in the Age of Giants,* (Johns Hopkins University Press, 2016).

[175] Patrick Moser, Jordan River could die by 2011, Phys Org. *www.phys.org/news/2010-05-jordan-river-die.html* (May 2, 2010) (August 22, 2017).

[176] See, for example, the English Standard Version or the Life Application Study Bible notes.

[177] J. Carballido, D. Pol, A. Otero, I. Cerda, L. Salgado, A. Garrido, J. Ramezani, N. Cúneo, M. Krause, A new giant titanosaur sheds light on body mass evolution amongst sauropod dinosaurs, *Proceedings of the Royal Society B* (August 9, 2017).

[178] Nathan P. Myhrvold and Philip J. Currie, Supersonic Sauropods? Tail Dynamics in the Diplodocids, *Paleobiology* 23 (December, 1997): 393—409; Benjamin Meyers, W. Wayt Gibbs, Did a Dinosaur Break the Sound Barrier before We Did? (*www.scientificamerican.com/video/did-a-dinosaur-break-the-sound-barrier-before-we-did/*) (November 3, 2015) (August 22, 2017).

[179] Ibid. (D. Sivam / P. Currie / N. Myhrvold).

[180] Dattatreya Mandal, *Hexapolis*, Physical Model To Show How Dinosaurs May Have Whipped Their Tails In Supersonic Speed (October 16, 2015). (*www.hexapolis.com/2015/10/16/physical-model-to-show-how-dinosaurs-may-have-whipped-their-tails-in-supersonic-speed/*) (August 23, 2017).

[181] David Lambert, *The Encyclopedia of Dinosaurs* (London: Bloomsbury Books, 1994), 26–27, published in association with the British Museum of Natural History. Reconstructed graphic provided by Dr. Tommy Mitchell, Answers in Genesis.

[182] Carl Werner, *Evolution: The Grand Experiment* (3rd Edition). New Leaf Press. Kindle Edition. (Kindle Locations 1473-1476)

[183] Werner, p. 116

[184] Werner, Kindle Locations 2597-2599.

[185] Most Biblical creationists hold that some dinosaurs lived after the Flood, but the vast majority of these likely went extinct rather quickly for a multitude of reasons.

[186] Peter D. Ward, *Out of Thin Air: Dinosaurs, Birds, and Earth's Ancient Atmosphere.* (Washington, DC: Joseph Henry Press, 2006).

[187] See 2 Peter 3:6; Genesis 1; and Romans 8:22.

[188] See Romans 5:12 and 1 Corinthians 15:22.

[189] Andrew A. Snelling, "Noah's Lost World," 2014; last featured May 3, 2015 (*https://answersingenesis.org/geology/plate-tectonics/noahs-lost-world/*) (Jan. 26, 2017).

[190] *The New Defender Study Bible* (Nashville, TN: World Publishing, 2006), states, "9:13 my bow. The rainbow, requiring small water droplets in the air, could not form in the pre-diluvian world, where the high vapor canopy precluded rain (Genesis 2:5). After the Flood, the very fact that rainfall is now possible makes a worldwide rainstorm impossible, and the rainbow "in the cloud" thereby becomes a perpetual reminder of God's grace, even in judgment." Several other Biblical Creation resources hold this view.

[191] Catherine Brahic, *New Scientist Daily News* (April 24, 2007). "Mystery prehistoric fossil verified as giant fungus": (*www.newscientist.com/article/dn11701-mystery-prehistoric-fossil-verified-as-giant-fungus/#.Uea7Qo2G18E*) (January 26, 2017).

[192] It is commonly taught in evolution-based textbooks that the oxygen levels during the "Carboniferous" era were 35%. See, for example: David Beerling, *The emerald planet: how plants changed Earth's history.* (Oxford University Press, 2007), 47. Peter D. Ward, *Out of Thin Air: Dinosaurs, Birds, and Earth's Ancient Atmosphere*, (Washington, DC: Joseph Henry Press, 2006), Chapter 6. See also: R. A. Berner, D. J. Beerling, R. Dudley, J.M. Robinson, R.A Wildman, Jr. "Phanerozoic atmospheric oxygen." *Annual Review Earth Planet Science*, 2003, pp. 31, 105–143.

[193] Jeff Hecht, November 6, 1993, "Last gasp for the dinosaurs." *New Scientist.* *www.newscientist.com/article/mg14018981-200-last-gasp-for-the-dinosaurs/* (January 26, 2017).

[194] *The Washington Post.* "Lack of Oxygen Blamed for Dinosaurs' Extinction." October 28, 1993

www.washingtonpost.com/archive/politics/1993/10/28/lack-of-oxygen-blamed-for-dinosaurs-extinction/84f102be-4264-4089-9e10-007b181476ee/?utm_term=.333d8cd2fefb (January 26, 2017). See also: R. A. Hengst, J. K. Rigby, G. P. Landis, R. L. Sloan. "Biological consequences of Mesozoic atmospheres: respiratory adaptations and functional range of Apatosaurus." In: Macleod N, Keller G, editors. *Cretaceous-Tertiary mass extinctions: biotic and environmental changes.* (New York: W.W. Norton & Co., 1996), pp. 327–347.

[195] Carl Wieland and Dr Jonathan Sarfati, "Some bugs do grow bigger with higher oxygen," *Journal of Creation* 25(1):13–14 (April 2011) (*http://creation.com/oxygen-bigger-bugs*) (January 26, 2017). See also J. Scheven, "The Carboniferous floating forest—an extinct pre-Flood ecosystem," *J. Creation* 10 (1):70–91, 1996.

[196] *Guinness World Book of Records,* The Jim Pattison Group, 2014, 27.

[197] Image Credit: Wikipedia.

[198] Gregory S. Paul, *Dinosaurs of the Air: The Evolution and Loss of Flight in Dinosaurs and Birds* (Johns Hopkins University Press, 2002), 472. See also: M.P. Witton and M.B. Habib. "On the Size and Flight Diversity of Giant Pterosaurs, the Use of Birds as Pterosaur Analogues and Comments on Pterosaur Flightlessness." *PLoS ONE,* 5(11) (2010). Other estimates place a range the weight range between 440 and 570 pounds: "That said, most mass estimates for the largest pterosaurs do converge, using multiple methods, around a 200–260kg [440–570lb] range at present, which represents decent confidence." (Ella Davies, BBC Earth, May 9, 2016) and "The biggest beast that ever flew had wings longer than a bus." (*www.bbc.com/earth/story/20160506-the-biggest-animals-that-ever-flew-are-long-extinct*) (January 26, 2017).

[199] Larry O' Hanlon, November 8, 2012. "This pterodactyl was so big it couldn't fly, scientist claims." *www.nbcnews.com/id/49746642/ns/technology_and_science-science/#.WH-U2_krKUn* (January 26, 2017).

[200] Mark P. Wilton, *Pterosaurs: Natural History, Evolution, Anatomy.* (Princeton University Press, 2013).

[201] Oxygen reported from within the amber bubbles are still debated among evolutionists.

[202] Ian Anderson, "Dinosaurs Breathed Air Rich in Oxygen," *New Scientist,* vol. 116, 1987, 25.

[203] Image Credit: Wikipedia.

[204] "No giants today: tracheal oxygen supply to the legs limits beetle size," was presented October 10-11 at Comparative Physiology 2006: Integrating Diversity (Virginia Beach). The research was carried out by Alexander Kaiser and Michael C. Quinlan of Midwestern University, Glendale, Arizona; J. Jake Socha and Wah-Keat Lee, Argonne National Laboratory, Argonne, IL; and Jaco Klok and Jon F. Harrison, Arizona State University, Tempe, AZ. Harrison is the principal investigator.

[205] Geological Society of America. "Raising giant insects to unravel ancient oxygen." *Science Daily,* October 30, 2010. *www.sciencedaily.com/releases/2010/10/101029132924.htm* (January 26, 2017).

See also: Gauthier Chapelle & Lloyd S. Peck (May 1999). "Polar gigantism dictated by oxygen availability." *Nature*. 399 (6732): 114–115. This article argues that higher oxygen supply (30–35%) may also have led to larger insects during the Carboniferous period: A.N. Nel, G. Fleck, R. Garrouste, and G. Gand, "The Odonatoptera of the Late Permian Lodève Basin (Insecta)." *Journal of Iberian Geology* 34 (1) (2008): 115–122.

[206] Simon J. Braddy, Markus Poschmann, and O. Erik Tetlie, "Giant claw reveals the largest ever arthropod," *Biological Letters.* (2008) 4 106–109 (Published February 23, 2008).

[207] M. G. Lockley & Christian Meyer. "The tradition of tracking dinosaurs in Europe," *Dinosaur Tracks and Other Fossil Footprints of Europe.* (Columbia University Press, 2013), pp. 25–52. See also: Donald R. Prothero, *Bringing Fossils to Life: An Introduction to Paleobiology.* Third Edition. (New York: Columbia University Press, 2015), p. 381.

[208] ThePaleobiology Database (Frequently Asked Questions): *https://paleobiodb.org/#/faq* (January 26, 2017)

[209] ThePaleobiology Database: *https://paleobiodb.org/navigator/* (January 26, 2017)

[210] RATE tested the assumptions using radiohalos and fission tracks. Both showed that the assumptions were violated (Larry Vardiman, Steven Austin, John Baumgardner, Steven Boyd, Eugene Chaffin, Donald DeYoung, D. Russell Humphreys, Andrew Snelling, *Radioisotopes and the Age of the Earth: Results of a Young-Earth Research Initiative.* The Institute for Creation Research).

[211] Ken Ham, "They Can't Allow 'It'!" AnswersinGenesis.org: *www.answersingenesis.org/articles/au/cant-allow-it* (January 1, 2014).

[212] Blake Edgar, "Dinosaur National Monument." *Dinosaur Digs.* (Bethesda, MD: Discovery Communications, 1999), 120.

[213] William A. Hoesch and Steven A. Austin, "Dinosaur National Monument: Jurassic Park Or Jurassic Jumble?" ICR.org: *www.icr.org/article/dinosaur-national-monument-park-or-jurassic-jumble/* (January 27, 2017)

[214] An articulated dinosaur skeleton means that a large number of the bones from an individual dinosaur were collected in close association, enough to reassemble the dinosaur.

[215] Werner, *Evolution: The Grand Experiment*, Kindle Locations 2598–2608.

[216] There is disagreement in the paleontology field as to whether the "dinosaur death pose" is due to choking while dying from drowning, or due to strong water currents arching the neck back after death. See: Achim G. Reisdorf & Michael Wuttke, "Re-evaluating Moodie's Opisthotonic-Posture Hypothesis in Fossil Vertebrates Part I: Reptiles—the taphonomy of the bipedal dinosaurs Compsognathus longipes and Juravenator starki from the Solnhofen Archipelago (Jurassic, Germany)," *Palaeobiodiversity and Palaeoenvironments* 92 (2012):119–168. Their findings stated, "From what has been presented above, it can be concluded that the formation of the 'opisthotonic posture' in *subaquatically deposited carcasses* of long-necked and long tailed reptiles is the result of a postmortem process…this posture must be seen as a normal phenomenon that occurs during subaquatic gradual embedding of these sorts of carcasses." See discussion: Drwile.com, "Arched Necks in Dinosaur Fossils: Is Water to Blame?" *www.blog.drwile.com/?p=7118* (February 16, 2016).

[217] D.A. Eberth, D.B. Brinkman, and V.A. Barkas, "Centrosaurine Mega-bonebed from the Upper Cretaceous of Southern Alberta: Implications for Behaviour and

Death Events" in *New Perspectives on Horned Dinosaurs: The Ceratopsian Symposium at the Royal Tyrrell Museum* (September 2007).

[218] *New Perspectives on Horned Dinosaurs: The Ceratopsian Symposium at the Royal Tyrrell Museum* (September 2007).

[219] Michael Reilly, "Dinosaurs' Last Stand Found in China?" Discovery.com: *www.news.discovery.com/earth/dinosaurs-last-stand-found-in-china.htm* (January 1, 2014).

[220] Michael J. Oard, "The Extinction of the Dinosaurs," *Journal of Creation* 11(2) (1997): 137–154.

[221] J.R. Horner & J. Gorman, *Digging Dinosaurs.* New York: Workman Publishing, 1988, 122–123.

[222] Credit: Caleb LePore. See: David Maxwell Braun, "Dinosaur Herd Found in Canada Named After Science Teacher." *National Geographic News.* National Geographic Society, October 2, 2008; Christopher A. Brochu, M. K. Brett-Surman. "Dinosaur Provincial Park." *A Guide to Dinosaurs.* (San Francisco, CA: Fog City, 2002), p. 220; John R. Horner and James Gorman. *Digging Dinosaurs.* (New York: Workman Pub., 1988), p. 131; Brett French, "New Finds, Old Site: Dinosaur Dig Revealing Insights into Montana 103 Million Years Ago." *Butte Montana Local News.* (August 23, 2015); Brett French, "Jurassic Starfish Discovery in South-central Montana Wows Researchers." *Independent Record.* (July 6, 2015); Blake Edgar, "Petrified Forest National Park." *Dinosaur Digs.* (Bethesda, MD: Discovery Communications, 1999), p. 104; Glendive Dinosaur and Fossil Museum, Glendive, Montana; Mike Dunham, "Scientists Identify Dinosaur That Roamed the Alaska Arctic." *Alaska Dispatch News.* Alaska Dispatch Publishing. (September 22, 2015).

[223] Tim Clarey, Ph.D. "Dinosaurs in Marine Sediments: A Worldwide Phenomenon." *Acts & Facts.* 44 (6) (2015).

[224] J. H. Hartman and J. I. Kirkland. "Brackish and marine mollusks of the Hell Creek Formation of North Dakota: Evidence for a persisting Cretaceous seaway." In *The Hell Creek Formation and the Cretaceous-Tertiary Boundary in the Northern Great Plains: An Integrated Continental Record of the End of the Cretaceous.* J. H. Hartman, K. R. Johnson, and D. J. Nichols, eds. Geological Society of America Special Paper 361, pp. 271–296. (2002); W. A. Clemens and J. H. Hartman. "From Tyrannosaurus rex to asteroid impact: Early studies (1901–1980) of the Hell Creek Formation in its type area." In *Through the End of the Cretaceous in the Type Locality of the Hell Creek Formation in Montana and Adjacent Areas.* Wilson, G. P. et al, eds. Geological Society of America Special Paper 503, 1–87. 2014.

[225] Jesse A. Sherburn, John R. Baumgardner and Mark F. Horstemeyer, "New Material Model Reveals Inherent Tendency in Mantle Minerals for Runaway Mantle Dynamics," *International Conference on Creationism* (2013).

[226] N. Ibrahim, et al. 2014. "Semiaquatic adaptations in a giant predatory dinosaur." *Science.* 345 (6204): 1613–1616.

[227] Horner & Gorman, *Digging Dinosaurs,* 128.

[228] Tim Clarey, Ph.D. "Dinosaurs in Marine Sediments: A Worldwide Phenomenon." *Acts & Facts.* 44 (6) (2015).

[229] We are thankful for the contributions made to this section by Brian Thomas and Pat Roy.

[230] *Creation Research Society Quarterly Journal* Spring 2015 (Volume 51, Number 4): *www.creationresearch.org/index.php/component/k2/item/118-2015-volume-51-number-4-spring* (January 27, 2017)

[231] Jeff Hecht, Daily News, "Blood vessels recovered from T. rex bone," NewScientist.com: *www.newscientist.com/article/dn7195-blood-vessels-recovered-from-t-rex-bone/* (March 24, 2005)

[232] Science via AP (*www.msnbc.msn.com/id/7285683/*) (January 27, 2017).

[233] See, for example: R. Pawlicki and M. Wowogrodzka-Zagorska. "Blood vessels and red blood cells preserved in dinosaur bones." Annals of Anatomy 180 (1998): 73–77; M. H. Schweitzer, J.L. Wittmeyer, J.R. Horner, and J.K Toporske. "Soft-tissue vessels and cellular preservation in Tyrannosaurus rex." *Science,* 307 (2005): 1952; M.H. Schweitzer, J.L. Wittmeyer, and J.R. Horner. "Soft tissue and cellular preservation in vertebrate skeletal elements from the Cretaceous to the present." *Proceedings of the Royal Society B* 274 (2007): 183–197; M.H. Schweitzer, W. Zheng, C.L. Organ, R. Avci, Z. Suo, L.M. Freimark, V.S. Lebleu, M.B. Duncan, M.G. Vander Heiden, J.M. Neveu, W.S. Lane, J.S. Cottrell, J.R. Horner, L.C. Cantley, R. Kalluri, and J.M. Asara. "Biomolecular characterization and protein sequences of the campanian Hadrosaur B. Canadensis." *Science,* 324 (2009): 626–631.

[234] M. Schweitzer and I. Staedter, *The Real Jurassic Park, Earth,* June 1997, 55–57.

[235] R. Pawlicki and M. Wowogrodzka-Zagorska. "Blood vessels and red blood cells preserved in dinosaur bones." *Annals of Anatomy* 180 (1998): 73–77; M. H. Schweitzer, J.L. Wittmeyer, J.R. Horner, and J.K Toporske. "Soft-tissue vessels and cellular preservation in Tyrannosaurus rex." *Science,* 307 (2005): 1952; M.H. Schweitzer, J.L. Wittmeyer, and J.R. Horner. "Soft tissue and cellular preservation in vertebrate skeletal elements from the Cretaceous to the present." *Proceedings of the Royal Society B* 274 (2007): 183–197; M.H. Schweitzer, W. Zheng, C.L. Organ, R. Avci, Z. Suo, L.M. Freimark, V.S. Lebleu, M.B. Duncan, M.G. Vander Heiden, J.M. Neveu, W.S. Lane, J.S. Cottrell, J.R. Horner, L.C. Cantley, R. Kalluri, and J.M. Asara. "Biomolecular characterization and protein sequences of the campanian Hadrosaur B. Canadensis." *Science* 324 (2009): 626–631; J. Lindgren, M.W. Caldwell, T. Konishi, L.M. Chiappe, "Convergent Evolution in Aquatic Tetrapods: Insights from an Exceptional Fossil Mosasaur." *PLoS ONE* 5(8) (2010): e11998.

[236] Barry Yeoman, "Schweitzer's Dangerous Discovery," Discovery Magazine: *www.discovermagazine.com/2006/apr/dinosaur-dna* (April 27, 2006) (January 27, 2017).

[237] M.H. Schweitzer, M. Marhsall, K. Carron, D.S. Bohle, S.C. Busse, E.V. Arnold, D. Barnard, J.R. Horner, and J.R. Starkey. "Heme compounds in dinosaur trabecular bone." *Proceedings of the National Academy of Sciences* USA 94, (1997), p. 6295.

[238] J.M. Asara, M.H. Schweitzer, L.M. Freimark, M. Phillips, and L.C. Cantley. "Protein sequences from mastodon and Tyrannosaurus rex revealed by mass spectrometry." *Science,* 316 (2007): 280–285.

[239] M. Armitage, "Soft bone material from a brow horn of a Triceratops horridus from Hell Creek Formation, MT." *Creation Research Society Quarterly,* 51 (2015): 248–258.

259

[240] M.H. Schweitzer, W. Zheng, T.P. Cleland, and M. Bern. "Molecular analyses of dinosaur osteocytes support the presence of endogenous molecules." *Bone,* 52 (2013): 414–423; M. Armitage, "Soft bone material from a brow horn of a Triceratops horridus from Hell Creek Formation, MT." *Creation Research Society Quarterly,* 51 (2015): 248–258; M. Armitage and K.L. Anderson. "Soft tissue of fibrillar bone from a fossil of the supraorbital horn of the dinosaur Triceratops horridus." *Acta Histochemica,* 115 (2013): 603–608; R. Pawlicki, "Histochemical demonstration of DNA in osteocytes from dinosaur bones." *Folia Histochemica Et Cytobiologica,* 33 (1995): 183–186.

[241] M.H. Schweitzer, et al. 2005. "Molecular preservation in Late Cretaceous sauropod dinosaur eggshells." *Proceedings of the Royal Society B: Biological Sciences.* 272 (1565): 775–784.

[242] G.D. Cody, N.S. Gupta, D.E.G. Briggs, A.L.D. Kilcoyne, R.E. Summons, F. Kenig, R.E. Plotnick, and A. C. Scott. "Molecular signature of chitin-protein complex in Paleozoic arthropods." *Geology,* 39 (3) (2011): 255–258; H. Ehrlich, J.K. Rigby, J.P. Botting, M.V. Tsurkan, C. Werner, P. Schwille, Z. Petrášek, A. Pisera, P. Simon, V.N. Sivkov, D.V. Vyalikh, S.L. Molodtsov, D. Kurek, M. Kammer, S. Hunoldt, R. Born, D. Stawski, A. Steinhof, V.V. Bazhenov, and T. Geisler. "Discovery of 505-million-year old chitin in the basal demosponge Vauxia gracilenta." *Scientific Reports.* 3 (2013): 3497.

[243] M. Helder, "Fresh dinosaur bones found," *Creation* 14(3) (1992): 16–17, www.creation.com/fresh-dinosaur-bones-found (January 27, 2017).

[244] "Fossils of new duck-billed, plant-eating dinosaur species found in Alaska, researchers say" (www.accesswdun.com/article/2015/9/337248) (September 22, 2015).

[245] Schweitzer, Wittmeyer, & Horner (2007), 183–197.

[246] Hirotsugu Mori, Patrick S. Druckenmiller, and Gregory M. Erickson, "A new Arctic hadrosaurid from the Prince Creek Formation (lower Maastrichtian) of northern Alaska." *Acta Palaeontologica Polonica* 61 (1), (2016): 15–32; A.R. Fiorillo, P.J. McCarthy, and P.P. Flaig "Taphonomic and sedimentologic interpretations of the dinosaur-bearing Upper Cretaceous Strata of the Prince Creek Formation, Northern Alaska: Insights from an ancient high-latitude terrestrial ecosystem." *Palaeogeography, Palaeoclimatology, Palaeoecology* 295 (2010): 376–388; R.A. Gangloff and A.R. Fiorillo, "Taphonomy and paleoecology of a bonebed from the Prince Creek Formation, North Slope, Alaska." *Palaios,* 25 (2010): 299–317; M.H. Schweitzer, C. Johnson, T.G. Zocco, J.R. Horner, and J.R. Starkey, "Preservation of biomolecules in cancellous bone of Tyrannosaurus rex," *J. Vertebrate paleontology* 17 (2) (1997): 349–359; M.H. Schweitzer, M. Marshall, K. Carron, D.S. Bohle, S.C. Busse, E.V. Arnold, D. Barnard, J.R. Horner, and J.R. Starkey, "Heme compounds in dinosaur trabecular bone," *Proceedings of the National Academy of Science* 94 (1997): 6291–6296; As stated in Helder (above): "An initial announcement was printed in 1985 in Geological Society of America abstract programs Vol.17, p. 548. Already in press at that time was an article describing the site and the condition of the bones (Kyle L. Davies, 'Duck-bill Dinosaurs (Hadrosauridae, Ornithischia) from the North Slope of Alaska', Journal of Paleontology, Vol.61 No.1, pp.198-200); M.H. Schweitzer, J.L. Wittmeyer, and J.R. Horner. "Soft tissue and cellular preservation in vertebrate skeletal elements from the

Cretaceous to the present." *Proceedings of the Royal Society B,* 274 (2007): 183–197.

[247] Barry Yeoman, "Schweitzer's Dangerous Discovery," Discovery Magazine: *www.discovermagazine.com/2006/apr/dinosaur-dna)* April 27, 2006) (January 27, 2017).

[248] Severo Avila, "Alan Stout is the Bone Collector," Northwest Georgia News: *www.northwestgeorgianews.com/rome/lifestyles/alan-stout-is-the-bone-collector/article_6b1268e7-3350-5dfd-a3dc-652dcf27d174.html* (April 11, 2010) (January 27, 2017).

[249] Alan Stout, Personal communication, January 16, 2017.

[250] Marshall Bern, Brett S. Phinney, and David Goldberg. "Reanalysis of Tyrannosaurus Rex Mass Spectra." *Journal of Proteome Research* 8.9 (2009): 4328–4332.

[251] Brian Thomas, "Original Biomaterials in Fossils." *Creation Research Society Quarterly,* 51 (2015): 234–347.

[252] Elena R. Schroeter, Caroline J. DeHart, Timothy P. Cleland, Wenxia Zheng, Paul M. Thomas, Neil L. Kelleher, Marshall Bern, and Mary H. Schweitzer, "Expansion for the Brachylophosaurus canadensis Collagen I Sequence and Additional Evidence of the Preservation of Cretaceous Protein." Journal of Proteome Research Article.

[253] See UPI News: *www.upi.com/Science_News/2017/01/23/Scientists-find-ancient-dinosaur-collagen/6091485202598/* (January 23, 2017).

[254] S. Bertazzo, et al. "Fibres and cellular structures preserved in 75-million-year-old dinosaur specimens," *Nature Communications,* 6, (2015).

[255] M. Buckley and M.J. Collins. "Collagen survival and its use for species identification in Holocene-Lower Pleistocene bone fragments from British archaeological and paleontological sites." *Antiqua,* 1 (2011).

[256] Robert F. Service, "Scientists retrieve 80-million-year-old dinosaur protein in 'milestone' paper," Science.com: *www.sciencemag.org/news/2017/01/scientists-retrieve-80-million-year-old-dinosaur-protein-milestone-paper* (January 31, 2017) (February 5, 2017).

[257] M. H. Schweitzer, et al. "Molecular analyses of dinosaur osteocytes support the presence of endogenous molecules." *Bone,* 52 (1) (2013): 414–423. S. R. Woodward, N. J. Weyand, and M. Bunnell. "DNA Sequence from Cretaceous Period Bone Fragments." *Science,* 266 (5188) (1994): 1229–1232.

[258] T. Lingham-Soliar, "A unique cross section through the skin of the dinosaur Psittacosaurus from China showing a complex fibre architecture." *Proceedings of the Royal Society B: Biological Sciences* 275 (2008): 775–780. T. Lingham-Soliar and G. Plodowski. "The integument of Psittacosaurus from Liaoning Province, China: taphonomy, epidermal patterns and color of a ceratopsian dinosaur." *Naturwissenschaften* 97 (2010): 479–486.

[259] Schweitzer, Zheng, Cleland, & Bern (2013): 414–423.

[260] Ibid.

[261] N.P. Edwards, H.E. Barden, B.E. van Dongen, P.L. Manning, P.O. Larson, U. Bergmann, W.I. Sellers, and R.A. Wogelius. "Infrared mapping resolves soft tissue preservation in 50 million year-old reptile skin." *Proceedings of the Royal Society B,* 278 (2011): 3209–3218.

[262] U. Bergmann, et al., "Archaeopteryx feathers and bone chemistry fully revealed via synchrotron imaging." *Proceedings of the National Academy of Sciences.* 107 (20) (2010), 9060–9065.

[263] S. Hayashi, K. Carpenter, M. Watabe, and L.A. McWhinney, "Ontogenetic histology of Stegosaurus plates and spikes." *Palaeontology* 55 (2012), 145–161.

[264] M.H. Schweitzer, W. Zheng, C.L. Organ, R. Avci, Z. Suo, L.M. Freimark, V.S. Lebleu, M.B. Duncan, M.G. Vander Heiden, J.M. Neveu, W.S. Lane, J.S. Cottrell, J.R. Horner, L.C. Cantley, R. Kalluri, and J.M. Asara. "Biomolecular characterization and protein sequences of the campanian Hadrosaur B. Canadensis." *Science,* 324 (2009): 626–631.

[265] M. Buckley and M.J. Collins. "Collagen survival and its use for species identification in Holocene-Lower Pleistocene bone fragments from British archaeological and paleontological sites." *Antiqua,* 1 (2011). Hypothetically, if dinosaurs include an unrealistically large mass of initial collagen, it may last as long as 1.7 million years (see Brian Thomas, "A Review of Original Tissue Fossils and their Age Implications," Proceedings of the Seventh International Conference on Creationism [Pittsburgh, PA: Creation Science Fellowship]). However, this upper estimate assumes that skin, muscles, and connective tissue collagen decays as slowly as bone collagen, which is not typically the case (Brian Thomas, personal communication, February 15, 2017).

[266] *Creation Research Society Quarterly Journal,* Spring 2015 (Volume 51, Number 4): *www.creationresearch.org/index.php/component/k2/item/118-2015-volume-51-number-4-spring* (January 27, 2017).

[267] Image Credit: Wikipedia: *www.commons.wikimedia.org/wiki/File:Edmontosaurus_mummy.jpg*

[268] Image Credit: Wikipedia: *www.news.nationalgeographic.com/news/2002/10/1010_021010_dinomummy.html*

[269] Image Credit: Dinosaur Mummy: *www.dinosaurmummy.org/guide-to-dinosaur-mummy-csi.html*

[270] Michael Greshko, "Hearts of Stone: A Fabulous Fossil Find," National Geographic: *http://news.nationalgeographic.com/2016/04/160421-fossils-hearts-fish-evolution-paleontology-science/* (April 21, 2016) (January 27, 2017).

[271] Nicholas St. Fleur, "First Fossilized Dinosaur Brain Found." New York Times: *www.nytimes.com/2016/10/28/science/first-fossilized-dinosaur-brain.html?_r=0* (October 27, 2016) (January 27, 2017).

[272] Image Credit: *www.ox.ac.uk/news/2016-10-28-fossilised-dinosaur-brain-tissue-identified-first-time* (January 27, 2017)

[273] Charles Gould, *Mythical Monsters,* W.H. Allen & Co., London, 1886, 382–383.

[274] Flavius Philostratus, "The Life of Apollonius of Tyana" (Vol. 1, Book III) (F. C. Conybeare, trans. New York: Macmillan Co., 243-247, 1912).

[275] The author pre-supposes the truth and accuracy of Scripture.

[276] Kenneth R. Miller and Joseph S. Levine, *Biology.* (Boston, MA.: Pearson, 2006), p. 466.

[277] This section was written by Roger Sigler and was carried over from: Daniel A. Biddle (editor), *Creation V. Evolution: What They Won't Tell You in Biology Class* (Xulon Press). Roger Sigler, M.S. is a licensed professional geoscientist in the State of Texas and has taught and published in the field of Biblical Creation since 1989.

[278] Gunter Faure, *Principles of Isotope Geology,* 2nd ed. (John Wiley & Sons, 1986), 41, 119, 288.

[279] A.O. Woodford, *Historical Geology*. (W.H. Freeman & Company, 1965): 191–220.

[280] Judah Etinger, *Foolish Faith*. (Green Forest, AR.: Master Books, 2003): Ch. 3.

[281] C.S. Noble and J.J. Naughton, *Science*, 162 (1968): 265–266.

[282] Data compiled and modified after Snelling (1998): Andrew Snelling, "The Cause of Anomalous Potassium-Argon 'Ages' for Recent Andesite Flows at Mt. Ngauruhoe, New Zealand, and the Implications for Potassium-argon Dating," in Robert E. Walsh (ed.), *Proceedings of the Fourth International Conference on Creationism* (1998), p. 503–525. See also: Andrew A Snelling, "Excess Argon": The "Archilles' Heel" of Potassium-Argon and Argon-Argon "Dating" of Volcanic Rocks. *www.icr.org/article/excess-argon-achillies-heel-potassium-argon-dating/* (February 3, 2016); Steve Austin, "Excess argon within mineral concentrates from the new dacite lava dome at Mount St Helens volcano," *J. Creation* 10 (3) (1996): 335–343 (see: *www.creation.com/lavadome)*. (February 3, 2016).

[283] Andrew Snelling, "Radiocarbon Ages for Fossil Ammonites and Wood in Cretaceous Strata near Redding, California." *Answers Research Journal*. 2008 1: 123-144. *www.answersingenesis.org/geology/carbon-14/radiocarbon-ages-fossils-cretaceous-strata-redding-california/*. (February 3, 2016).

[284] Ibid.

[285] See earlier note regarding biblical genealogies and dating Creation and the Flood.

[286] Thanks to Jeffrey Tomkins, Ph.D., Jerry Bergman Ph.D., and Brian Thomas, M.S. for this section.

[287] Jonathan Silvertown (ed), *99% Ape: How Evolution Adds Up* (University of Chicago Press, 2009): 4.

[288] Bruce Bagemihl, *Biological Exuberance: Animal Homosexuality and Natural Diversity* (1999). St. Martins Press. New York.

[289] R.J. Rummel, "Statistics of Democide: Genocide and Mass Murder Since 1900," *School of Law, University of Virginia* (1997).

[290] Jerry Bergman, *Hitler and the Nazis Darwinian Worldview: How the Nazis Eugenic Crusade for a Superior Race Caused the Greatest Holocaust in World History*, (Kitchener, Ontario, Canada: Joshua Press, 2012).

[291] J. Tomkins, "Separate Studies Converge on Human-Chimp DNA Dissimilarity." *Acts & Facts* 47 (11) (2018): 9.

[292] See Human assembly and gene annotation: *http://useast.ensembl.org/Homo_sapiens/Info/Annotation*

[293] Many attempts have been made and all have failed. See Kirill Rossiianov, "Beyond Species: Ii'ya Ivanov and His Experiments on Cross-Breeding Humans with Anthropoid Apes." *Science in Context*. 15 (2) (2002): 277–316.

[294] See the U.S. Department of Health and Human Services (*https://optn.transplant.hrsa.gov/*) (February 1, 2016).

[295] Credit: Wikipedia

[296] Tomkins, 2018.

[297] Various sources will show minor differences in these comparisons. These are for example only.

[298] S. Kakuo, K. Asaoka, and T. Ide, "Human is a unique species among primates in terms of telomere length." *Biochemistry Biophysics Research Communication*, 263 (1999): 308–314

[299] N. Archidiacono, C.T. Storlazzi, C. Spalluto, A.S. Ricco, R. Marzella, M. Rocchi, "Evolution of chromosome Y in primates." *Chromosoma* 107 (1998): 241–246.

[300] Answers in Genesis: "What about the Similarity Between Human and Chimp DNA?" *www.answersingenesis.org/articles/nab3/human-and-chimp-dna* (January 14, 2014).

[301] J. Bergman & J. Tomkins, "Is the Human Genome Nearly Identical to Chimpanzee? A Reassessment of the Literature" *Journal of Creation* 26 (2012): 54–60.

[302] Ibid.

[303] J. Tomkins, "How Genomes are Sequenced and why it Matters: Implications for Studies in Comparative Genomics of Humans and Chimpanzees," *Answers Research Journal* 4 (2011): 81–88.

[304] I. Ebersberger, D. Metzler, C. Schwarz, & S. Pääbo, "Genomewide Comparison of DNA Sequences between Humans and Chimpanzees," *American Journal of Human Genetics* 70 (2002): 1490–1497.

[305] "Human-Chimp Genetic Similarity: Is the Evolutionary Dogma Valid?" Institute for Creation Research: *www.icr.org/article/6197/*

[306] Chimpanzee Sequencing and Analysis Consortium, "Initial Sequence of the Chimpanzee Genome and Comparison with the Human Genome," *Nature* 437 (2005): 69–87.

[307] J. Tomkins, "Genome-Wide DNA Alignment Similarity (Identity) for 40,000 Chimpanzee DNA Sequences Queried against the Human Genome is 86–89%," *Answers Research Journal* 4 (2011): 233–241.

[308] J. Prado-Martinez, et al. "Great Ape Genetic Diversity and Population History," *Nature* 499 (2013): 471–475.

[309] J. Tomkins, & J. Bergman. "Genomic Monkey Business—Estimates of Nearly Identical Human-Chimp DNA Similarity Re-evaluated using Omitted Data," *Journal of Creation* 26 (2012), 94–100; J. Tomkins, "Comprehensive Analysis of Chimpanzee and Human Chromosomes Reveals Average DNA Similarity of 70%," *Answers Research Journal* 6 (2013): 63–69.

[310] Nathaniel T. Jeanson, "Purpose, Progress, and Promise, Part 4*," Institute for Creation Research: http://www.icr.org/article/purpose-progress-promise-part-4* (September 2, 2015).

[311] Tomkins & Bergman, 63–69.

[312] Tomkins, 2011.

[313] R. Buggs, "How similar are human and chimpanzee genomes?" Posted on Richardbuggs.com July 14, 2018, accessed August 9, 2018.

[314] Tomkins & Bergman, 63–69.

[315] Subsequent analyses revealed an anomaly in the BLASTN algorithm used for determining the 70% figure and the revised estimate (88%) has been included in this chapter. See: Jeffrey P. Tomkins, "Documented Anomaly in Recent Versions of the BLASTN Algorithm and a Complete Reanalysis of Chimpanzee and Human Genome-Wide DNA Similarity Using Nucmer and LASTZ," (October 7, 2015), Answers in Genesis: *https://answersingenesis.org/genetics/dna-similarities/blastn-algorithm-anomaly/*

[316] Tomkins, 2011.

264

317 E. Wijaya, M.C. Frith, P. Horton & K. Asai, "Finding Protein-coding Genes through Human Polymorphisms," *PloS one* 8 (2013).

318 New Genome Comparison Finds Chimps, Humans Very Similar at the DNA Level, 2005, National Human Genome Research Institute (*www.genome.gov/15515096*)

319 Christine Elsik. et al. The Genome Sequence of Taurine Cattle: A Window to Ruminant Biology and Evolution. *Science*. 324:522-528.

320 Source is Pontius, Joan. et al., 2007. Initial Sequence and Comparative Analysis of the Cat Genome. *Genome Research*. 17:1675–1689 (*www.eupedia.com/forum/threads/25335-Percentage-of-genetic-similarity-between-humans-and-animals*).

321 Background on Comparative Genomic Analysis (December, 2002) (*www.genome.gov/10005835*).

322 NIH/National Human Genome Research Institute. "Researchers Compare Chicken, Human Genomes: Analysis of First Avian Genome Uncovers Differences Between Birds and Mammals." ScienceDaily (December 10, 2004).

323 J. Tomkins & J. Bergman, "Incomplete Lineage Sorting and Other 'Rogue' Data Fell the Tree of Life," *Journal of Creation* 27 (2013): 63–71.

324 Brian Thomas, "Where Are All the Human Fossils?" (August 31, 2018). Institute for Creation Research: *www.icr.org/article/where-are-all-the-human-fossils/* (November 5, 2018).

325 Dinosaur Provincial Park-World Heritage Site (*www.albertaparks.ca/media/4499676/dinosaur_pp_-_fact_sheet.pdf*) (November 5, 2018).

326 Fossilworks.org as of October 19, 2018.

327 J.D. Morris, *Is the Big Bang Biblical?* (Green Forest, AR: Master Books, 2003): 108–109; and J.D. Morris, *The Young Earth* (Green Forest, AR: Master Books, 1994): 70. Statistics provided by paleontologist Kurt P. Wise, Ph.D. Geology (Paleontology).

328 T.L. Clarey & D.J. Werner, "Use of sedimentary megasequences to re-create pre-Flood geography." In Proceedings of the Eighth International Conference on Creationism (ed. J.H. Whitmore) Pittsburgh, Pennsylvania: Creation Science Fellowship (2018): 351–372.

329 T.L. Clarey, "Local Catastrophes or Receding Floodwater? Global Geologic Data that Refute a K-Pg (K-T) Flood/post-Flood Boundary." *Creation Research Society Quarterly*, 54 (2) (2017): 100–120.